KU-725-692

Educational Innovation in Developing Countries

Case-Studies of Changemakers

Edited by

Keith M. Lewin

Reader in Education
University of Sussex

with

Janet S. Stuart

Lecturer in Education
University of Sussex

© Keith M. Lewin and Janet S. Stuart 1991

All rights reserved. No reproduction, copy or transmission of
this publication may be made without written permission.

No paragraph of this publication may be reproduced, copied or
transmitted save with written permission or in accordance with
the provisions of the Copyright, Designs and Patents Act 1988,
or under the terms of any licence permitting limited copying
issued by the Copyright Licensing Agency, 90 Tottenham Court
Road, London W1P 9HE.

Any person who does any unauthorised act in relation to this
publication may be liable to criminal prosecution and civil
claims for damages.

First published 1991 by
THE MACMILLAN PRESS LTD
Houndmills, Basingstoke, Hampshire RG21 2XS
and London
Companies and representatives
throughout the world

Typeset by
Footnote Graphics, Warminster, Wiltshire

ISBN 0–333–58663–8

A catalogue record for this book is available
from the British Library.

Printed in China

Reprinted 1993

Contents

List of Maps   vii
List of Tables   viii
List of Figures   ix
Acknowledgements   x
Notes on the Contributors   xi

Introduction
Keith M. Lewin   1

1 Changemakers and Change Models: Educational
Innovation in Developing Countries
Keith M. Lewin   7

PART I   CURRICULUM INNOVATIONS   21

2 Modernising the Geography Curriculum in Post-1976
China
Julian Leung Yat-ming   23

3 Science Education as a Development Strategy in
Nigeria: a Study of Kano State Science Secondary Schools
Abdalla Uba Adamu   61

PART II   TEACHER DEVELOPMENT PROJECTS   93

4 Inservice Training in Malaysia for the New Primary
Curriculum (KBSR)
Noor Azmi Ibrahim   95

5 Classroom Action Research in Africa: a Lesotho Case
Study of Curriculum and Professional Development
Janet S. Stuart   127

PART III   INSTITUTIONAL CONTEXTS   153

6 Perception Gaps in Technical Assistance Projects:
the Sudanese Case
Fiona Leach   155

7 School Climates in The Gambia
Baboucarr Sarr with Keith Lewin   185

Contents

PART IV   SYSTEMS REFORMS 215

8 Vocationalising Secondary Education: A Study of the
Junior Secondary Schooling Innovation in Nigeria
Florence Nwakoby with Keith Lewin 219

9 The National Youth Service in the Seychelles
Ian G. Haffenden 256

10 Postscript
Keith M. Lewin 281

Bibliography 304

Index 320

List of Maps

Map of China   24
Map of Nigeria showing Kano State   63
Map of Malaysia   96
Map of Africa with Lesotho   128
Map of Sudan   156
Map of The Gambia   186
Map of Nigeria showing Anambra State   220
Map showing Seychelles   257

List of Tables

2.1   Test structure of the first edition of Senior Middle School Geography Textbooks, June 1982   42

2.2   Distribution of questions according to different levels of intellectual abilities in geography papers of the Unified National Higher School Examination   50

3.1   Kano State manpower strength in science and technological disciplines, 1968–71   68

3.2   Science teaching in Kano State Science secondary schools   79

3.3   Science schools general GCE ordinary level examination passes, 1980–86   85

3.4   Course distribution of science school students in ABU, BUK and UNISOK, 1984–86   86

4.1   Structure of KBSR   97

4.2   Interview respondents   102

4.3   Details of KBSR courses   102

4.4   KBSR course contents   108

4.5   Time spent on different course activities   109

4.6   Use of course time by key personnel and participants   110

4.7   Teachers' responses to statement, 'I would prefer not to be chosen for KBSR courses', according to age groups   112

4.8   Cross-tabulation of variables 'Bored' and 'Alknow'   115

4.9   Comparison between grouping of skills suggested and skills taught: Subject: B. Malaysia, grade 5   120

7.1   Students' intentions on leaving   196

List of Figures

4.1 Organisation chart of KBSR implementation   99
4.2 Dissemination and training model: KBSR   105
5.1 Basic action research cycles   130
5.2 Outline of project and action research cycles   134
5.3 Comparisons of pupil participation in classroom dialogue at beginning and end of project   138
7.1 Summary of field-work activities   193
8.1 List of subjects in the JSS curriculum   221
8.2 Nigerian Federal Ministry of Education: organisational chart   235
8.3 Lesson profile, Hillside School   245
9.1 Evolution of the educational organisation   276

Acknowledgements

The contributors to this book all deserve recognition for the work they put in, often at very busy times and under less than ideal circumstances. Various organisations – the Commonwealth Scholarship Commission, the International Development Research Centre of Canada, the Malaysian Ministry of Education, Macmillan publishers – have provided financial support for the different studies. Individual authors dug deeply into their own pockets when assistance was not forthcoming. Special recognition should be given to the organisations and individuals in different countries who had the vision, confidence and openness to allow the research to take place. I am indebted to my co-editor for her painstaking work and to Fiona Leach for her careful proofreading and indexing, and to other colleagues at Sussex who assisted in the development of the ideas in this book.

Keith Lewin
Hove
1991

Notes on the Contributors

Abdalla Uba Adamu is Lecturer in Science Education at Bayero University, Kano, Nigeria. He has researched and published in the area of cultural dimensions of science-teaching in development countries, and his publications include monographs focusing on aspects of teaching and learning science in developing countries.

Ian G. Haffenden is Staff Tutor in the Department of Educational Studies at the University of Surrey. Having taught in secondary, further and adult education, both in England and abroad, he has published many articles and is currently co-editing a book entitled *International Perspectives on Youth, Development and Education* (with Karen Evans).

Noor Azmi Ibrahim is Principal Assistant for Research and Evaluation at the Curriculum Development Centre, Malaysia. He has taught and worked as an education officer at State level. He holds a Master's degree and doctorate from Sussex University.

Keith Lewin is Reader in Education and Director of Research Studies at the University of Sussex. He was previously a research officer at the Institute of Development Studies, and has published widely on education and development. His books include *Education in Austerity: Options for Planners* and *Doing Educational Research in Developing Countries: Qualitative Strategies* (with G. Vulliamy and D. Stephens).

Fiona Leach has spent 11 years working overseas on British aid-funded projects in English-language teaching and teacher training. She holds an MA in Education in Developing Countries and is currently completing a doctorate at the University of Sussex.

Florence Nwakoby is Deputy Director of Education and Acting Head of Educational services at the Ministry of Education, Nigeria. Her publications include *Problems and Prospects of Educational Technology* and *Organising Resource Centre Materials for Use*.

Baboucarr S. Sarr is Co-ordinator of Research and Evaluation at the National Curriculum Development Centre, The Gambia. He has an

MA from the University of Sussex, which led to further research for his doctorate.

Janet S. Stuart taught Social Studies in London from 1968–79, and then worked in Lesotho for six years, training Development Studies teachers. In 1988 she took up her present position as Director of the Overseas B.Ed at the University of Sussex. Her published books include *The Unequal Third* and various articles on education in Lesotho.

Julian Leung Yat-Ming is Teaching Consultant and Lecturer in the Department of Curriculum Studies at the University of Hong Kong. His research interests are concerned with curriculum development and teacher training in Hong Kong and China and he has published a number of articles on these subjects.

Introduction

This book is about the problems which confront politicians, planners, curriculum developers and teachers, in enacting innovations in the education and training systems of a variety of developing countries. It is a collection of case studies that have been produced from research undertaken at Sussex University over the last five years. In all cases the contributions are drawn from research theses which go well beyond the depth which can be encapsulated here.

We have written with five audiences in mind. These are policy makers and planners working in developing countries; international development agency staff; graduate students in education, development studies and the social sciences; the educational research community; teacher trainers in developing countries.

The case studies presented here are organised in four groups. The first group consists of studies of curriculum change; the second focuses on changes centred on teachers; the third explores the institutional climates within which change takes place; and the fourth is concerned with system level reforms. A general pattern has been adopted in presenting the case studies which considers the rationale for the case study; the research approach adopted; description, interpretation, analysis and comment on the initiation, development, implementation, and effectiveness of the innovations identified; and finally some reflections on the research process used.

GENESIS

The inspiration for this book grew from a number of events. Since the early 1970s the University of Sussex and the Institute of Development Studies (IDS) developed several international research projects to examine different aspects of educational reform in developing countries. The first of these at the IDS took up the challenge provided by dominant development thinking at the time that educational systems could provide 'the engine of growth' by developing human capital to complement investment of physical capital. If only, many thought, neo-colonial education systems could throw off their inheritance and provide educational experiences tailored to developmental needs, a 'judo trick' could be performed to channel the overwhelming demand

1

for educational participation down tracks that would balance the interests of individuals in selection with those of nation states in providing adequate supplies of educated personnel.

As a result, the IDS project on selection and qualification in the education systems of developing countries was established. Research was undertaken in seven countries; Japan, England, Ghana, Mexico, Sri Lanka, Malaysia and China. This produced two books (Dore 1976, Oxenham ed. 1984), a film (Dore and Little 1982), and many research reports and articles (see also Dore *et al* 1975, Little 1978, Brooke *et al* 1978, Deraniyagala *et al* 1978, Brooke and Oxenham 1980, Unger 1982, Boakye and Oxenham 1982; SLOG 1987).

In 1979 a Masters programme was established at the University of Sussex that built on the fruits of this and other research. It was targeted specifically on the professional education and training needs of curriculum developers and system managers working in developing countries. This programme quickly attracted a steady flow of mid-career professionals embedded in the operational problems of educational innovation in developing countries. These colleagues challenged our imagination as analysts of change and encouraged us to develop our skills as process helpers in educational innovation. Desmond Hogan and I developed a distinctive approach to the study of education and development problems taking advantage of the inter-disciplinary environment promoted by the IDS and the University of Sussex.

The programme that evolved linked exploration of the role of education in national development with the analysis of organisational structures in order to gain insights into how planned change might best be managed. It therefore went beyond the orthodoxies of many traditional postgraduate programmes in curriculum development. The intention was to take participants on a journey that first opened their minds to broad issues and to the re-examination of taken-for-granted assumptions about the nature and form of educational provision and innovation, through the development of specific analytical skills, to design exercises in innovation. The latter sought to integrate specific educational ideas with implementation strategies grounded in the real world of the organisations that delivered educational services.

The activities of the Sussex education cluster broadened to culminate in the establishment of the Centre for International Education (CIE). From small beginnings our research activity has expanded to incorporate a D.Phil programme, alongside funded research and operational support for development project, and this collection results from the work of colleagues who have all been based at Sussex. It has been my privilege to act as an adviser to all but one of these studies, the exception being Nwakoby's work which was supervised by Desmond Hogan. (Colin Lacey cosupervised Haffenden's study). To be able to create such a collection as this is testimony to the efforts of those who were stimulated by the Sussex academic environment.

There is an often repeated criticism that there are few documented examples of studies of educational change grounded in developing countries to use as a basis for formulating future policy. This is at best a half-truth. There is a long record of studies of educational development and attempts to innovate extending well back into the colonial age. No doubt its quality is mixed, some is very partial, and much adopts unfashionable approaches to research, but it does exist. In many, but not all, developing countries there is an accumulation of national literature and reports which offer insights into patterns of educational development, the motivations of those involved, and the impact attributed to reforms. To deny this is to do violence to the efforts of those who have toiled to contribute to these literatures. It is true, however, that much of this material is difficult to access, diffusely located, and poorly catalogued. Only very small portions enjoy international publication. It is this that can lead to the superficial impression that it is absent.

As a consequence of this, much of the educational innovation literature available internationally for teaching purposes is based on studies undertaken in the countries of the North. The insights and models derived from these, it might be felt, are at best to be treated with caution; at worst they are positively misleading when applied cross-culturally to the education systems of developing countries. Even those studies which are orientated to developing countries' experience are frequently authored by 'first world' nationals writing about countries they have worked in. Critics argue that these accounts are sometimes not recognised as authentic by those the studies claim to speak for, since the authors stand at a distance from contextual nuances.

I believe that one of the challenges for the future is to meet these criticisms. This book tries to begin the process of redressing the balance. Half the contributors are not UK nationals and their research cannot be tainted with a neo-colonial flavour except by a contorted leap of the imagination. Hopefully the UK-based contributors are not susceptible to this either, since we have tried to develop a strong tradition at Sussex of working cross-culturally with, rather than on, developing country education systems.

THE COLLECTION

This collection has a special character that differentiates it from other case study collections and the evaluative project reports produced by stakeholders in particular innovations. All the accounts included are the product of individual researchers working over sustained periods of up to four years – far longer than is normal for contract research and evaluation. All have spent long periods in the field working closely with informants. This lends a depth of penetration that is unusual. The authors have a strong claim to be able to provide disinterested critiques and insights not conditioned directly by operational involvement in the objects of study. Of course, intensive research brings its own involvement and interaction with the parts of systems under study, especially where, for example, action research methods have been chosen. But none of the contributors were working with relationships to sponsors that might strongly influence the nature of their analysis. This sets them apart from much of the existing literature based on studies of innovation and change related to development.

Having explained what this book is and how it came about, it is important to indicate what it is not. It does not try to present a single coherent theoretical perspective on education and development. It is a view shared by the authors that the search for such an overarching theory is an elusive chimera. Since the 1970s, when the general debate on education and development reached its zenith, it has become much clearer that the developing countries are not a simple homogeneous grouping. They cannot all be referred to in the same breath as if they had common structural features, shared colonial experiences, similar educational and cultural traditions, and convergent expectations of the roles that education can play in contributing to development. The chapters in this book make this clear. The Chinese educational system is the polar opposite to that of the Seychelles in terms of size. The resourcing constraints on innovation in Malaysia are a world apart from those in Nigeria or the Sudan. For those unconvinced that developing countries have such important differentiating characteristics three recent books on development highlight how the room to manoeuvre in education policy, as in other fields, is conditioned by very different features in different countries (Seers 1983, Lewin 1987a, Toye 1987).

This book is also not a book on research methods for intending researchers. Elsewhere I and other colleagues have written accounts bearing on the process of educational research undertaken in several developing countries (Vulliamy, Lewin and Stephens 1990). This, we hope, contributes to the beginnings of a literature which addresses some of the specific problems confronting the intending researcher in developing countries. We hope also that it can serve as the stimulus for more accounts by nationals of research practice and problems that can be made more widely available and which will provoke a debate about the universality or cultural and contextual specificity of methods of enquiry and research strategies.

The case studies do represent a range of approaches. Several have used illuminative (Parlett and Hamilton 1977) and responsive (Guba and Lincoln 1981) approaches to evaluation. One is an action research study (McNiff 1988). Some have used more systems-orientated frames of reference (Havelock and Huberman 1977), others have more of the flavour of ethnographic accounts (Woods 1986). All utilise both quantitative and qualitative data collection and interpretation. Techniques for enquiry have been chosen that reflect the nature of the research problems identified by the authors. Thus there is no doctrinaire attachment across the case studies to a particular research paradigm (such as positivist or interpretive), or to particular data collection methods (survey methods, questionnaires, interviews, observational techniques). Rather, choices have been made based on those techniques that seem most promising and feasible in exploring particular questions.

If there has been an overriding concern across the studies it has been to attempt to ground research questions in those things that are thought important by different actors in the education systems studied and thus strike a balance between emic and etic concerns. All the researchers have taken pains to explore the perceptions of those they researched and to use these as an important input to define research questions, rather than prescriptively deciding what questions should be explored at the outset of the research without reference to the concerns of actors involved. Equally all contributors have attributed significance to the wider literature which bears on the issues that they pursue and to their own predilections in identifying research questions.

None of the research reported here would have been possible without several kinds of support. First the sponsors of the authors, which range from governments and donor agencies to the families of individual researchers, should be commended on their generosity. Second, many faculty at Sussex have contributed ideas in different ways to the development of the studies. Non-academic staff have kept the wheels of the production process oiled. Third, my co-editor Janet Stuart has worked tirelessly editing copy and helping to finalise the manuscript in its present form. Fourth, and perhaps most importantly in a period when it is becoming more difficult to protect academic freedoms, recognition is due to the contributors who have had the courage to search out insights that may not always be palatable to particular interest groups. This collection owes everything to their efforts, perception and hard work in persisting with the difficult task of completing a substantial piece of research.

A continued commitment to open, sensitive and rigorous research and debate on innovation in education in the context of development is a high ideal. It is one that is essential to effective future policy-making and attempts at planned change that take as a starting point what *is*, and not what *ought* to be.

Keith M. Lewin
Hove

1 Changemakers and Change Models: Educational Innovation in Developing Countries

Keith M. Lewin

This book takes up the challenges to understanding presented by attempts at planned change. It examines those who plan change, the changemakers, the assumptions and models that help interpret their practices; and some of the most important effects of what they do. In a postscript some structuring ideas and commentary are provided to make links between the case studies and two areas of theoretical debate – the literature on innovation and that on education and development. These accounts deliberately stop short of offering a comprehensive development of ideas, to keep them more accessible to the non-specialist reader, and to allow the case studies to speak for themselves. If these tentative observations provoke debate and provide some of the intellectual yeast to stimulate deeper reflection on the significance of the case studies they will have served their purpose.

Chapter 1 has three parts. First, it has a preamble that introduces the case studies and explores the reasons for undertaking them. Second, a discussion of value issues is included because any discourse with an evaluative flavour involves values. Third, a paradox is presented that those involved in attempts at planned change in developing countries might like to consider as they read the case studies.

PREAMBLE

The eight case studies presented fall loosely into four groups. These are: curriculum reform within a subject area; innovations to support change amongst teachers; the institutional contexts of change; innovation at the whole system level.

The first group focuses on the introduction of a new geography curriculum in China and on the development of new provisions for science education in Kano State, Nigeria. Leung Yat-ming traces the development of thinking at the national level that led to the implementation of a geography curriculum throughout China in the 1980s. From fieldwork data he is able to explore the curriculum in action in selected sites and arrive at judgements about the effectiveness of its development and its impact on teaching and learning. Abdalla Uba Adamu charts the origins of the special Science Schools in Kano State, the development and new characteristics of the curriculum that they offer, and assesses the impact of two phases of their development on science education and on the supply of qualified personnel indigenous to Kano State.

The second case study group contains two very different approaches to the promotion of changes in teaching methods in support of curricula goals. Noor Azmi offers an account of the inservice training programme mounted to accompany the introduction of a new national primary school curriculum (KBSR) in Malaysia. This analyses the form and content of the training provided, empirically accumulates different perspectives on particular inservice courses, and follows up trainees into schools to assess the value of the support given to teachers in adopting new teaching methods. In contrast, Janet Stuart mobilises the techniques of action research to work very closely with a group of development studies teachers in Lesotho as a process helper. One of her major objectives in this was to facilitate the conditions under which teachers could assess their own practice in their own terms, experiment collaboratively with innovations new to them, and evaluate the effectiveness of these.

The third group is concerned with the institutional contexts in which change takes place. Fiona Leach's case studies concentrate on the interrelationships between expatriate and national staff in donor-financed projects in the Sudan. This provides new insights into an under-researched area where often casual empiricism is all that informs debate. She traces the operational characteristics of three projects. Her analysis explores the staff perceptions of key constructs, such as those concerned with the socio-cultural dimensions of working relationships, consultation and decision-making, and organisational style. This offers observations on a dimension of planned change which bears centrally on judgements of the success or failure of the projects. Baboucarr Sarr's work on the institutional climate for reform in The Gambia illustrates some of the gulf between policy and practice in developing and sustaining two types of secondary schooling. Despite a long record of attempts at reform the resilient tradition and prestige associated with the academic high schools seems to have precluded movement towards goals identified as desirable. In contrast, the secondary technical school studied illustrates the power of resource constraints, prevalent conventions, and ambiguous goals to limit effective innovation.

The last group of studies are directed towards two system level reforms. Florence Nwakoby takes on the task of appraising the introduction of the new Junior Secondary School (JSS) curriculum in Anambra State in Nigeria. The case study reported here is restricted to the vocationalised aspect of this system level innovation. In it Nwakoby portrays the pitfalls of the implementation process and gives vivid accounts of how its demands overstretched the capacity of infrastructure available to support it. The consequences of this become clear from her school level data on the curriculum in action. Ian Haffenden's work concludes the book with his analysis of aspects of the National Youth Service (NYS) in the Seychelles. System level reform came about in the Seychelles as a result of new political alignments which saw the restructuring of the education system along socialist lines as a central policy priority. The small system, with its relatively well-resourced base and short communication channels, provides a contrast to the Nigerian case study. Haffenden's work therefore highlights some of the problems that arose from other sources, and echoes some of the earlier contributions in its analysis of the social dynamics of the development of the NYS.

There are five reasons why the case studies presented here are timely. First, the literature on educational innovation in developing countries is beginning to mature. The long and extensive history of the study of innovation in general and educational innovation in particular originating in the experience of industrialised countries is being complemented by accessible material based on the experience of developing countries.

Several of the contributors to this book break new ground. Leung contributes the first case study we are aware of which focuses on curriculum development and implementation in the People's Republic of China. This he argues is part of the 'third generation' of studies on China that probe directly into policy-making processes. Stuart's study of Lesotho teachers is one of very few examples of attempts to employ action research techniques to educational innovation in an

African country. Leach's analysis of perception gaps between expatriates and local staff offers new insight into the human relations of development projects. Sarr's work is the first of its kind to attempt to explore institutional climates in two types of secondary school in The Gambia. Haffenden's Seychelles study explores system innovation in a small socialist state which has few parallels, with the possible exception of work on Grenada.

The other case studies offer equally interesting food for thought through their illumination of attempts to innovate and their consequences which are grounded in empirical evidence from the field. Adamu's study in Kano State shows how the advocates and critics of the new Science Schools he researched did not base their arguments on evidence or a detailed consideration of curricula proposals. Their casual empiricism allowed decision-making to proceed without any grounded theory behind it. Noor Azmi's study illustrates how difficult it is for systems to learn from experience, in his case study concerned with organising inservice courses for teachers to support the new Malaysian primary school curriculum (KBSR). Nwakoby's analysis in Anambra State is a perceptive and independently undertaken account of a major system level change, drawing attention to the gulf between intention and reality.

Second, effective educational innovation has, if anything, become an even more difficult problem than in the past in many developing countries. The 'World Educational Crisis' identified by Coombs in 1968 has not been resolved, by Coombs' own account (Coombs 1985) as well as those of others. The problems of static or diminishing resources available to meet expanding demand have been exacerbated by economic recession, growing debt and by a policy-making climate that favours reductions in public sector spending (Lewin 1987a) and 'cost recovery' through the charging of fees (Lewin and Berstecher 1989). The apparent 'failure' attributed to many educational innovations has accumulated, causing some loss of confidence and ambiguity towards further attempts at change. The conservatism that this has evoked looks backwards rather than forwards for solutions and, arguably, can result in the identification of policy options that analysis suggests are the cause of present problems rather than their result.

Amongst the case study countries Sudan, Nigeria, The Gambia and Lesotho all have economic problems of varying severity that restrict the resources available for innovation to very low levels. Other countries have avoided the worst effects of recession on public sector investment in the social sector; however, cuts in expenditure were a reality in the mid-1980s in Malaysia, and the Seychelles economy has always been vulnerable to the vagaries of the world market, where small events can have a disproportionate impact on demand, be it for spices or package holidays. China's education system has historically been resourced at levels below those of most other countries (in relation to the proportion of GNP allocated), and its relative efficiency is all the more remarkable for this.

Third, the climate for educational research related to policy in some countries has not been improving. Resource availability plays its part in this. In addition, though it is difficult to find evidence for this except through individual examples, academic freedom, research funding, and research approval have arguably become subject to more rather than less restriction. Many decision-making systems have become more politicised; the power of professionals and their influence has been eroded. Research which uncovers the unpalatable may be seen as embarrassing and inconvenient to those who take the ideological high ground and seek to manipulate evidence and opinion for ends unrelated to the fruits of rigorous analysis. A major defence of 'open societies' (Popper 1966) against prejudice, manipulation, self-serving decision-making, and the tyranny of factionalism, is the free flow of information and disinterested analysis of events. It is to this that the academic world can contribute.

Fourth, much has been made of the apparent failure of educational innovations to deliver the developmental benefits promised in their initiation. Failure in relation to ambitious expectations is seen as no success at all when in reality often much has changed for the better. 'Change without change' (Lewin 1985) fuelled by project cultures and budgetary systems that promote quick fixes, idealistic appraisals of the rate of change sustainable, and exaggerated expectations of the impact of educational change on development problems, are seen by some as evidence of the futility of further innovation. This view needs to be challenged and the successes given as much prominence as the failures; this especially where benefits were not anticipated and may therefore be easily overlooked in narrowly-focused evaluations.

In all the case studies here changes have occurred as a result of the efforts to innovate. Not all those identified coincide with those planned. The Chinese case study shows that geography has been resurrected in the curriculum, though in ways that fall short of many of the original expectations. Surface adoption rather than implementation seems to have characterised the process. A central concern for 'fidelity' of implementation seems to clash with the apparent need for 'mutual adaptation' to reflect the different client groups and circumstances of use (Fullan 1982, Marsh and Huberman 1984) and there seem some parallels with developments in other curriculum areas, for example science (Lewin 1987b). Nwakoby and Adamu both show how in Nigeria real changes have taken place. In the first case vocationalised elements of the Junior Secondary programme are operating in recognisable form in some schools; in the second the original group of Science Schools seem to have produced outcomes in line with some of the expectations for them. Stuart's work shows how real changes can be promoted which affect classroom practice, albeit in circumstances that are small-scale and relatively resource-intensive. Her success in catalysing action research seems to have paid dividends and to have left a legacy on which to build.

Leach's study indicates that success is relative to the expectations of different groups. Task cultures create different expectations to role cultures and the tension between these is often at the heart of problems arising between expatriates in transient technical cooperation posts and those in permanent bureaucratic employment. Confusion and conflict of purposes is apparent from Sarr's study. This appears at least part of the explanation for the lack of change that he observes. The institution of the NYS in the Seychelles continues eight years after its founding. It has changed its form and the study shows that the radical curricular innovations proposed did not all survive. But enough of them have done so for the NYS to retain a distinctive identity which breaks with past patterns and seems to offer a genuine alternative to the previous system.

Fifth, whatever the record of success and failure, the fact remains that most developing countries allocate the largest or second largest shares of public expenditure to educational provision directly and indirectly. Requests for educational services are overwhelming and growing in all the countries in which the case studies were completed. Changes in the global economy and the development of new technology stimulate educational change to reflect changes in the environment in which development takes place (Lewin 1988b, Lewin 1989). Effective demand is stronger than for most other things amongst rich and poor alike. All the more important then that the quality of what is delivered and the processes through which this is improved are understood. The case studies contribute to this end.

A NOTE ON VALUES

At the outset we need to remind ourselves that development is a process of change. The consequences of change will always be open to controversy since judgement of both ends and means involves values that will differ as a result of ideology, culture and the aspirations and responsibilities of those who express them. Changes in social systems, in which educational provision is embedded, are not wholly rational or predictable, as those involved know only too well. Many interests have to be balanced, mobilised and reconciled. In the process meanings are renegotiated and purposes modified to reflect and promote outcomes that are durable and represent real rather than cosmetic changes. How these case studies are received will therefore depend on value positions taken in relation to the wider debate on education and development, some aspects of which are treated in the postscript.

The editors of the book take a view of effective educational change that is *client-centred, purposive* and *evolutionary*. The flavour of the case studies suggests that this is shared by most of the contributors. Our basic value stance is that change is for the benefit of the clients of education systems (students, parents, employers, communities) and those who work in them (teachers, administrators, planners and policy-makers). Our judgement of the research literature, including that reviewed here, is that the weight of evidence on effective change supports the view that innovations where consultation with clients is marginalised and their interests and motivations are not recognised rarely lead to durable change which is recognised positively by clients. This does not imply commitment to a particular form of organisation of education systems – for example we hold the view that decentralised structures are not necessarily the most appropriate ways of ensuring client-centred innovation. But we are orientated towards democratic traditions that value participation, consultation and negotiation of meanings rather than prescription, autocracy and imposition of solutions to problems that are not grounded in the needs of clients.

Our view of change as purposive is at the core of the rationale for studies of educational innovation of this kind. It might be possible to study change as a purely responsive phenomenon, and to describe the development of systems from this perspective. But our interest in change, and that of the professionals with whom we are trying to share experiences, is to learn more of the process in order that future attempts can build on the experience of the past. Managing *planned* change is a central concern of those concerned with quantitative and qualitative improvements in the education systems in developing countries. The price of failure may be higher and the rewards of success greater than in well-resourced systems that can provide many highly differentiated pathways to satisfy the needs of the communities and individuals that they serve. Purposive change is the goal of policy-making systems and the source of professional satisfaction to educators, whether it be concerned with individual learning, the development of effective schools, or in enhancing the contribution of schooling systems to national development needs.

Evolutionary change we take to mean change built on and beyond existing practices, values and needs perceived by clients. Revolutionary change, in contrast, we characterise as breaking dramatically with the past and representing fundamental reappraisals of social relations well beyond those embedded in education systems. Revolutions may, of course, be of the political right or of the political left. Some of the problems that the case studies address are not simply those of educational change but are deep-rooted in political and socio-economic structures that arguably have to change before meaningful educational innovation is possible. Some of the innovations studied have taken place in conspicuously post-revolutionary environments – the Seychelles and China.

Recognising evolutionary change, rather than revolutionary change, may imply to some that we do not have the courage of our convictions that far-reaching socio-economic changes are both desirable and necessary. There are four answers to that. Firstly, to take an evolutionary stance is not to abandon radicalism. Indeed, radical change may sometimes best be achieved by small-scale demonstration of its benefits to encourage more widespread voluntary adoption.

Second, revolutionary change strategies have within them the seeds of a contradiction. If they succeed they must confront future development in an evolutionary way or seek to 'renew' the revolution through sporadic upheavals that, by definition, challenge their original premises. The least attractive outcome is that of the ossification of revolutionary rhetoric and attachment to structures which outlive their original usefulness.

Third, education systems are complex social systems which have considerable inertia and do not respond to the stroke of the policy-maker's pen in ways which some other arms of government might do.

Examples are legion of attempts at fundamental change, neutralised
at the level of implementation, where the interests of their progenitors are not shared, or are actively opposed, by those with the power
to change educational practice at the point it is delivered. The case
studies provide yet more examples of these. Educational systems are
people systems where participation in most of what is valued is
voluntary. Their effective operation and changes in practice are the
result of the motivations, enthusiasms and commitment of their
members. These are unlikely to respond to revolutionary initiatives
unless these build on existing aspirations and offer solutions to
teaching and learning problems that are recognisable and feasible
from the perspective of existing practitioners.

Finally we take an evolutionary view of change for pragmatic
reasons. In many of the countries from which the case studies are
drawn stability and continuity of educational provision cannot be
taken for granted. Exogenous factors – political alignments, the
development of new technologies, terms of trade and global economic recession – all have unpredictable knock-on effects on education.
Indigenous factors – population growth and distribution, the competition for jobs, the enhancement of national identity through new
curricula – fluctuate in their impact on policy. Both affect the *ability*
and *willingness* to support educational provision (Lewin 1987a).
Evolutionary change strategies that build on what exists, however
inadequate it may seem, have the prospect of reaching out to those
parts of the system where needs are most acute, a basis for action
already exists, and consolidation can take advantage of continuity
with established practice. The history of development shows the
importance of stability to a degree which is independent of its
political complexion.

THE PLANNER'S PARADOX

Planners are not renowned for their humour. They are often the butt
of blame for failed innovations since somehow 'they did not get it
right' and overlooked what in retrospect proved to be the key factors
that undermined attempts at change. Their business, it could be wryly
observed, substitutes *error* for *risk*. With no plan there is simply the
risk of judgement. With a plan there is a probability of being wrong.
Planners are usually subordinate to politicians. As was said of a
former US President, he took full responsibility but not the blame for

the events that ultimately led to his demise. The blame fell on his subordinates. Hence, perhaps, the unhappy lot of the planner.

A theme that runs through many of the case studies that is worth formalising concerns a paradox of attempts to innovate and this is the serious point to be made. The planner's paradox created by change can be stated very simply: it is that innovation is needed in education systems which fail to deliver equitably an acceptable quality of service. Innovation is disruptive, resource-consuming, and unevenly implemented. As a result it is likely to adversely affect the equitable delivery of a service at an acceptable level of quality.

There are some parallels here with the economic theory of the second-best (Toye 1987). The introduction of policy measures designed to improve a particular state of affairs may actually result in less net benefit than would no action at all. This is partly because the impact of changes on a particular group may be positive, but may be adverse when a population as a whole is considered. There may be some cases where it is better to do nothing than the policy measures taken.

There are often many good reasons advanced to support innovations to improve access and quality in education. High rates of change can, however, penalise those parts of the system that most need its benefits. In many educational systems in developing countries the losers in the change process are those clients on the margins of the existing system. Rural children and teachers in isolated, under-resourced, and neglected schools, with many unqualified teachers and little access to information, are those least prepared for change. This is interpreted by some as rural 'conservatism'. In reality it may be ignorance of alternatives and lack of understanding of the purposes the changes are directed to. These are linked to lack of capability and confidence in implementing change. High rates of change in these systems are disruptive of fragile delivery systems that at best succeed in enrolling most children for most of the time and make as much use as they can of whatever teachers are available.

The need for system maintenance at the most basic level can be overlooked in the flood of enthusiasm that often accompanies innovations and siphons off the most capable administrators and educators to more exciting pastures. If the concern of the innovator is to improve the quality of an educational service to those most disadvantaged by existing structures, the larger and more frequent the innovations the less the infrastructure in place will be able to cope. This argues in favour of evolutionary approaches with continuity and sensitive phasing sympathetic to the absorptive capacity of institutions and individuals for change.

There is evidence for all these propositions in the case studies which draw further attention to this planner's paradox. In China attempts to re-establish geography have apparently benefited parts of the Keypoint School system where implementation has occurred in a form close to that intended. But this has to be balanced by the evidence from more typical schools where implementation has been partial and has created new difficulties. The initial reaction to the proposal of Secondary Science Schools in Kano State from the Ministry of Education was negative. The schools were seen to detract from the maintenance and improvement of science education in the system as a whole. It may be that their short-term impact has had such negative consequences. In a somewhat contradictory development it seems that the success the schools have had quantitatively has not been matched by the qualitative changes in teaching and learning that were seen as an essential feature of the schools. Taking a broader brush Nwakoby's work shows that the vocationalised aspects of the Junior Secondary School (JSS) restructuring only affected a minority of the schools. The planner's paradox seems to apply here since considerable disruption and unclear conceptualisation, lack of co-ordination between parts of the Ministry, and the poor level of preparation of teachers for change, combined to create a climate of uncertainty amongst teachers about what to do and how to do it. It is not necessary to fall into the innovator's trap of paralysis by analysis, to infer that so little analysis of need and capacity was undertaken that the infrastructure would collapse under the weight of demands made on it.

The Sudanese case studies illustrate how the complexities of human relationships cross-culturally can exacerbate the 'organisational pain' of innovation. Conflicting expectations and aspirations, and the goal displacement that occurs in organisations under stress, led in some of the projects to worsening of performance and, for various reasons, the frustration of all involved. The Gambian case shows how attempts to innovate may have at least temporarily disadvantaged some of those that they were designed to help. The plight of the below-average enrolled into the high schoool whose needs are subordinated to those likely to be successful in examinations shows this. So also does the under-resourcing of the secondary technical school which compromises its effectiveness. Initial reactions to the NYS show that some established groups felt that their interests were being directly threatened. Performance in the new system was inferior, as measured by the examination-orientated criteria of the old system. But this misses the point that it was designed with radically different outcomes in mind. Initial problems with staffing and management do seem to have adversely affected progress towards the goals established for the NYS, but stability now seems to be allowing some of the benefits to take root.

Noor Azmi's study illustrates a slightly different type of paradox. In order to support implementation it was necessary for key personnel to be identified to organise inservice courses. Because KBSR and its teaching methods were new, few trainers had direct experience of integration, flexibly organising activities, using group work and so on. A consequence of the insecurity some trainers felt in presenting the new pedagogy and curriculum without active experience of it was that KBSR inservice sessions involved a lot of formal lecturing and information giving. In the eyes of a significant number of participants this exposed the limitations of the key personnel and undermined their credibility and effectiveness as change agents.

Stuart's study illustrates an exception to the paradox. The changes her group introduced on the basis of reappraisal of their own practice were apparently valued and effective. They were not disruptive, partly because they were small-scale and at the level of the classroom. But they did involve significant personal costs in time and effort to those involved and depended on a sense of professionality to lead to the levels of commitment necessary. This may be one way forward, though it must be remembered that the teachers were a self-selected group who were prepared to live through the uncertainty and short-term inefficiencies of adopting and evaluating new practices, some of which had to be abandoned.

To suggest that there is a planner's paradox is deliberately provocative. The idea is unsettling to those who see planned change as basically a technical problem where difficulties can be resolved by sufficient control over all the variables that are thought to be salient. It suggests not only that innovations intended to make things better may make things worse, but also that in some circumstances this is a necessary short-term cost that should be weighed alongside others. One purpose of injecting this into the debate on planned change is precisely to retain a focus on the needs of the most vulnerable groups as a whole, rather than those segments identified as the target group of special intervention programmes which are transient and often not generalisable. The valuing of the vulnerable (Lewin 1988c) that this implies resurrects a very respectable tradition in development planning, variously identified as a basic needs approach, poverty-focused planning, or redistribution with growth, and neatly captured in the title of a recent book in development studies – *Rural Development: Putting the Last First* (Chambers 1983).

A further observation gives insight into why it has become increasingly difficult to avoid the short-term consequences of the planner's paradox for the marginalised. It can be illustrated by a remark made at a recent conference. The suggestion was made that in the current economic climate in the United Kingdom, assessment items of the kind, 'If a farmer has 150 chickens that lay on average one egg every 30 hours, the cost of food grain is 150p for 1Kg, chickens consume 250g a day, and overheads on a chicken shed are £100 a month, what is the cost of an egg?' are likely to be answered with the riposte 'Buying or selling?'. Market indicators, it is implied, are the best if not the only criteria for allocating scarce resources. But markets only function well if they do not suffer serious distortions and if real choices are available – unrealistic conditions in many educational systems. For most educational innovations, in any case, valued outcomes cannot be simply reduced to cost-benefit equations. And those without purchasing power are those most likely to be excluded from the educational market place.

Finally, we may note another aspect of the paradox. Decisions have to be made without the availability of enough information to allow a rational choice between options to be made, and before the effects of previous decisions can be assessed. Innovations may then build on bedrock which is the sand of previously unimplemented change. Worse, they may result in unintended consequences which are unrecognised, since these mature over a period longer than that available to collect data on their effects. An extreme form of this situation can be characterised as 'crisis management'. The compulsion of today's problems drives out consideration of medium-term strategies. It thus precipitates tomorrow's crisis and so on, *ad infinitum*, and changes the social psychology of decision-making (Lewin 1987a). This draws attention to a related problem – the lack of phasing between the time cycles of political decision-making and those of educational planners working in large complex systems. Several of the case studies offer evidence of the consequences of this kind of mismatch.

All this may sound depressing for the intending planner of change. On the down-side some solace can be taken from a poster that has graced our building at Sussex for many years, which shows a worried individual peering anxiously from behind a protecting wall and is captioned: 'Just because you are paranoid, it does not mean that they are not watching you'. This neatly encapsulates the double bind of the planner, caught within the expectations of rational strategies for planned change which depend on assumptions that do not hold in the real world of educational provision. On a more optimistic note, forewarned of some of the pitfalls is forearmed. If these case studies enrich our understanding of the processes at work they will enhance the capacity to plan, develop and implement educational innovations more effectively in the future. The scene is now set for the reader to digest the contributions and judge whether the claims made for the collection serve this purpose. Like the innovators we describe, we *risk* failure but we have not made an *error* in trying.

Part I
Curriculum Innovations

These two chapters deal with different aspects and types of curriculum innovation in two very different contexts: China and Nigeria. Yet there are interesting similarities. Both show, though in different ways, the interweaving of political with educational issues; both demonstrate how the problems of implementation – of resources, teacher qualifications and attitudes – can prevent the intentions of curriculum developers from penetrating to the classroom.

Leung Yat-ming's study concerns the huge unwieldly education system of the People's Republic of China, where the national style of curriculum development is centralised and power-coercive. He describes the changes that took place after the end of the Cultural Revolution and how Deng Xiaoping, in attaining power, focused attention on the need for modernisation, a central element of which was modernisation of the curriculum.

Leung takes as an example the new Geography Curriculum for the Senior Middle Schools, showing how it was designed and put into action. He details the struggles among the various interest groups such as politicians, academics, bureaucrats, teacher educators and curriculum developers, each with varying backgrounds and orientations, before a syllabus was agreed and textbooks produced. He then shows how although the curriculum was 'adopted' for immediate use in schools, in most places it could not be 'implemented' in the sense of altering practice in the classroom because of critical barriers, such as the lack of clarity about the planned changes, the mismatch between the developers' intentions and school realities, the backwash effects of public exams, and the shortage of geography teachers.

Abdalla Adamu's study concerns innovation in a much smaller political unit – Kano State in the north of Nigeria, with its population of ten million compared to China's billion people. Yet similar concerns about the need to produce indigenous manpower trained for development led to the establishment of special 'Science Schools' to produce doctors, engineers and scientists. Interestingly this was at first a purely political decision; indeed, the educational bureaucracy opposed it and only the fortuitous move of a powerful Commissioner from Economic Planning to Education enabled the project to go ahead. It was not until eight years later that the educationists, independently of the Science Schools Project, produced a new science curriculum geared to helping students to understand scientific processes, with the aim of assisting in the socio-economic transformation of society.

Adamu details the processes by which the decision to set up the schools was taken, and the kinds of opposition it faced. He then examines how far these schools were, at a later stage, able to implement the practical 'process' approach to teaching and learning recommended by the new science curriculum. He found that even though so much investment of resources and personnel had gone into these Science Schools, the teaching remained didactic and abstract, apparently due to shortages of equipment as well as to the experiences and attitudes of the teachers. He concludes that although the Science Schools Project was producing more science graduates who could pass exam hurdles and go on to higher education, thus providing a potential indigenous manpower pool, the quality of these graduates might be questioned; there was little evidence at classroom level of changes in students' understanding of science and it was not clear how far development processes were being helped by such training.

Both these studies use an 'illuminative evaluation' framework to study the changes through the perceptions of the actors involved. Interviews were extensively used, and both authors observed classrooms as a counterpoint to the views of teachers and bureaucrats, though neither were able to collect students' perceptions.

The studies both show how curriculum development was being strongly influenced by convictions about the role of science and technology in the modernisation process and how the education system could be used to produce the scientifically trained cadres necessary to play leading roles in development. Both indicate the importance of a strong lead from the top, and how a change of personnel in even one crucial role can alter the direction of innovation. Both identify the limitations that mediate the translation of planned changes at the system level into new practices at the level of the classroom.

2 Modernising the Geography Curriculum in Post-1976 China

Julian Leung Yat-ming

INTRODUCTION: RATIONALE AND METHODS

Rationale for the Case Study

1976 was a watershed in the history of the People's Republic of China (hereafter called China). After the death of Mao Zedong and the downfall of the 'Gang of Four', the new Chinese leadership gradually abandoned the ultra-leftist policy of 'permanent revolution' (*buduan geming*) and shifted its attention to achieving the four modernisations (*sege xiandaihua*) of China – a set of vague development goals grouped as the comprehensive modernisation of agriculture, industry, national defence and science and technology. A growth-oriented national development goal was put forward by Deng Xiaoping which, in operational terms, aimed at reaching a per capita GNP of $US800 by the year 2000.

The Chinese leadership conceived of China as being still in the stage of 'underdeveloped socialism' (Su and Feng 1979) and falling 20 years behind the world's most advanced countries in science and technology. The 'Ten Years Cultural Revolution' (*shi nian wen ge*) had deprived one million qualified senior middle school graduates of higher education opportunities and China was in need of 800 000 qualified manpower (*rencai*) at all levels to launch the initial modernisation programmes (Liu 1980). The Chinese leaders placed high expectations on the contribution that educational expansion and curriculum innovations could make in overcoming manpower shortages and enabling the nation to catch up with the advanced countries.

Vigorous curriculum development activities took place in China between 1979 and 1983. It was reported (*Xinhua News*, 4 October 1984) that Deng Xiaoping ordered the Ministry of Education to organisé several hundred experts and scholars from different fields to update primary and secondary textbooks by making reference to

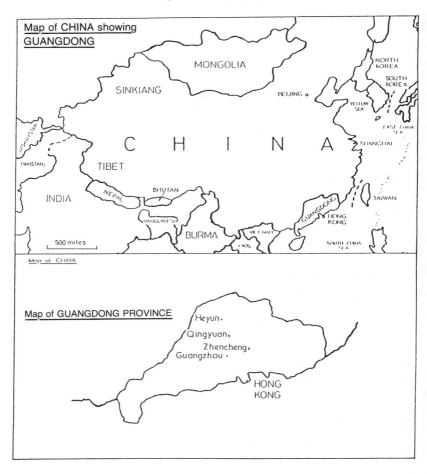

imported foreign textbooks. The purpose was to enable Chinese pupils to master quickly the newest scientific knowledge for China's modernisation needs. The policy of borrowing advanced foreign knowledge for China's benefit was in line with the principle of 'using foreign things to serve China' (*yang wei zhong yong*) put forth by Chinese modernisers ever since the humiliating 'opening' of China to foreign occupation in 1840.

Such a goal-directed approach to curriculum development and modernisation typically is similar to practice in other countries where a pressing need has been identified to reorientate the school curriculum to the needs and aspirations of national development (Pilder

1968, Kelly 1975). In the developing countries, Woodhouse (1984) succinctly argues that:

> the newly-founded sovereign state requires both loyalty and modernisation of the agrarian economy, thus national consciousness and identity, combined with scientific technological development, are to be developed by means of education. The curriculum reflects both of these aims in bringing about the required change in society at large.

The experience has been that there is always a gap between the large scale, top-down curriculum development initiatives at the central level and implementation outcomes at the grassroots of the school system. The 'change without change' and 'intention becoming façade' syndromes of curriculum innovation (Lewin 1981, Crossley 1984, Morris 1985, Guthrie 1986) described in the experiences of other countries are also recognised in post-1976 China. For example, after 1976 English was made a major second language and all school children were officially encouraged to learn English in the 'whole country learns English' (*guan min xue ying yu*) campaign. But most schools, especially those in the countryside, could not actually offer English due to the lack of qualified English teachers. Many other subjects also remained non-implemented or cosmetically implemented after 1976 because of the lack of supporting resources, for example, laboratory equipment, wall charts and even the required textbooks. Moreover, it was later acknowledged by the Ministry of Education that mathematics, chemistry and physics were too academically and theoretically oriented and that watered-down versions had to be produced to meet the ability level of most pupils (Ma Li 1985). The overall relevance of the school curriculum to the majority of rural children was also questioned by educators and local community leaders (He 1985, Wang 1986).

It is exactly this 'intention becoming façade syndrome' of curriculum innovation that stimulated the inquiry of this study. It is hypothesised that the pattern of rhetoric and the lack of impact of curriculum change in post-1976 China resulted from her national style of curriculum development. Specifically two factors operated to undermine the achievement of the new intentions for the curriculum. First, the highly centralised political system, together with its strong element of personality cult (of Deng Xiaoping), led to a power-coercive approach to curriculum innovation, resulting in the hurried production of highly academic and monolithic school curricula that lacked flexibility and relevance to meet the wide variations in conditions in different parts of the country. Second, the process of curriculum innovation was contentious because the educational objectives and strategies identified as essential for achieving modernisation goals through the curriculum were interpreted differently by different stakeholders. This made the redefinition of school subjects highly controversial in practice. Furthermore, different school subjects scrambled for status and resources (time allocation, examination emphasis and so on) in competition with each other. As a result, the end-product of this politicised process of curriculum change was limited in its impact and failed to take into account the realities of implementation in typical, rather than exceptional, school environments.

Nature and Worth of the Case Study

This study seeks to verify the diagnosis offered above by investigating, through case study methods, the development and implementation of the Senior Middle School Geography Curriculum (SMSGC). The key research question was:

> How was the SMSGC, as a typical example of post-1976 curriculum innovation in China, designed and developed to correspond to the nation's development goals and to what extent do curriculum intentions and implementation realities match?

The key research question was refined into five subsidiary questions, namely:

(a) What roles were assigned to education development and curriculum development for meeting the national leaders' interpretation of national development goals of China after 1976?
(b) What strategy of curriculum development was used?
(c) What factors influenced various stakeholders during the innovation process which eventually shaped key features of SMSGC at the design stage?
(d) How was the SMSGC transacted in the school system and how was it perceived by its users?
(e) What factors can be identified to account for the mismatch between curriculum intentions held by curriculum innovators and the actual implementation of the SMSGC?

This study is a policy analysis of a curriculum innovation (SMSGC) that reflects the change of educational and curriculum policy in China after 1976. In the literature there is so far no study that analyses in detail a specific curriculum innovation process in the People's Republic of China and links it up with implementation problems. This contrasts sharply with a rich international literature that investigates the styles and processes by which different educational systems have promoted curriculum innovation, dissemination and implementation (OECD/CERI 1972, APEID 1976, Berman and McLaughlin 1976, 1979, Becher and MaClure 1978, Watson 1979). This study is based on a first-hand and in-depth research hoping to fill in a blank area of curriculum development research by revealing the 'blackbox' of curriculum innovation processes in China. It is influenced by the belief that 'reform and innovation should be viewed by examining the complex, economic, political and social forces and processes through which they are generated, adopted and implemented' (Papagiannis 1982). It falls into what Harding (1984) calls the 'third generation of Chinese political studies' which is characterised by the possibility of probing into Chinese policy processes directly.

The study is an *ex post facto* one. It investigates retrospectively how the SMSGC was designed and put into action in 1982. It tries to trace the rationales and socio-political forces behind the stability and change of middle school geography education in China, with particular emphasis on the period 1979–82 during which the SMSGC was revived. This kind of research into the history of school subjects is typified by the works of curriculum historians like Waring (1979), Stenhouse (1980), Lewin (1981), Ball (1982), Goodson (1983), Cooper (1984), Lillis (1984, 1985) and Reid (1986), all of whom take views consistent with Lillis that:

> the complex interrelationships among the actors involved, the processes of adoption and development, the nature of the curriculum content, and the nature of the infrastructure are important determinants of the nature of the change process.
>
> (Lillis 1985: 96)

This study leans towards an illuminative case study which focuses on the description and interpretation of a curriculum innovation in a very specific context of time and place, rather than on measurement and judgement of implementation results. It is an account of what has happened (the innovation process) and what is happening in some selected sites of the school system into which the SMSGC has been introduced.

Major findings of this study indicate the generalisability of selected curriculum theories across cultural and socio-political systems. Data collected in the study will be interpreted and discussed in the light of a collection of rich yet conflicting views of curriculum innovation mostly derived from research conducted in non-communist systems, both in developed and developing countries. In this respect this analysis will enrich the scope of comparative curriculum studies.

Research Design and Methods

A pragmatic multiple-methods approach was adopted for this study. Research methods were chosen upon the basis that they best addressed the following research focuses:

(a) the reformulation of educational and curriculum goals in post-1976 China;
(b) the innovation process of SMSGC;
(c) intrinsic features of SMSGC;
(d) the implementation and assessment patterns;
(e) the barriers to implementation.

Altogether five major research methods were used, namely:

(a) documentation analysis;
(b) semi-structured interviews and informal discussions;
(c) intrinsic curriculum materials analysis;
(d) field visits to schools;
(e) examination analaysis.

There are two advantages of following this multiple-methods approach. First, it enables the researcher to collect data from a wide range of sources on different aspects of the study. For example, some key actors in the innovation process were first identified in published materials and then targeted for interview. During the interviews more source materials and informants were recommended. Second, it was possible to use triangulation for cross-checking data to ensure higher research reliability and validity. The five methods used were supplementary to each other. For example, analysis of conference papers distributed at important stages of the innovation process filled information gaps caused by informants' fading memory or self-interested interpretation of events. Users' comments on the short-comings of SMSGC were supplemented by intrinsic materials analysis and verified by classroom observations.

Documentation analysis included an intensive search of available primary and secondary source materials related to this study. Primary source materials covered official documents, internally circulated materials, official publications and officially published curriculum materials. Secondary source materials mainly referred to professional and academic publications circulated in China. A wide range of papers and books written by scholars outside China on Chinese education were consulted. In this way viewpoints of both the 'insiders' and 'outsiders' were accommodated.

Eighty-one people were formally interviewed, mostly individually but some in groups, between October 1985 and March 1988. The interviewees comprised officials (15 per cent), professionals (40 per cent), administrators (23 per cent) and teachers (22 per cent). Twenty-three of them were key actors in the innovation and were directly involved in decision making. The others were users. Four types of semi-structured interview questions were asked, namely, information-seeking, perception-seeking, problem-seeking and triangulation questions. They were constructed with reference to a checklist of refined questions developed from a preliminary review of literature available for analysing curriculum innovation and implementation. Before each interview, the key interview questions were sent to the interviewees for their consideration and preparation. This ensured greater efficiency, and more time could be saved for emergent questions arising during the interviews. From a protocol point of view this procedure was also desirable. All interviews were hand-recorded, then fully reconstructed and coded immediately after every interview for cross-referencing. The researcher's participation in a conference on geographical education enabled him to hold informal discussions with over 30 geographers and teachers from different parts of China. This supplemented formal interviews and provided insights into different issues.

Field studies were undertaken in five schools: one urban keypoint[1] middle school in Shanghai, one rural keypoint middle school in Zhenchang Xian (county) in Guangdong Province, one urban non-keypoint school in Guangzhou and two rural non-keypoint middle schools in Qingyuan Xian in Guandong. These schools were chosen to represent an urban/rural and keypoint/non-keypoint cross section of school structures in China. The school visits were aimed at revealing implementation patterns in different school settings and identifying barriers to implementation. The duration of visits ranged from four days to one day, depending on the willingness of the school's authorities to be studied. During these visits, 11 geography classes were observed, and 13 school administrators and 12 geography teachers were interviewed. The Sussex Scheme of Curriculum Materials Analaysis (Eraut *et al.* 1975) was adapted to analyse, quantitatively and qualitatively, the first edition of SMSGC, published in 1980, to illustrate its main intrinsic features and the extent to which curriculum goals were matched by content arrangement. Teaching References of SMSGC published by People's Education Press (PEP) in 1983 were analysed to identify the officially recommended teaching approaches and resource implications. Amendment notices issued by PEP every year between 1980 and 1986, and revised versions of SMSGC were analysed to show the types and rationales of modification made on SMSGC. Data generated from these analyses were then used to verify the users' comments on the SMSGC and implementation problems identified during field visits.

Geography examination papers in the Unified National Higher School Examination (UNHSE) between 1978 and 1986 were analysed to reveal their major characteristics, such as the composition of different types and cognitive levels of questions. These data were matched with official guidelines on examination to disclose the change over time. The negative backwash effects of the NUHSC on the implementation of SMSGC in schools were identified by an analysis of internal examination reports, teachers' comments and field study data.

BACKGROUND AND CONTEXT FOR THE INNOVATION

Education and Modernisation Post 1976: The Conditions of Change

Ball (1987) calls for attention to the conditions of curriculum change – the political and economic context, the ebb and flow of public opinion, which provide both a material frame and social climate for curriculum change. In China, the definition and elaboration of an official ideology as the basis for a claim to legitimacy is very significant in all types of policy changes (Schram 1984). In the context of educational changes, post-1976 China witnessed a controversial debate in which political leaders reinterpreted and redefined the relationship between education and China's modernisation goals in a series of political confrontations. The core of this struggle between the neo-Maoists, led by Chinese Communist Party chairman Hua

Guofeng, and pragmatic modernisers, led by Deng Xiaoping, involved a gradual disposal of Mao Zedong's revolutionary model of education that was based on a dogmatic Marxist 'superstructure' viewpoint of education. According to this the primary role of education was to serve as a powerful tool for consolidating proletariat dictatorship by reproducing citizens loyal to Mao Zedong thought. As Depierre (1987:204) accurately remarks 'the ultimate aim of the Maoist revolution was less the transformation of the world than the transformation of human persons'.

After 1976 the function of education in China's national development was redefined. In the first half of 1977 criminal charges were made against the Gang of Four for ruining Chinese education and purging intellectuals. Deng Xiaoping began to stress the manpower production function of education which had been strongly advocated by modernisation and human capital theorists in the West since the 1960s. After his second return to power in May 1977 Deng started to redefine the function of education in a number of speeches to members of the Central Committee of the Chinese Communist Party. Firstly he put science and technology as the top priority of the four modernisations, saying that 'the key to achieving modernisation is the modernisation of science and technology' (Deng 1977). Secondly, he assigned education a primary role in upgrading China's level of science and technology as a driving force of China's four modernisations and in producing the needed manpower. Thirdly, he proposed an elitist and discriminative approach to manpower production by restoring the meritocratic examination system and the keypoint school system.

At the National Science Conference held in March 1978 Deng Xiaoping stated that scientists served the revolution best by their professional excellence, possibly spending all their time on professional work instead of 'studying stacks of books on political theory, joining in numerous social activities and attending many meetings not related to their work' (Deng 1978a). Deng also wished to open China to Western influences. He advocated better prestige and material rewards for a first class scientific élite that could build up extensive interaction with the international academic community and carry out technological transfer so as to bring China forward into the front ranks of the world. This was bitterly opposed by Hua who was less prepared to accept any dilution of Maoist values. In the closing speech, Hua bluntly refuted Deng's excessive emphasis on professionalism by saying that 'far from being weakened, political and ideological work should be strengthened' (Hua 1978). He also insisted on a populist and nativist approach to modernisation, and called for relying on the united strength of the masses.

Deng Xiaoping also played an overarching role in defining the concept of curriculum modernisation (*kecheng xiandaihua*). In August 1977 he instructed that 'teaching materials are crucial. Teaching materials must reflect the advanced level of modern technology and match the conditions of our country' (quoted in Pu 1985). The central idea of curriculum modernisation was outlined at the National Congress of Education held in April 1978. Deng expounded that:

> if we wish to catch up with the world's advanced level of science and technology, not only must we raise the quality of higher education, we must also raise the quality of middle and primary education. Enrich the contents of middle and primary education with advanced scientific knowledge according to the level of acceptance of pupils (Deng 1978b).

This instruction then became the guideline of curriculum development at all levels of schooling.

In August 1977, Deng instructed the People's Education Press to organise a team of two hundred scholars from tertiary institutions to produce new primary and middle school textbooks for use in the academic year 1978. They used a Beijing hotel as headquarters to finish this blitz task. The team was given $US10 000 to import primary and middle school textbooks from the United States, UK, France, West Germany and Japan for this curriculum modernisation exercise (Tang 1985).

The political triumph of Deng came at the third plenum of the 11th Chinese Communist Party (CCP) Central Committee in December 1978. Deng became vice-chairman of the CCP and many of his supporters secured important posts. Hua's faction crumbled and his chairmanship was put under 'collective leadership'. The Plenum called on the CCP to shift its energies to the task of economic production. In April 1979 it was officially announced that science and technology was the key and education the foundation for the implementation of the Four Modernisations (Guanming Ribao, 25 April 1979). In January 1980 an Education Work Conference held in Beijing endorsed the view that education must be geared to the needs of socialist construction and modernisation, and the proportion of expenditure on and investment in education must be adjusted and raised. Deng's notion of education modernisation (*jiaoyu xian-daihua*) was by then fully adopted.

Degeneration of Geographical Education in China 1862–1976

Geography (*Dili*) as a formal curriculum first appeared during the so-called Tong Zhi Restoration between 1862–67 which aimed at strengthening the declining Manchu Dynasty by learning Western knowledge. It was taught in the third year of the Tong Wen Guan (Foreign Language Institute) to a small group of selected Confucian scholars and the main content was about geography of other countries. Geography became a middle school subject in 1903 when China adopted the Japanese model of education and since then it has been treated differently by governments of different time periods. Between 1903 and 1949 geography was mainly a descriptive subject, heavily influenced by regional description and environmental determinism. Nevertheless it occupied a reasonable proportion of the overall middle school timetable, ranging from 5.4 to 8 per cent of the total teaching time (Chu and Sun 1982).

After 1949 geography in the middle school curriculum was heavily influenced by political changes. Russification of China's education system began in 1953 and led to the transplant of Russian geography syllabuses and teaching approaches into China. In particular physical geography and world geography were taught at junior middle level while economic geography was taught at senior middle level. Curriculum content was politically oriented. Primarily it aimed at promoting patriotism and preaching the achievements of socialist construction. Physical geography enjoyed a high status because China was in great need of geologists, meteorologists and surveyors. Human geography was condemned as a 'capitalist' discipline and banned. Geographers who challenged the relevance of the Russian approach or advocated human geography were purged.

After 1958 the importance of geography in the school curriculum further declined. In 1959 Mao started the first education revolution, which strengthened political and labour education at the expense of the academic curriculum. Geography was cancelled at the senior middle level. It was only taught at the junior middle level. The time allocated to geography in the middle school timetable dropped to 1.7 per cent as compared with 6.3 per cent in 1953. Geographical education was given a fatal blow during the Cultural Revolution. Mao's wife, Jiang Ching, openly stated that geographical knowledge was useless. Geography was labelled as a bourgeoise discipline because it encouraged travelling and sightseeing. So it was completely scrapped from the middle school and university curriculum. Teachers were either dismissed or forced to teach other subjects. Geographers in universities were sent to the countryside to be 're-educated'.

In 1977 the Ministry of Education announced a *Draft Teaching Outline for Full-time 10 year Schools* which was basically a restoration of that of 1962. Geography was initially revived. *Zhongguo Dili* (geography of China) was to be taught in junior middle one, for three lessons a week; *Shijie Dili* (world geography) in junior middle two, for two lessons a week. But geography was not restored at the senior middle level because it did not exist in the 1962 Teaching Outline. Geography occupied just 1.7 per cent of total teaching time.

Initiation of Change by the Academic Community

Between 1977 and 1980 the official status of the science and technological community was elevated to its highest level since 1949 because national leaders saw science and technology as the key to China's four modernisations. This subsequently changed the politics of modernisation by providing new channels for the representation of professional interests in Chinese politics (Suttmeier 1981). The intellectual community soon used its newly acquired status to speak for its interests.

The trigger influence on restoring senior middle school geography came from geographers in tertiary institutions. Based on the Russian model, geography had enjoyed high esteem as a science discipline in higher education institutions in China before the Cultural Revolution. Geographers wished to revive this tradition. In July 1979 the Ministry of Education commissioned the China Geographical Association to hold a conference at Wuxi in Jiangsu Province. The main theme was to discuss curriculum objectives and content of geography at universities and tertiary level teacher training institutions. Seventy-five delegates attended the Wuxi Conference and 65 per cent of them were from tertiary institutions. They unanimously stressed the contribution of geography to China's modernisation needs and called for more resources and staffing for geography education at tertiary level.

The delegates then examined the problem of curriculum linkage between universities and middle schools. Three acute problems were pinpointed. First, geography was not taught in senior middle schools in 1978. Second, it was anomalous that in the newly restored university entrance examination geography candidates took an examination paper that was based on junior middle school geography while other subjects were based on the senior middle school curriculum. Third, there was a great mismatch between university entrance examination and recruitment policy: tertiary geography specialities recruited science candidates but only arts pupils could take geography in the examination. The deepest concern of the academics was to ensure that their specialisms could recruit pupils with a solid background knowledge of geography.

At the end of the Wuxi Conference it was proposed that geography should be taught successively at primary (general geographical knowledge), junior middle (regional and physical geography) and senior middle school (earth science and economic geography) levels. The amount of teaching hours for geography should be raised from 1.7 per cent to about 6 per cent of the total teaching time. The training of geography teachers should be speeded up to overcome the severe shortage of geography teachers in China.

The Second National Conference on Science and Technology held in April 1980 provided geographers with an external stimulus to help thaw the frozen situation. In the opening speech Hu Yaobang, who later replaced Hua Guofeng as CCP General Secretary, emphasised the importance of science as 'a great force that pushes history forward. The mastery of the most advanced technology of the contemporary world is a fundamental problem related to the future of China' (Hu 1980). Dr Wu Chuanjun, vice-president of the China Geographical Society and a senior member of the Academia Sinica, felt that it was a golden opportunity to make national leaders aware of the problem of geography education in schools. He therefore drafted a *Proposal on the Strengthening and Popularisation of Earth Science* which served two purposes: first, to argue for the importance of earth science in China's modernisation programme; second, to make earth science a legitimate school curriculum subject in primary and middle schools. The *Proposal* was jointly signed by the China Geographical Society and ten other related professional societies as an open petition at the end of the Conference. This was an unprecedented action which reflected a new tactic used by the intellectual community to press for policies which it felt, in its expert judgement, would be the best for the four modernisations and for the prestige of the academic community as well.

Shaping the Senior Middle School Geography Curriculum at the Hangzhou Conference, December 1980

Both the Wuxi Conference and the Second Conference on Science and Technology challenged the arrangement of geography teaching in schools in the *Draft Teaching Outline for Full-time 10 year Schools* and called for improvement. In particular the ten-year schooling system, which was a Cultural Revolution legacy, was considered too short for teaching the newly revised science curriculum that was generally overloaded with 'advanced' concepts.

In September 1980, the political climate in China further relaxed with the downfall of Hua Guofeng. Hu Yaobang was elected as General Secretary of the Chinese Communist Party. A campaign to 'liberate the mind from subjectivism' (*si xiang jie fang*) was launched which aimed at breaking away from Mao's ideological constraints. The Cultural Revolution was completely negated and condemned as a national disaster. Mao's widow was put on public trial and convicted. In the field of education the Ministry of Education began to plan to extend the schooling system from 10 years (5–3–2) to 12 years (6–3–3) and further revise the school curriculum. The Ministry of Education organised study tours to visit the United States, Europe and Japan to bring back experiences of curriculum reforms in the advanced countries, hoping that these would provide shortcuts to curriculum modernisation in China.

In December 1980 the China Geographical Association held a two-week conference at Hangzhou in Zhejiang Province to discuss the objectives, content and teaching hours of the senior middle school curriculum. The Conference was still dominated by geographers from tertiary institutions (64 per cent) and government officials (13 per cent). Middle school teachers were only 23 per cent of the delegates and most of them were from keypoint middle schools in key cities.

There was a consensus among the delegates that geography education in China was both backward in approach and inadequate in teaching time. But opinions differed greatly on evaluating the contribution of geography between 1949 and 1976. There were three groups of opinions. The first group outspokenly accused the 'ultra-leftist' inclination and the Russian model of geography education. They argued that geography education was merely political propaganda that preached biased viewpoints and closed-mindedness. Geography was taught to promote patriotism and socialist beliefs but it greatly ignored the backward aspects and problems of China. Geography had not contributed to national development because, by following the Russian practice of condemning human geography, it led to pupils' ignorance of the importance of environmental conservation and ecological balance. Only by emancipating geography from political dogma could meaningful geography be taught in schools. The second opinion group was apolitical. It only attacked some technical shortcomings of the geography curriculum after 1949, such as the reduction of teaching time and over-emphasis of physical geography. The third group followed an eclectic viewpoint, saying that the approach of geography education was basically acceptable between 1949–62, and only after that was geography education damaged by the political intervention of the ultra-leftists.

The main area of dispute at the Hangzhou Conference was in the approach of the Senior Middle School Geography Curriculum. There were three groups of actors each advocating a particular approach and content arrangement for the intended SMSGC:

Earth science (Di-xue) *advocates*
The earth science advocates were mainly represented by Beijing Normal University, Hebei Normal University and Shanxi Normal University, all of which were prestigious keypoint universities that produced lecturers for China's tertiary institutions. Naturally they stressed the academic relevance of geography more than anything else. They argued that earth science (*dixue*) enjoyed higher academic status than geography (*dili*) because earth science was one of the six foundation sciences (mathematics, physics, chemistry, astronomy and biology) in the contemporary world. Therefore, pupils who studied earth science could master advanced scientific knowledge, such as plate tectonics, remote sensing, geophysics, spatial analysis and chemical analysis. In this way it was possible to prepare pupils for advanced studies at university level. It was obvious that the earth science advocates narrowly interpreted Deng Xiaoping's idea of curriculum modernisation, that is, enriching the content of the school curriculum with advanced scientific knowledge. They also represented a major concern of the keypoint normal universities to raise the status of geography education by giving it a distinctive scientific outlook and label. This was in line with what was petitioned in 1980.

A set of trial earth science textbooks, which was produced by the Beijing Normal University after the Wuxi Conference in 1979 and piloted in its two attached keypoint middle schools, was introduced to the conference participants as a concrete example of what a senior earth science curriculum should look like. It contained 23 chapters of 314 pages in two volumes. 96 teaching hours were recommended to teach the two books. But when the delegates examined the books they found that there were a lot of different concepts, equations and complicated calculations which were beyond the abilities of most pupils in China. One participant pointed out that the chapters were highly condensed from university course books and hastily compiled together as a middle school curriculum. Hebei Normal University also produced a proposed earth science syllabus which was heavily oriented to physical geography.

Man land relationship (ren-di guanxi) *Approach Advocates*
They were mainly represented by the Nanjing Teachers' College, Beijing Teachers' College and Guangzhou Teachers' College which trained middle school teachers. The most influential leader of this group was the late professor Li Xudan of Nanjing Teachers' College. Li was a human geographer who had studied at Cambridge University in England in the 1930s. In 1957 he was denounced as a 'rightist-reactionary' when human geography was condemned as 'anti-Marxist'. Since then he had been deprived of teaching and publication rights. In 1976 his reputation and teaching duties were restored. He then wrote many articles to revive the reputation of human geography and attacked the Russian model of geographical education. In August 1980 he attended the 24th International Geographical Conference held in Tokyo. Because of his seniority and personal experience Li became a charismatic figure at the Hangzhou Conference.

Li gave an opening speech at the conference. He introduced his impression of the 24th International Geographical Conference to the audience. The message was that Japan was a highly industrialised and urbanised country but Japan took serious measures to protect the environment and conserve the countryside. Also the world trend of geographical education was to study the interaction between man and the physical environment (Li 1980a).

In another conference paper Li (1980b) argued that the most important role of geography education was to increase its social relevance, addressing it directly to China's development problems such as agricultural land use, urban planning, industrial planning, natural conservation and population growth. Li also advocated that geography pupils should be made fully aware of China's developmental constraints, such as the lack of farmland and uneven distribution of energy resources.

But the man-land relationship advocates failed to produce any proposed curriculum of their own to convince the participants. Beijing Teachers' College just distributed a translated version of 'High School Geography' used in Japan to illustrate the content of the man-land approach, while Madame Huang Defen of Guangzhou Teachers' College introduced the Hong Kong A-level geography curriculum that was based on a framework of man-environment interactions.

Earth science and economic geography advocates
These advocates were mainly represented by geographers from Shanghai. In 1979 Shanghai took the lead nationally in reforming the ten-year schooling system and decided to extend one-third of Shanghai's senior middle schools from two to three years. The Shanghai Bureau of Education assigned East China Normal University, Shanghai Teachers' College and Shanghai Institute of Education to produce a *Text Writing Outline for Senior Middle School Earth Science and Economic Geography*, which was published in February 1980 for nationwide comments. In general it was a modification of the 1958 curriculum arrangement which taught physical geography and economic geography at senior middle level. In a sense this was just a revival of the Russian model.

At the Hangzhou Conference the Shanghai delegates explained their reasons. The first was to enable pupils to master systematically fundamental knowledge about the physical world and to cultivate their interest in further studies in earth science. The second was to enable pupils to understand the economic factors governing patterns of human activities (Chu and Sun 1980). They also claimed that the earth science and economic approaches were based on a survey of the world's major patterns of middle school geography, as reflected by geography syllabuses and textbooks used in Singapore, Hong Kong, Japan, France, UK, Rumania and Russia in the early 1970s. A sixty-page document containing translated versions of these syllabuses was distributed at the Conference as evidence.

All three groups of advocates were academics from tertiary institutions. They tried to press for a particular approach to senior middle school geography based on their own perception of its academic and social relevance and with reference to their partial understanding of geography education in some developed countries. But on a whole there was little discussion on the feasibility of implementation in the school system. Some middle teachers (Tien, Wang and Li 1980) pointed out possible difficulties encountered by arts pupils in studying earth science. The delegates from Shenxi Institute of Education advocated that any approach to senior middle school geography should meet the needs of the 96 per cent of middle school graduates who would join the working force.

Despite the difference of viewpoints and approaches, innovation actors at the Hangzhou Conference were unanimous on two points: that SMSGC should occupy between 6 to 9 per cent of the total teaching time at the senior middle level of general education; and that it could be taken by both arts and science candidates at the national university entrance examination.

THE PROCESSES OF THE INNOVATION

Formulation of the Senior Middle School Geography Curriculum

No decision was made in the Hangzhou Conference on the title, approach, content and timetable arrangement of the proposed senior middle school curriculum. It only provided an occasion for different opinions to be voiced. The authority of curriculum change was vested in the Ministry of Education and the People's Education Press.

On 17 April 1981 the Ministry of Education announced that senior middle school geography was to be restored both in five-year and six-year middle schools for 64 teaching hours in both systems. SMSGC was to be an examination subject only for arts candidates but schools were encouraged to teach SMSGC to science pupils. These decisions had two significant implications on the development of SMSGC. First, five-year and six-year middle schools differed greatly in student intake and resources but they had to implement the same senior middle geography curriculum. Second, if SMSGC was only for arts candidates it was unlikely that schools would teach it to science candidates because of examination pressure. Moreover, the content of SMSGC should be adjusted to fit arts students.

In China the production of teaching materials (*jiaocai*) is exceptionally important in the process of curriculum development. Politically, *jiaocai* are 'the main tool for educating millions of Chinese youths to

become successors of the socialist revolution' (Zhang 1985). Pedagogically, *jiaocai* are the 'physical foundation of teaching and learning'
(Chen and Chu 1983). The People's Education Press was established
in September 1950 as a central agency for producing nationally
unified textbooks (*jiaokeshu*) of the highest quality by qualified
subject experts who were recruited as full time editors in PEP.
Curriculum uniformity was stressed because there was a deep-rooted
belief that nationally unified syllabuses and textbooks could ensure
the standards of schools, teaching schedules and quality of teaching
(Wu 1986). In this respect curriculum development is synonymous
with the production of textbooks as standardised teaching materials.

The geography editorial board of the People's Education Press was
directly responsible for writing standardised textbooks for all pupils
in China. Specifically, its chief editor Mr Chen Erzou was empowered
to make the final decision on content and approach. Mr Chen was a
graduate of the Central University at Nanjing (now the Nanjing
University) in the 1940s. He joined the underground communist
party and became a PEP editor in the early 1950s. Like Professor Li
Xudan he was denounced as a rightist in 1957 because he advocated
that pupils ought to understand both the greatness and limitations of
China in geography lessons. He was removed from PEP and exiled to
Inner Mongolia. There he was an eye-witness of the blind conversion
of the Mongolian grassland into rice fields which led to large scale soil
erosion. In 1979 he returned to PEP and headed the geography
editorial board. When the Hangzhou Conference was held he was
studying geographical education in Japan. He heard a report of the
Conference and read all the papers to find out the main controversies. But he was personally inclined to support the man-environment
approach because of his personal experience and his study tour of
Japan.

On 20 July 1981 Mr Chen, on behalf of the PEP, produced an
Explanatory Note on the Outline of Senior Middle School Geography
which finalised the title, approach, content and guiding principles of
writing the restored SMSGC. The title 'geography' (*dili*) was chosen
instead of 'earth science' (*di-xue*) because China could not follow
Japan and USA's example of offering an independent earth science
option. The man-land relationship approach was adopted because it
addressed both contemporary world problems, such as environmental pollution, and China's development problems like deforestation
and overpopulation.

As far as content selection was concerned, the *Explanatory Note* spelled out specific guidelines. The level of difficulty of those teaching materials related to physical geography would not exceed those of the existing senior middle mathematics, physics and chemistry; those related to human geography would not exceed the level used in existing Chinese languages, politics and history materials. The latest geographical knowledge was to be included. Pupils were encouraged to apply theories and concepts of the man-land relationship. The skills of observation, judgement, extrapolation, comprehension and analysis were particularly stressed. Titles of the eleven proposed chapters (see Table 2.1 below) indicated that PEP had reached compromises with the three schools of thought at the Hangzhou Conference.

A full-time writing team composed of seven PEP geography editors and one human geographer seconded from Beijing Institute of Education was responsible for producing the first edition of SMSGC within nine months. An official deadline was set for March 1982. The writing team divided the job among themselves and exchanged manuscripts for comments. Individual chapters were sent to relevant experts for comments. For example, Chapter 8 on agricultural

TABLE 2.1   *Test structure of the first edition of Senior Middle School Geography Textbooks, June 1982*

Chapter	No. of pages	Column cm of text	No. of diagrams	Teaching hours*	Pages/ hour
1 Earth in Universe	35	302	30	9	3.8
2 Atmosphere	45	374	44	8	5.6
3 Water	29	276	15	7	4.1
4 Earth Movement	45	412	43	8	5.6
Book One sub-total	154	1364	132	32	5.1
5 Biosphere & Natural Regions	33	336	16	5	6.6
6 Natural Resources	29	294	9	5	5.8
7 Energy Problems	26	239	14	5	5.2
8 Agriculture & Food Problems	28	334	5	5	5.6
9 Industrial Problems	30	320	9	5	6.0
10 Population & Urbanisation	31	288	15	5	6.2
11 Man & Environment	6	67	2	2	3.0
Book Two sub-total	183	1878	86	32	5.7

*One teaching hour equals 45 minutes.

production and problems was reviewed by agricultural experts in the Ministry of Agriculture. PEP claimed that there was enough communication between the editorial board and professional geographers during the process of writing and editing. Mr Chen Erzou was the overall editor of the two volumes of textbooks which were printed in July 1982.

Immediate Implementation of SMSGC

Immediate implementation of SMSGC was expected in September 1982, without any pilot schemes to try it out. The strategy of implementation was top-down and coercive though the official rhetoric encouraged flexibility and adaptation to the realities of local schools. The Ministry of Education and PEP believed that standardisation of the national school curriculum would guarantee quality and avoid the kind of anarchy experienced during the Cultural Revolution. The Unified National Higher School Examination excluded the possibility of local modifications of SMSGC.

In July 1982 the Ministry of Education officially issued a circular *On Offering Senior Middle School Geography* to local education bureaus. It quoted Premier Zhao Zhiyang's government report delivered at the Fifth National Congress that 'schools at various levels must strengthen the teaching of Chinese history and geography as a major aspect of inculcating patriotism among pupils'. This signified that national leaders strongly supported geography teaching but at the same time implied that the implementation of SMSGC was a political task that ought to be carried out locally. The circular recognised the problem of shortage of qualified geography teachers so it suggested the implementation of SMSGC by stages. It announced that SMSGC was to be examined in 1984 and only arts candidates could take geography at the Unified National Higher School Examination. It also stated that only PEP textbooks were to be used. This meant that Beijing, Shanghai and Tientsin had to withdraw their experimental senior middle school geography textbooks already in use.

Strong pressure for implementation was exerted on schools which hoped to prepare their arts candidates for the first SMSGC examination in 1984. They had no alternatives because geography was one of the six compulsory subjects. It then became clear that some schools were capable of preparing geography candidates while others were not. This intensified the discrepancies between schools because keypoint and urban schools could easily recruit qualified geography teachers to implement SMSGC. For example, in the summer of 1982 Guangdong Bureau of Education organised 15 sessions of seminars to promote the implementation of SMSGC and it was found that only about one-third of middle schools in the province, mostly keypoint schools and established urban schools, could implement SMSGC in the new academic year. Non-keypoint schools and rural schools in particular were disadvantaged because they had greater difficulty in recruiting qualified teachers. They had to wait until freshly trained geography teachers from the teacher training institutions were available.

A *post factum* examination of SMSGC was made at the Xiamen Conference in September 1982. It was attended by 103 delegates, 39 per cent of whom came from tertiary institutions while 24 per cent were teachers. There was criticism of the lack of vertical linkage between the geography textbooks used at primary, junior middle and senior middle levels. In particular the first edition of senior middle geography textbooks was strongly criticised for:

> overloading with difficult content. Many difficult teaching points and concepts are beyond the competence of the majority of senior middle school geography teachers. There are lots of mistakes in texts and diagrams which need revision (China Geographical Association 1982).

But these comments could only be minuted for future improvement because the textbooks were already in use in schools. Delegates also expressed great disappointment with the teaching time given to geography. They wished to increase the teaching time from 64 hours to 96 hours. They also pointed out that it was unreasonable to make SMSGC an examination subject only for arts candidates while in fact geography specialities at tertiary level only recruit science candidates.

The Xiamen Conference showed that SMSGC was produced in a rush without enough consultation with teachers on its 'teachability' (teaching hours and ability level of geography teachers) and 'learnability' (level of difficulty) in schools. The strong dissatisfaction expressed was a criticism that the initiation of SMSGC came from professional geographers who wished to legitimise its scientific status in the school curriculum and to secure a bigger share of teaching time for the purpose of resolving the mismatch between university entrance examination arrangements and recruitment policies. But in the end none of these objectives were met. In the scramble for status in the school curriculum the 'Big Three' (mathematics, physics and chemistry) maintained their supremacy by squeezing geography out of the domain of science.

ANALYSIS, FINDINGS AND REFLECTIONS

Problems and Patterns of Implementation of SMSGC

There is a clear distinction between implementation and adoption. Implementation is a referent concept to imply a process over time by which people, events and resources determine whether or not practice is altered when something new is attempted (Fullan 1985a). Adoption only represents a decision to use a new programme and does not imply implementation. Implementation is perceived as a multidimensional and multilevel phenomenon (Hall and Loucks 1977, Leithwood 1981). Perfect implementation is unattainable as there is always an 'implementation gap' which leads to little implementation or even non-implementation (Gunn 1978). One of the major concerns in innovation literature is to examine the factors that account for the acceptance or rejection of an innovation. Internal attributes or 'pre-conditions' are matched with external attributes or 'co-conditions' pertaining to implementation (Rogers and Shoemaker 1971, Zaltman *et al* 1973, Havelock and Huberman 1977, Dalin 1978, Adams and Chen 1981).

In a vast and heterogeneous country like China the nature of curriculum implementation is far more complicated than central curriculum planners have envisaged. The Ministry of Education follows a simplistic model of implementation, viewing the adoption of an impending change by schools as being the final stage in the curriculum innovation process. After all, once a standardised curriculum is produced, in the form of nationally unified textbooks, the remaining problem is to boost the supply of qualified teachers and to upgrade teachers for the gradual adoption of the intended curriculum innovation. The unified national university examination is taken as a powerful yardstick to manipulate implementation. However there are four critical barriers that have undermined the implementation of SMSGC in the school system, namely: the lack of clarity about change, the mismatch between curriculum intentions and school realities, the backwash effects of public examination, and the great shortage of geography teachers.

The first problem is related to the lack of clarity about change and what is involved in it. In the case of SMSGC, the change means more than restoring a geography curriculum at the senior middle level since its cancellation in 1957. It involves the adoption of a man-environment approach which is an epistemological and pedagogical approach in geographical education still subject to controversy in the Western world (Long and Robertson 1972, English and Mayfield 1972, Schools Council 1979), and with varied practices between countries. In China it requires a departure from the Russian model of geographical education and there was very great reluctance to do this among geographers trained in the 1950s on the Russian model. Therefore, in requiring geography teachers to follow a new educational approach, it is essential for curriculum designers to describe in detail all the implications of change, in language the users can understand. The lack of explicitness may hoodwink the users and lead to uncertainty or even scepticism (Pratt 1980).

In 1982 the communication of the goals and nature of the innovation to teachers was weak at the early stage of implementation. Neither the *Explanatory Note* issued by PEP in July 1981 nor the official circular of the Ministry of Education sent to local educational bureaus in July 1982 spelt out the objectives of the man-land approach. There was no separate curriculum guide on SMSGC to explain the innovation as textbooks were the *de facto* curriculum. A short paragraph in the preface of senior middle geography textbooks summarised the goal of SMSGC:

> the guiding principle of this book is to study the relationship between man and the environment. Firstly to equip pupils with the foundation knowledge about the physical world, then pupils learn how to correctly utilise and conserve the environment so as to make the physical environment more advantageous to human activities and production (PEP 1982).

The preface further spelled out some teaching objectives in different paragraphs, namely:

> (a) enable pupils to recognise the inter-relationship between the essential physical elements;
> (b) enable pupils to understand the physical conditions for production and human activities provided by nature, and the impact of human activities on nature;
> (c) help pupils to build up comprehensive viewpoints on natural resources, population and environment;

(d) develop pupils' ability to analyse problems comprehensively;
(e) promote patriotism and dialectic materialism.

It was claimed that SMSGC provided the prerequisite scientific and cultural knowledge for pupils to continue studying or for participation in modernisation construction. In-service seminars were organised by local teacher training institutions to explain the man–land paradigm to teachers. Special explanatory articles also appeared in the leading academic journals on geography teaching. However, teachers' understanding of the recommended man–land approach mostly derived from their perception of the nationally unified textbooks which exactly specified the teaching sequence and number of teaching hours in the preface. Unfortunately, the intrinsic features of the textbooks induced teachers to treat physical geography and human geography separately.

Firstly, the content arrangement suggested only a mechanical collation of physical geography and human geography with a concluding chapter trying to explain the importance of striking a balance between human activities and the physical environment. As the analysis in Table 2.1 shows, the first four chapters in Book One are devoted entirely to physical geography as the physical foundation, with an average of 5.3 pages per suggested teaching hour. Book Two includes seven chapters on human geography, with an average of 5.7 pages per teaching hour. In the interviews geographers and teachers generally felt the theme of man–land interaction was not distinctive.

Secondly, both the presentation form of the textbooks and the suggested teaching time are unfavourable for teaching and learning. In general the texts are written in a highly condensed and encyclopaedic language that is 'dry and unimaginative for arousing pupils' interest' (Ge 1986). For example, Book One has 8.2 column cm of text per page and 42 column cm per teaching hour; Book Two is even more congested, with 10.8 column cm per page and 62 column cm per teaching hour. In particular, teachers expressed great difficulties in teaching Book One which contained many difficult concepts like the celestial system, obliquity of the eliptic, atmospheric circulation, plate tectonics and geological evolution. An analysis of the composition of texts on physical geography revealed that teachers had to explain 3.5 new geographical concepts every five minutes, which was actually an impossible task! To compensate for the insufficiency of teaching hours for physical geography, it was a common practice by teachers, which was evidenced in all the five schools visited, to squeeze teaching hours from Book Two. Pupils were asked to read this book by themselves because the texts were considered as purely descriptive and could be easily understood. Teachers' backgrounds also contributed to this practice. Many qualified teachers were trained in the 1950s and early 1960s when physical geography dominated the field of geography. It was natural for them to put more efforts into Book One.

The second barrier to implementation arises from the great mismatch between the resource implications for effective implementation of SMSGC and the realities of resource allocation in schools. While textbooks are nationally unified, there is no concerted effort to guarantee the provision of resources to schools. According to suggestions listed in the official *Teaching Reference* (*Jiaoxue Cankou*), which was written by geographers of Beijing Normal University and published by the People's Education Press in January 1983, different types of visual teaching aids are recommended to facilitate the effective teaching of Book One on physical geography. These include the use of 50 wall maps and charts, six physical models, two sets of rock and mineral specimens, two sets of slides, films and many display pictures. These teaching resources were produced by different agencies, such as the Cartographical Press, Geological Press and many local factories. Usually the numbers produced fell short of real demand. There was no proper channel for informing schools of the availability of these materials. Geography teachers in the rural schools complained to the researcher that they did not know where to purchase teaching resources even if they had the funds.

Middle schools in China were generally ill-equipped due to the lack of funds. According to a survey conducted in 1982 in 14 coastal provinces, only 4.1 per cent had the required teaching equipment to fully implement the official curriculum. Eighty-seven per cent of middle schools had an acute shortage of teaching facilities, including blackboards and pupils' desks (Liu 1987). Rural and non-keypoint schools are particularly disadvantaged. The field studies confirmed this disparity between schools. For example, the geography department of East China Normal University No. 2 attached middle school has managed to secure a yearly funding of 3000 yuan and it therefore has acquired all the needed teaching aids, with the luxury of having one 12-inch globe for every pair of pupils, and one set of rock specimens for every four pupils. There is a separate resource room to accommodate the teaching aids and hardware, such as slide projector, overhead projector, television and video-recorder. But a rural keypoint middle school in Zhencheng *xian* (county) of the same pupil population only allocates 300 yuan to geography a year and there is just one cabinet to accommodate all its resources. In one school located in a hilly rural area in Quingyuan *xian* there is not even a globe to show to pupils. Rural geography teachers complained that they could only rely on chalk and talk to explain abstract concepts. At the same time local teachers have no incentives to make home-produced teaching aids because there is little support from local education authorities. They are also ill-prepared for making teaching aids as educational technology is a very weak component in teacher training programmes in China.

The third barrier to implementation comes from the public examination which exerts negative backwash effects on the implementation of SMSGC in schools. In the entire innovation process of the SMSGC no consideration at all was given to its internal and external assessment strategies. The Department of Student Affairs of the Ministry of Education monitors the Unified National Higher School Examination (UNHSE), which plays two important roles at the terminal year of middle school education: as an effective selection instrument and as a reliable test of the terminal competencies of pupils. But there is no independent and professional examination agency which is capable of ensuring the quality of tests, analysing test results and feeding this information back into the school system in constructive ways. *Ad hoc* examination paper setting teams composed of university scholars are appointed every year to set examination papers for different subjects. To prevent test leaking the teams are usually very small in size, with little or no representation of middle school teachers, and work in a secretive manner. Pre-testing and item bank building are not practised. After the examination, papers are marked locally at provincial level following a standardised marking scheme. Each province sends a confidential report based on random sampling of its candidates to the Ministry of Education. However, teachers only know their provincial performance through internal and informal feedback. The official explanation for concealing the national performance is that variation between provinces is so great that public announcement will cause embarrassment and unjustified comparison. Pupils are given a raw score (a maximum of 100 marks) for each of the six compulsory subjects. Tertiary institutions then set their enrollment marks (600 being the maximum) for admission.

The geography examination paper setting team is composed of five to six university geographers. Since 1978 the team has had the difficult job of striking a balance between discriminating candidates for university enrollment and ensuring a proper rate of passing. The conventional practice is to guarantee that up to 60 per cent of the marks in the examination paper can be safely secured by thorough study of the textbooks, while the remaining 40 per cent come from more mind-stretching questions to allow for discrimination. The result is that, as Table 2.2 shows, the percentage of lower-order types of questions fluctuates between 55 and 85 per cent. This induces textbook-based learning and question spotting. Even so, the general performance of geography candidates is far from satisfactory. Three kinds of general weaknesses are identified by the chief examiner: a weak foundation of geographical knowledge, poor geographical skills and poor analytical skills (Sun 1985). Geographers in China complained that the geography examination papers produced candidates with 'high marks but with low skills' (*gao fen di neng*).

TABLE 2.2 *Distribution of questions according to different levels of intellectual abilities (by % of total marks) in geography papers of the Unified National Higher School Examination*

| Year | Lower-order types | | | Higher-order types | | |
	Recall	Comprehension & application	Total	Synthesis & analysis	Evaluation	Total
1978	60	25	=85	15	0	=15
1979	45	35	=80	20	0	=20
1980	30	40	=70	30	0	=30
1981	35	35	=70	30	0	=30
1982	30	42	=72	20	8	=28
1983	25	30	=55	39	6	=45
1984*	31	34	=65	26	9	=35
1985	24	46	=70	20	10	=30
1986	22	40	=62	33	5	=38

*SMSGC was first examined in 1984.

The teaching of SMSGC in schools is further undermined by examination requirements that bewilder school teachers. Firstly, the examination requires geography candidates to demonstrate their mastery of the 'double foundations' – foundation knowledge and foundation skills. Yet teachers are uncertain of what constitutes geographical skills in the SMSGC. The PEP has stressed the skills of observation, judgement, extrapolation, comprehension and analysis in the *Preface* of the textbooks. But ironically the pupil exercises encourage rehearsal and regurgitation of textbook information: of the 150 pupil exercise questions included in the textbook, 67 per cent belong to recall types. The majority of marks in the public examination also come from recall types of questions. Secondly, teachers are given conflicting advice on preparing the candidates. The chief examiner openly calls upon teachers to help pupils master basic knowledge and skills integratively instead of disrupting teaching with drilling exercises and question-spotting activities (Sun 1985). On the other hand, articles in the more influential journals like *Geography Teaching* (*Dili Jiaoxue*) frequently report success stories of how some schools achieved excellent examination results by drilling and question analysis (spotting). For example, it was suggested that 'pupils should grasp textbook knowledge tightly; not a drop of water should leak away – study everything in the book, no matter the texts, maps, footnotes, read them all' (Hu Yongfai 1986).

The geography paper requires candidates to revise all the junior middle school textbooks on world geography and Chinese geography. About 50 per cent of marks in the examination paper came from junior middle school geography. This greatly increases the burden on candidates and teachers.

In China it is publicly acknowledged that examination is the 'conduct baton' (*zhi fai bang*) that orchestrates teaching and learning. The reputation and material rewards of a school are measured by its performance in public examination. Therefore, the general pattern of teaching and learning of SMSGC, as observed in field studies, is one that is strait-jacketed by the textbooks and examination requirements. In keypoint schools with better pupil intake and abundant facilities, like the East China Normal University Attached No. 2 Middle School which the researcher visited, geography teachers use home-designed worksheets to promote enquiry-oriented learning and carry out extracurricular activities to enhance learning. But field observations in the other four schools reveal a common teaching pattern: teachers follow the textbook very closely, and mostly rely on chalk and talk to spoonfeed the pupils. Time is always constrained. Teachers rush along to complete the SMSGC in one year, then spend the second year revising junior middle school geography and drilling pupils. Teachers have to rely on past examination papers and mock examination questions available on the market to prepare their candidates. Local education bureaus also encourage drilling. For example, in 1987 the geography section of Guangzhou Education

Bureau supplied schools in Guangzhou with a set of test units of 63 pages on important topics. The official in charge took this as an obligation to help schools to perform better in examination (interview, May 1987).

Shortage of qualified geography teachers still remains the greatest factor that cripples the implementation of SMSGC. In 1982 there were about 16 000 senior middle school teachers in China and most of them were in the cities. One-third of them were unqualified. Training and inservice education of geography teachers were speeded up but could never satisfy demand. For example, in Zhenzheng *xian*, a fairly prosperous rural area adjacent to Guangzhou city, only one keypoint middle school out of the 20 middle schools in the whole *xian* managed to implement SMSGC in 1982. The number increased to three in 1987. Rural middle schools which cannot offer the six compulsory arts or science subjects in full simply abstain from joining the UNHSE. In 1986 PEP conducted a survey trip to the border regions in Northwest and Southwest China. It was admitted that there was little chance of implementing SMSGC in these regions due to the severe shortage of qualified teachers (Guo 1987). Unfortunately in the last five years the morale of the teaching profession has dropped rapidly due to low wages and poor social status. Many experienced teachers have left the teaching profession because of poor incentives. For example, between 1979 and 1985 about 50 per cent (6 300 teachers) of Liaoning Province's backbone teachers switched to administrative and commercial jobs (He 1986). In 1987, teacher training institutions in Beijing failed to recruit the expected number of students and there was a cry of alarm (Su and Zhang 1987). The president of Guangdong Teachers' College frankly admitted that the rate of brain drain in the teaching profession far exceeded the rate of teacher supply, and that the problem of teacher shortage was unlikely to be resolved until the next century (interview, March 1988).

Significant Findings

From this case study it can be seen that the main impetus of the modernisation of the senior geography curriculum came from the national leaders' conception of education's role in modernisation and the importance of curriculum for this purpose. Curriculum changes were aimed at having an impact on the four modernisations through improvements in the production of the needed manpower by selective examination and expansion of higher education. This typically resembles the second curriculum development cycle gone through by developing countries in the early 1970s, which was oriented towards the adaptation of foreign innovations and the updating of antiquated materials, with most attention focused on the design of written materials at secondary school level (Lewin 1985). Modernisation of the geography curriculum meant updating the restored senior geography curriculum and adoption of a man-land relationship approach that was believed to be a fashionable approach in the world trend of geographical education as well as socially relevant to China's development problems.

The innovation process was highly political. The external politics of curriculum change were synchronised with the change of political climate in post-1976 China. The internal politics involved debates on the rationale, approach and content of the intended SMSGC between three groups of stakeholders possessing different academic status in the intellectual community, and reflected how different interest groups held competing values about what to teach. The decision-making process about knowledge and participation in curriculum planning were dominated by professional geographers from tertiary institutions. Participation of school teachers in the innovation process was insignificant because teachers had a low professional status in the academic hierarchy.

The highly centralised curriculum development system induced a 'convectional' pattern of change that was also policy-directed (Archer 1984). Curriculum controversies related to the nature of SMSGC were passed to the decision-making centre, that is the Ministry of Education and the PEP, and negotiated there through political interaction between the dominant subject groups. Then the decision was transmitted downwards to the school system as a decree. The execution of change was nationally uniform in conception and application, allowing little variations to meet local conditions or for adaptation in response to changing circumstances. Implementation of SMSGC simply meant the adoption of nationally unified textbooks with specified teaching schedules and teaching hours, and orchestrated by the Unified National Higher School Examination. School teachers were perceived as passive adopters faithfully conforming to official requirements of the curriculum change.

Nevertheless, the top-down and power-coercive implementation strategy did not itself guarantee effective implementation. On the contrary, co-ordination was poor and sometimes self-conflicting between those agencies that were responsible for curriculum arrangements, curriculum development and assessment. As a result, many inhibiting factors were imposed on the school system. For instance, the official decision that SMSGC was to be taken only by arts candidates was self-defeating because, in an examination-oriented school system, it confined the study of SMSGC to about 25 per cent of arts candidates who took part in the UNHSE. This also counteracted the planners' idea that the man–land relationship approach was addressed to China's development problems and was socially relevant to all pupils. SMSGC was perceived by teachers as epistemologically undistinctive, pedagogically inflexible and functionally difficult. The mismatch between teaching objectives and assessment objectives, between resource implications and resource allocation realities, baffled teachers at the grassroots level. Due to the great disparities between schools and regions in terms of teacher supply and resources the implementation of SMSGC demonstrated a polarised pattern: it was either implemented or non-implemented in the school system.

A cumbersome 'stop-go pattern of change' is also exhibited in the process of curriculum modernisation in post-1976 China. Universal reforms are followed by a period in which grievances build up and finally result in another universal reform (Archer 1984). Problems resulting from the lack of basic and applied research in curriculum development were fully exposed and acknowledged by the Ministry of Education and PEP immediately after the SMSGC was produced and put into operation in the school system. Responding to feedback from teachers, PEP revised SMSGC in its second editions in 1984. The general trend was to delete many geographical concepts that were considered too difficult. In November 1984 a conference was held at Taiyuan in Shanxi province on the vertical relationship between primary, junior middle and senior middle school geography. It discussed Deng Xiaoping's latest instruction that 'education must be oriented to modernisation, to the outside world and the future'. It also reinterpreted Deng's guidelines for curriculum modernisation laid down in 1977 but the emphasis was put on taking account of realities in China (Chu 1985).

But it was not until May 1985 that the Central Committee of the CCP made a decision to restructure education. One important agenda in this restructuring exercise was to emphasise basic education by the promotion of a nine-year system of compulsory education, which is perceived as 'a hallmark of modern civilization . . . a matter of vital importance for the improvement of the quality of the nation and for the prosperity of the country' (CCP 1985). In October 1985 the newly established State Education Commission (SEC), which replaced the Ministry of Education, gave a verdict on the first phase of curriculum modernisation between 1979–81, stating that:

> the implementation of the teaching plans of 1981 reveals that textbooks are geared to keypoint schools. They are divorced from the realities in the majority of regions and schools in the country. Haste makes waste – neither can teachers teach well nor pupils follow. This is disadvantageous to raising the quality of the entire generation of learners. (Yang 1986)

The State Education Commission decided to design a core curriculum appropriate for the nine-year basic education programme and a deadline for implementation was set for 1990.

The immediate policy implication for geographical education is that the man–land concepts socially relevant to China's development problems should be acquired by primary and junior middle pupils. The practice of curriculum development has also been changed. Curriculum development is to be clearly divorced from textbook production. The State Education Commission will produce a nationally standardised geography syllabus, with clearly specified objectives, teaching points, basic geographical concepts and skills. Based on this, both the PEP and local geographers could produce geographical textbooks which are to be scrutinised and approved by SEC textbook review committees. Schools then choose approved textbooks relevant to their needs. It is expected that devolution of curriculum control will encourage greater teacher participation in curriculum innovation and local initiatives. At the same time the examination system will change. It has been proposed that the United National Higher School Examination will only test pupils' basic numerical and language skills, leaving the other subjects to be examined at the provincial level by local examination agencies which award graduation certificates to middle school leavers. Geography then becomes a subject for all school leavers (Lewin and Wang 1988).

The effectiveness of this revised approach to curriculum development can only be evaluated in 1990 when the new curriculum is implemented. It is hoped that curriculum developers and geographers have learned enough lessons from the first phase of curriculum modernisation that was over-concerned with borrowing advanced scientific knowledge from the developed world, and narrowly focused on the selection of university candidates at the senior middle school level. The first lesson is that curriculum modernisation should not overlook the reality that China possesses the world's second largest number of illiterates, and that the illiteracy rate in the age groups 12 to 40 ranges between 18 and 45 per cent in the country (Zhongguo Jiaoyu Bao, 25 February 1988). The provision of nine years of basic education to 200 million school children (one-fifth of the country's population) is a tremendous task unmatched by any other country in the world. This has considerable implications for textbook writing and the presentation of curricula.

The second lesson is, as vice-director He Dongchang of the State Education Commission acknowledges, that since 1976 too much attention has been paid to studying the educational experiences of urbanised foreign countries while ignoring China's rural realities. The State Education Commission has ruled that curriculum development must be oriented to the 80 per cent of pupils in the countryside (He 1988). The third lesson is that curriculum development should be viewed as 'systems engineering' (*xi tong gongcheng*). In the words of Ye Lequn, director of PEP, better coordination needs to be made between the main educational agencies involved in curriculum arrangements, curriculum development, curriculum evaluation, teaching training and resource allocation. A research-development-dissemination approach to curriculum change would gradually replace the mandatory top-down approach (Ye 1987).

Reflections on the Research Methods

In selecting research methods for this case study research, the researcher has followed the advice given by Husen (1985) that research methods should be selected according to the nature and necessity of research, rather than being embedded in paradigmatic confrontations.

In retrospect the multi-method research approach and the five major research techniques adopted in this research have proved to be effective. Documentation analysis and semi-structured interviews, which are commonly employed by policy researchers in education and curriculum historians, were useful for reconstructing the in-novation process of SMSGC and soliciting divergent viewpoints of different groups of curriculum stakeholders inside China. Intrinsic curriculum materials analysis, examination analysis and field observa-tions, which have a strong qualitative flavour and are widely used in research on curriculum evaluation and implementation, provided strong evidence to illuminate problems of implementation. In fact, the five methods were complementary to each other. Five methodological constraints were encountered by the researcher in the research process. The first constraint was on the representation of the interviewees and field study sites. Not all the key innovators were interviewed because they lived in different parts of China. Moreover, the most influential innovator, Professor Li Xudan of Nanjing Teachers' College, passed away before the researcher could meet him. However, leading figures of the three groups of advocates were interviewed, and Professor Li's contribution was reconstructed by an analysis of his papers distributed at the Hangzhou Conference and interviewing his colleagues and supporters.

The sample of schools was not a very satisfactory one in terms of number and distribution. It had proved to be very difficult to conduct in-depth school visits in China because schools generally felt unsure about being closely studied, unless the visitor was perceived as a 'friend' through internal referral (*Guanxi*), and accompanied by someone trusted by the school. It was also up to the school's leadership to decide how much they wanted to entertain the researcher's requests. The researcher's experience was that the disadvantaged rural and non-keypoint schools were very reluctant to disclose data related to pupils' performance in public examinations. In these schools, the duration of the study was confined to one or two days. The unqualified geography teachers did not turn up for interviews. Neither were their lessons arranged for observation. Most probably there was embarrassment on the part of the school or the teachers. Nevertheless, such a phenomenon was itself a true reflection of disparities in China's schooling system.

The five schools where field visits and classroom observations were undertaken were chosen to include urban/rural and keypoint/non-keypoint schools. As case study sites they were not identified using statistical methods and could not be a representative sample. The five schools were located in the prosperous coastal region of China and therefore did not reflect realities in the remote and backward regions. The minority regions were not represented. The small sample size and limited geographical representation may induce accusation of 'low population validity' – the extent to which generalisations can be made from the research sample to other populations (Crossley and Vulliamy 1984). However, it had never been the researcher's intention to provide an overall generalisation of implementation of SMSGC in China. Rather, the field visits were intended to give 'snapshots' of implementation in schools with different contextual backgrounds. Luckily, all the informants in the five schools were extremely frank in voicing their difficulties and grievances which helped to illuminate the barriers to implementation of SMSGC.

The second constraint arose from the confidentiality of information, which caused difficulties in collecting source materials in the research process. Although the political climate had relaxed greatly in post-1976 China there were unclear guidelines on what constituted confidentiality. Yet the consequence of breaking confidentiality could be as severe as imprisonment. Therefore, informants inside China took great precautions against giving primary source materials (conference papers, internal publications, examination reports) to an outsider to avoid possible accusations. The dilemma in this research was that the closer one got to the picture of the innovation process the greater the danger of breaking 'confidentiality'. One typical example was gaining access to the lists of participants at various conferences in the innovation process. These lists would provide important evidence to illustrate the level of participation of different groups of stakeholders. The researcher was very keen to have them but several key innovators who were interviewed openly declined to disclose the name lists saying that these were treated as confidential matters. The same difficulty occurred in collecting conference papers and official documents. Fortunately one retired professor was sympathetic to the researcher and secretly gave him name lists that were copied by hand. Also when the researcher became aquainted with geographers in China through academic exchange activities the confidentiality constraint was reduced. Ultimately the researcher managed to collect all important source materials. Important statistics on the number and composition of candidates in past Unified National Higher School Examinations were directly obtained from senior SEC officials when the researcher took part in a curriculum materials analysis workshop conducted by Dr Michael Eraut and Dr Keith Lewin of Sussex University at PEP in September 1987. As external examiner of one master's degree candidate from East China Normal University, who wrote on examination reform in geography since 1949, the researcher also obtained valuable information on the evolution of examination papers. It is obvious that the establishment of mutual trust with Chinese professionals is beneficial to conducting in-depth first-hand academic research in China.

Reliability of information given by interviewees was undermined by several factors. All informants had de-emphasised the heated debates between the three groups of advocates at the Hangzhou conference. One possible reason was that harmony was treasured after the Cultural Revolution. Wrong dates and names were sometimes given due to fading memories in recollection of events. Personal prejudices or self-interest of some informants caused a mixture of facts and gossip, or deliberate omission of important details. The role status of the interviewees also affected reliability. Central government officials usually kept to party and government lines when responding to the researcher's questions. As a whole they were less outspoken than principals and teachers at the grassroots level.

Special attention had been paid to increasing the reliability of interviews. These included increasing the number of interviewees until 'views of the processes and the main issues proved to be so consistent with each other that more interviews began to produce a "diminishing return"' (Kogan 1975: 21). Triangulation was used to detect contrasting facts and fill in gaps of missing information. Whenever possible source materials were used as evidence to verify assumptions and support interpretation of events.

Admittedly the greatest limitation in this research was the lack of communication with pupils. In one urban middle school the researcher participated in extra-curricular activities for geography and therefore managed to talk with pupils informally. In other schools there was little chance to talk to pupils due to shortage of time. Even if a few pupils were approached they were too passive and gave general answers. Therefore this research has not illuminated how pupils perceive the usefulness and interest of SMSGC.

In studying China a researcher is easily caught in the dilemma between 'pseudo-sophistication' and 'Chinese exceptionism' (Harding 1984). The former refers to the misuse of Western social science models, concepts or hypotheses in explaining Chinese affairs. The latter implies that China is so unique that she cannot be explained by any 'Western' theories, but this often leads to 'English versions of Chinese official explanations'. Other writers have challenged the applicability of Western theories of curriculum innovation and implementation to developing countries because of differences in cultural context (Mohr 1969, Broadfoot 1980, Hurst 1983). A further complication is that the language of policy processes in communist states and in capitalist states differs a lot and makes cross-reference difficult (Holmes 1984, Ham and Hill 1984).

In this research it has been proved that purposeful reference to an international literature of curriculum innovation and implementation is beneficial and necessary. Insightful discussions raised by previous researchers provided a useful frame of reference within which focused observation could be made, particularly when little was known about curriculum innovation processes in China. A basic literature review enabled the researcher to arrive on the scene with a considerable 'theoretical baggage' (Kirk and Miller 1986) to enable a more systematic and efficient examination of the innovation process of SMSGC. It also provided a useful frame of reference for the interpretation and discussion of research findings. Moreover, differences in cultural context and language could only be identified in an analysis which offers the opportunity to contrast perspectives. The researcher enjoys an advantage that he is a Chinese who is familiar with the academic literature on curriculum innovation in the Western world, and yet he has no direct interest or prejudice in the success or failure of the innovation of SMSGC. There is also no intention to develop or test any theories. On the other hand, Chinese curriculum developers and policy makers are very keen on knowing how outsiders view their performance. They are also very sincere in wanting to know about foreign experiences and accept constructive suggestions for improvements in curriculum innovations in China. It is therefore possible to establish professional dialogue between the researcher and professionals in China based on mutual understanding and genuine exchange of viewpoints.

NOTE

1. Keypoint schools: special institutions which enjoy more favourable resourcing – more money for equipment, lower staff-student ratios – than ordinary schools. They enrol, through selective entrance tests, some 4 per cent of the secondary school population, and most of these students will continue to higher education.

3 Science Education as a Development Strategy in Nigeria: a Study of Kano State Science Secondary Schools

Abdalla Uba Adamu

INTRODUCTION

The early 1960s and early 1970s witnessed massive science education reform activities aimed at a more utilitarian interpretation of science education for pupils in both developed and developing countries. Two basic strategies can be identified. The first, which was predominant, focused attention on the nature of the science curriculum. The second focused on improving teaching and learning in schools and other institutions without large-scale reform of materials. Reforms of the first type were carried out mainly as science teaching projects aimed at improving school science curricula through reform in content and methods of teaching.

Such reforms occurred in both developed and developing countries such as Japan (Imahori 1980), Thailand (Sapianchai and Chewprececha 1984), Malaysia and Sri Lanka (Lewin 1980), Lebanon (Za'rour and Jirmanus 1977), Australia (Lucas 1972), Germany (Millar 1981), Holland (Hondebrink 1981), Malawi (Moss 1974), Nigeria (Ivowi 1982), and Canada (Ste-Marie 1982). However, the science education reform activities were not without their critics, who analysed the extent to which these reform activities did what they set out to do, and urged a clearer distinction between academic rhetoric and the socio-political realities of the project in action (Tisher *et al* 1972, Jackson 1983 and Lazerson *et al* 1984).

An added dimension to this strategy in both developed and developing countries (although more so in the latter), was an emphasis on an orientation to the labour market in some of the reforms, aimed at national self-reliance in scientific and technological disciplines through science education. This was inspired by the view that only a radical reform in science education could lead to national development and self-reliance (Bude 1980, Commissiong 1979, Knamiller 1984 and Maddock 1981a). Many school administrators and political leaders saw this as particularly important because it was expected that the students produced by these reforms would constitute a source of highly skilled manpower in science and technology, especially after having passed through higher education institutions.

The second science education reform strategy focused not on the science curriculum directly, but on the improvement of the conditions of schooling aimed at achieving similar goals to the project-based curricular reforms. This second approach, usually part of long-term educational planning, was aimed at the continuous production of school leavers with positive inclinations towards science as a subject of study, and consequently as a career. Examples of this category of science education efforts included the Turkish Science Lycée (Maybury 1975), the Philippines Science Education Center (now the Institute for Science and Mathematics Education) (Maddock 1981b), the Fitz-mat Preparatory Science School in the Soviet Union (Baez 1976), and the Kenya Science Teachers College (Gumo and Kann 1982).

In Kano State, Nigeria, a science education development strategy belonging to this last category was introduced by the state government in September 1977. This was the Science Secondary Schools Project, created to offer science education to specially selected senior secondary school students (Grades 10–12) under different conditions from conventional senior secondary schools in the state. The main objective of establishing the Science Schools was to provide an educational framework where Kano State students with a high inclination and aptitude for science and technology disciplines could be developed into a large stock of skilled manpower for the effective social development of Kano State.

This chapter traces the development of the project from two perspectives. The first is the genesis of the Science Schools Project as an educational change strategy. In this respect the chapter investigates the rationale and mechanism behind the establishment of the Science Schools. The second focus analyses the implementation of the project with reference to the classroom dynamics in the schools. This provides the opportunity to investigate the institutional realities of the Science Schools and to examine the extent to which the Science

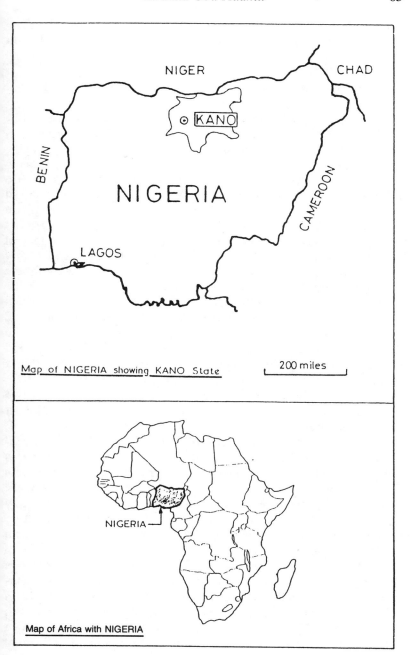

Map of NIGERIA showing KANO State   200 miles

Map of Africa with NIGERIA

Schools have contributed, or can be made to contribute, to the development of skilled indigenous manpower in science and technology for Kano State.

Considerations of Method

The overall data collection procedures for the study were inspired by the illuminative research tradition as proposed by Parlett and Hamilton (1972). Illuminative evaluation as an approach to studying educational innovations is rooted in social anthropology and seeks to describe and interpret, rather than to measure and predict. It also takes into account the contexts in which educational innovations must operate. The approach is characterised by a process of three-phase progressive focusing.

In the first, exploratory, phase investigators observe the general process and become familiar with the context of the change in a fairly unstructured and open way. The second phase begins with the selection of a number of phenomena and themes associated with the change, which emerge from the perceptions of the actors and from their actions, for a more sustained, focused and intensive study. The third phase consists in seeking general principles underlying the organisation of the change process, by spotting patterns of cause and effect within its operation and placing individual findings within a broader explanatory context (Parlett and Hamilton 1972).

In general terms therefore the defining features of the illuminative approach are to study the innovatory project; how it operates, how it is influenced by the various school situations in which it is applied, what those directly concerned regard as its advantages and disadvantages, and how students' intellectual tasks and academic experiences are most affected. It also hopes to discover and document what it is like to be participating in the scheme, whether as a teacher or pupil, and in addition to discern and discuss the innovation's most significant features. Thus the illuminative approach seeks to inform those with an interest in the innovation and assist those who have to make decisions about it.

The basic limitation associated with the illuminative approach is the subjectivity imposed by its interpretative nature. The interpretative paradigm of analysis, according to Burrell and Morgan (1979) is informed by a concern to understand the world as it is, to understand the fundamental nature of the social world at the level of subjective experience. It seeks explanation within the realm of individual consciousness and subjectivity, within the frame of reference of the participant as opposed to the observer of the action.

Thus lack of objectivity – or more appropriately, predominance of subjectivity – and assumed potential research bias are the main weaknesses of this approach. Some researchers who have used this approach, especially in evaluating science education programmes, have attempted to rationalise the process by introducing what they see as 'objective' elements in their strategies in order to balance out the subjectivity of the approach. For instance, Boud *et al*. (1985) used this tactic in an evaluation of the Western Australian Physical Science course. In explaining their analytical approach, they stated:

> Although attracted by this novel and different approach [of illuminative evaluation], we were reluctant to eschew elements of the established, traditional positivist methodologies. We were also acutely conscious of the possible charge of subjectivity, which is frequently leveled at interpretative research and from the very inception of the project took a number of steps to counteract this possibility. We tended, for example, to validate our impressions and observations by the collection of quantitative data if appropriate. Visits to schools were made on rotational basis by each of us in turn, major interviews were undertaken by two of us together. (Boud *et al*. 1985:88)

Further steps taken include separate preparation of field notes on observations, interviews and perceptions so that they can be cross-checked. A basic flaw in all these precautions is the implicit assumption that objectivity is evidenced by masses of quantitative data. In any event, subjectivity does not imply lack of empirically verifiable evidence. Subjective insights often capture the essence of different people speaking with different views. Moreover, some projects can be more effectively analysed from a subjective perspective, rather than from a standpoint which distances the researcher from the mechanism of the process.

Nevertheless, due to its flexibility, the illuminative approach can incorporate a wide range of techniques, which provide a powerful tool in conducting any enquiry with significant emphasis on social dimensions.

Using this framework, data for this study was obtained during seven months' fieldwork in Kano State, Nigeria, during which four schools – two Science Schools and two non-science – formed the main focus of the study. Structured classroom observations in these four schools, and interviews with science teachers, school administrators and policy initiators of the project all contributed to providing primary insights into the development of the project (see Adamu 1988).

THE GENESIS OF THE SCIENCE SCHOOLS PROJECT

Kano State was created in 1968 out of the then Northern Region of Nigeria. With a population of 10 million (Kano State 1981), of which 97 per cent were Muslim (Kano State 1970), the state emerged as the most populous and one of the most Islamic in Nigeria. However, the creation of the new state in 1968 was not without some problems for the state administration, because Kano State lacked the indigenous (that is, of Kano State origin) expert scientific and technical manpower considered essential for social development.

This situation arose because modern schooling, as the main agency for manpower training in Kano, was still to gain wide acceptance among the populace. This was caused by historical antecedents which linked the development of modern education in Nigeria with Christian missionary activities (Williams 1960, Graham 1966). Education therefore was viewed with suspicion as a forum for conversion to Christianity in a predominantly Islamic society (Kano State 1976, 1983). From 1968 to 1978 two successive Kano State governments had tried all sorts of strategies to ameliorate the situation. These included the provision of generous scholarship facilities for any student from Kano State to study any discipline of their choice, virtually free education at all levels of education, and even open threats of incarceration if parents did not allow their children to go to school. But despite these measures, the eventual educational output – both in its quantity and quality – was far less than that which the state government wanted, especially in scientific and technological disciplines.

This was the situation in Kano when the oil boom era exploded in Nigeria in the early 1970s, which saw the initiation of massive projects, based on the new-found wealth and aimed at the rapid social transformation of Nigerian society. The Kano State government, as part of this process, launched a very ambitious development plan in 1971. The strongest feature of this plan was its attention to agriculture and industrial development. As stated in the introduction to the Plan:

It is a farmers' plan; and this is as it should be considering the fact that agriculture is the backbone of Kano State economy.... But, while agriculture is given due priority, it is realized that industry is the hope for the future considering the density of population and the natural limitation of horizontal expansion in agriculture.... Industry is therefore given equal priority with agriculture in the belief that only balanced growth could serve our desired economic and social objectives.   (Kano State 1971:4)

The responsibility for the implementation of the development Plan was given to the Kano State Ministry of Economic Planning. However, the major obstacle – or 'bottleneck' – to these ambitious plans was expert manpower, especially in the scientific and technological fields necessary to guide the implementation of these projects. With the vibrant Nigerian economy of the early to late 1970s, the Kano State Civil Service Commission could afford to recruit the required manpower from overseas, but the government was also aware such manpower could not be relied on to remain for a long period.

To compound the situation, local personnel (especially those from Kano State) that could be relied on to stay on a permanent basis were not available either in the number required or in the necessary disciplines. This is reflected in the overall manpower situation in Kano State at that time, shown in Table 3.1, which reveals a shortage of indigenous manpower in all fields necessary for social and economic development in Kano State since its creation in 1968.

What was politically disturbing to Kano State policy makers at the time was the awareness of the vulnerability of the various development projects in Kano, should all the expatriates and other Nigerians decide to withdraw their services for whatever reason – as did indeed happen during the Nigerian Civil War (1966–70).

This situation was complemented by the general feeling among government officials in Kano that schooling was not functioning in a way which matched the hopes for social and economic development. As a Kano State Government document stated in referring to the situation in the 1970s:

The acute shortage of manpower in Kano State results largely from the lack of the right kind of educational facilities. In most of our secondary schools, the available science teaching facilities, laboratories, equipment, materials compared against actual school requirements are far too inadequate. In almost all secondary schools

TABLE 3.1   *Kano State manpower strength in science and technological disciplines, 1968–71*

Occupation	1968/69				1969/70				1970/71			
	KI	ON	NN	TOT	KI	ON	NN	TOT	KI	ON	NN	TOT
Doctors	3	–	22	25	3	–	28	31	5	1	29	35
Pharmacists	5	6	–	11	5	6	–	11	7	8	–	15
Architects	–	1	3	4	–	1	3	4	–	1	8	9
Surveyors	1	–	2	3	–	–	1	1	–	–	3	3
Engineers												
Civil	1	–	5	6	1	8	–	9	–	2	13	15
Water	–	–	4	4	–	–	2	2	–	2	10	12
Electrical/												
Mechanical	–	–	4	4	–	1	4	5	–	2	5	7
Irrigation	–	–	1	1	–	–	1	1	–	–	6	6
Agric.	–	1	–	1	–	1	–	1	–	1	–	1
Agriculture												
Vet. officers	–	–	2	2	–	–	3	3	2	1	4	7
Animal husbandry	1	–	–	1	3	–	–	3	3	1	–	4
Agric. officers	1	1	3	5	5	2	2	9	8	2	3	13
Pest control	–	3	1	4	1	3	1	5	1	3	1	5
Total	12	12	47	71	18	22	45	85	26	24	82	132

KI = Kano indigenes
ON = other Nigerians
NN = non-Nigerians
TOT = Total
SOURCE   Kano State 1970.

there is a general shortage of qualified science teachers. The students going into secondary schools do not appear to appreciate the career prospects of personnel with the needed science qualifications.   (Kano State 1979:138)

It was under these circumstances that a new military government came to power in Nigeria in 1975. One of the first acts of the newly appointed governor of Kano State was the reorganisation of the Kano State civil service. But because of the importance of the Ministry of Economic Planning in the implementation of the various projects in the state, its functions were further widened to include a ministerial committee called the Manpower Development Committee (MDC).

   In the few months immediately after its establishment, this Committee concentrated on monitoring the implementation of the various development projects that had been started. During the meetings of the Committee in late 1975, it eventually emerged that in every project there was a conspicuous lack of scientific and technical manpower, especially from Kano State. The agenda of the Committee began to focus on this problem by attempting to determine the most viable strategy for producing more technical manpower from Kano on a long-term basis, to provide leadership for such projects as might arise in the future. During one of their meetings, as the then Chairman of the Committee recalled:

> A member of the Committee just suggested that one of the best ways of dealing with this kind of situation potentially is to set up a Science Secondary School which will be a specialist school with nothing but concentration in science training ... so that instead of dissipating all resources in all the secondary schools, we would have a concentration of science students.　　(Interview 7/1/87)

Based on this rather spontaneous suggestion during a meeting, the Committee arrived at the tentative consensus that extensive and specialist schooling in secondary science education, which would be structurally different from the existing conventional schooling in Kano State, was the most viable solution to the problem of manpower development, although the Committee was not exactly sure what form it would finally take.

In arriving at the decision to propose the establishment of the Science Schools as a longer-term scheme for manpower production, the strategy set a precedent in that it was the first of its kind in Nigeria. But interestingly, the Science Schools emerged not out of professional dissatisfaction with the science curriculum – which was a major reason for the large-scale science education reforms in many other countries in the 1960s – or the way it was taught, but with the political need to increase the output of students with extensive science backgrounds from Kano State. As the Chairman of the Committee further explained:

> Many of us in the [Manpower Development Committee] were not science graduates. We were simple teachers of Arts and so on. Our main interest was to provide a situation where you give yourself the chance to select the best students that are endowed in science and develop that so that they could now perform better than they used to. The idea of being dissatisfied with the teaching of science at that time was not in anybody's mind. We were only dissatisfied with the

performance ... we didn't bother ourselves even to look at the [teaching methods, equipment or syllabuses] because we were not experts. Our expertise is only in provisions.   (Interview 7/1/87)

But this unorthodox origin of a major science education change strategy was not totally surprising since the decisions to establish the project were made not at the Ministry of Education, but at the Ministry of Economic Planning, which gave the project a different focus from those of the general science curriculum reform movements. Thus the Science Schools Project was determined directly by economic and political pressures, rather than by academic learning priorities. And although similar pressures contributed to the first generation science education reform activities in the United States (Harms and Yager 1981) and England (Waring 1979), nevertheless a significant focus of such science education activities in these countries, which provided models for the rest of the world, was on a radical reinterpretation of science teaching and its effects on the general development of the learner (Dowdeswell 1967, Gatewood and Obourn 1963, Goodlad *et al* 1966, Kelly 1963).

But although the Kano State Manpower Development Committee (MDC) had arrived at the decision that specialist training facilities were needed in Kano to produce the quantity and quality of scientific manpower needed, the Ministry of Economic Planning was not responsible for education or training. That was the responsibility of the Kano State Ministry of Education. As the next step, in early 1976 the Ministry of Economic Planning sent a memorandum to the Ministry of Education stating the recommendations of the MDC that scientific manpower training and production in Kano should be carried out by establishing Science Secondary Schools. The memorandum was discussed at a professional level at the Ministry of Education and, according to the Chairman of the MDC:

they came back and said they were not interested. In fact they were kind of saying well this is not your business: this is our business and we know what we are doing. So the idea almost died at that time.   (CTV 21/2/1986; also Interview 7/1/1987)[1]

And because the Ministry of Education had indicated its non-willingness to consider the proposals establishing the Science Schools, and since there was no other mechanism for implementing the idea, that would effectively have been the end of the project in Kano.

It was at this point that other, more arcane and little understood aspects of educational innovations, not often included in theoretical models of educational reform, began to have their influence on the development of the Science Schools, providing further insights into the mechanism of educational policy evolution in Nigeria.

The events were as follows: in April 1976 the Commissioner for Education in Kano resigned. The Military Governor of the State then appointed the Commissioner for the Ministry of Economic Planning, who was incidentally also the Chairman of the Manpower Development Committee, as the new – at first acting – Commissioner for Education. As he recalled:

> So from April/May 1976 I was holding these two responsibilities [Education and Economic Development, although later he moved completely to Education], and of course the initial memo that I sent to the Ministry of Education [about the Science Secondary Schools] which was almost killed, was resuscitated at that time for me. But I discovered at that time there was a lot of opposition, both in the Ministry [of Education] and in the Kano State Executive Council because people were arguing that that kind of idea was not for us here. They said it was a elitist kind of thing. What we needed to do, they said, was actually to improve science in all the secondary schools. (CTV 21/2/1986)

But this rationale was not acceptable to those who supported the establishment of the Science Schools. As the new Commissioner for Education further recalled:

> The argument was of course weak. I said things were extremely limited. The science teachers that you can find now are of course not available. It would be impossible for us to man all the secondary schools, provide excellent equipment in science and excellent teachers. (CTV 21/2/1986)

But now having total executive control over the Ministry of Education, it became possible for the new Commissioner to present his proposals for the establishment of the Science Secondary schools at the Kano State Executive Council meeting. Before presenting the idea, however, he wrote to the major universities in Nigeria with the proposal for their assessment and comments. As he further recalled: 'We had to go to Universities, get professors to examine it and tell us what they thought about the system. They were in favour of it' (CTV 21/2/1986). Even though the proposal was now firmly a Ministry of

Education concern, this remained the only time an attempt was made to gain an academic assessment of the project. And when the necessary and favourable comments were received, the proposal was placed on the agenda of the Kano State Executive Council meeting in late 1976. But it was not easy to get it accepted because of strong, and anticipated, opposition from the Executive Council generally, and the Ministry of Education in particular. This was all the stronger because of the nature of the proposal concerning the Science Schools.

There were four main points of the proposal. Firstly, a new body called the Science Secondary Schools Management Board would be created to implement the project, and it would be independent of the Ministry of Education in most aspects of its operations. As the then Commissioner for Education rationalised:

> In order to avoid the problems of the Ministry of Education, the government bureaucracy, and to give the scheme the best chance of success, we said the best way is to take it out of the system. Not to operate it within the Ministry of Education, but to create a parastatal that would be independent of the Civil Service and the bureaucracy of the Ministry of Education ... We realized we couldn't get the best teachers, the best equipment under those conditions of the Ministry of Education.   (Interview 7/1/1987)

However, financial control of the Board would be under the Commissioner for Education, who would have to approve its estimates before submitting them to the Ministry of Finance. To provide a legal backing to this Board, a Science Secondary Schools Management Board Edict was to be promulgated with effect from 1 January 1977. The Science Schools Management Board was to be controlled by its members which would include an Executive Secretary and Chairman.

Incidentally, the choice of the first members of the Board demonstrates the powerful effect of fellowship network interactions on the development and maintenance of the policy in Kano. As the new Commissioner for Education further stated:

> The first Chairman [of the Board] was Dr Sadiq Wali [a medical doctor], a science person, Dr Abdullahi [a mechanical engineer] who was a Commissioner later was also a member, and that had good repercussions later, because during the political days [1979–1983] the idea would have been killed again, if not for the fact that we had these people who had become Commissioners in the State.   (CTV 22/2/1986)

Secondly, the Ministry of Education was to provide three secondary schools which would be converted into Science Schools. Two of these schools would be for boys and one for girls. All the schools should have boarding facilities. This was to provide the students with full opportunities for concentrating on academic work under structured supervision. The Ministry of Education would also, in future, have to release any school the Science Board might wish to take over for the purposes of conversion into a Science School as part of their expansion.

Thirdly, the Science School students would be drawn from academically excellent students selected from the Form II cohort of all secondary schools in Kano, after a selection examination. This meant the Science Schools, starting with Form III, would be Senior Secondary Schools under the newly envisaged National Policy on Education (Federal Republic of Nigeria 1981) which split secondary education in two tiers of Junior and Senior Schools, each of three years duration. At the end of the Senior years, the students would take the General Certificate of Education Ordinary Level examinations (replaced in 1990 by the Senior Secondary School Certificate Examination).

In the initial stage, each of the Science Schools was expected to have 720 students when fully operational, with 240 students in each of the three years. The proposal further stipulated the teacher-student ratio should be 1 teacher per 20 students (instead of 1 teacher per 35 students as in conventional schools). And subsequently, each of the Science Schools should have eight laboratories (instead of the three for the main science subjects available in conventional secondary schools), two each for biology, chemistry and physics, and in the boys' schools a technical drawing studio and a geography room.

Finally, each student would have to offer the following subjects only: biology, chemistry, physics, mathematics, English, geography, Hausa language or Islamic religious knowledge, and for girls, food and nutrition. Boys would take one elective chosen from technical drawing, further mathematics, or agricultural science. Interestingly, it was this rigid curricular offering that would characterise, in the main, the Science Schools.

The Kano State Executive Council accepted this proposal with all its attendant conditions, but persistent opposition was quite strong, mainly from the Ministry of Education. The latter, hitherto the sole educational power in Kano State associated with restrictive and conservative tendencies, saw its power base being eroded by the

Science Board over which it had no immediate control. The first Executive Secretary of the Science Board (1976–78), analysed the nature of this opposition as follows:

> All the opposition we had in the Ministry of Education at that time – and there was very very strong opposition – was surprisingly from people who should not oppose the idea of Science Secondary Schools at all. Their opposition, I am sure, had nothing to do with science being anti-Islamic. I think the opposition was primarily because they think we were trying to hijack some bright students from their schools and putting them in these prestigious schools – schools that one of us called elitist because he said we were only going to put the sons of who and who in the schools. This, when I know very well they themselves represent elitism in this country!
>
> (Interview 22/2/1987)

Despite the opposition to the concept, the Military Governor of Kano State accepted the proposals to establish the Science Schools. As he announced in April 1977 during a policy broadcast to the State:

> Two existing secondary schools have already been converted to schools of science. These schools will emphasise science in their curriculum so as to enable us to compete in gaining university places in the field of science in which we are very deficient.
>
> (Kano State 1977:4)

The Establishment and Functions of the Board

Based on the recommendations of the Kano State Executive Council, the Science Secondary Schools Management Board was established in March 1977 by the Kano State Government. The Science Secondary Schools Management Board Edict was published in January 1977 (but it later became the Science and Technical Schools Board Law in 1982 [Kano State 1982]), and the Science Schools started operations in September 1977. Once the Science Board was established as an administrative organisation, its objectives became much more clearly formed. According to an internal communication of the Science Board dated 5 April 1984, the Board is vested with:

> the responsibility for providing science education at secondary level, with the following hopes and aspirations in mind:
> (a) that more secondary school leavers with science backgrounds will eventually be produced;

(b) that the majority of those so produced will proceed to higher institutions of learning;
(c) that in the long run, a crop of high level manpower (doctors and engineers) will be available;
(d) that the expected insignificant few that might not necessarily be doctors and engineers might find themselves in the polytechnics for HND/OND courses in: (i) engineering (civil and mechanical); (ii) agro-allied, food technology and lab technology fields; health and nursing care.

It is significant to note the nature of the expectations placed on the Science Schools by the Kano State Government. These objectives must be kept in mind when analysing the development and outcomes of the Science Schools Project in Kano, as they become the criteria against which the outcomes are judged.

The Science Secondary Schools

(a) Initial preparations
The first two boys' schools selected for conversion into Science Schools were the secondary schools at Dawakin Kudu (originally established in 1975), and Dawakin Tofa (1972). Each of these schools was well built and located in a pleasant rural pasture land. The Dawakin Kudu School was also relatively new at the time (1977) and built with financial assistance from the United Nations Development Project. But most significantly, both were exactly the same short distance away from the Kano metropolitan area (32 kilometres). This was important to the planners of the Science Schools Project because they did not want to locate the schools too far from Kano which would make them unattractive places to work for teachers, especially expatriate staff. As the first Executive Secretary of the Science Board explained:

The two schools (Dawakin Kudu and Dawakin Tofa) were selected because we wanted schools that were very close to Kano, where we can literally leave the office now and get there within the next twenty minutes. And we needed centres where you can put international staff without them having to worry about coming to Kano. We also needed easy access to Kano because we thought if our laboratories could not operate we bring our staff and students to laboratories in Bayero University [in Kano] – because we were not prepared to allow anything to stop us from operating.
(Interview 22/2/1987)

(b) The Students

There was no area in the establishment of the Science Schools in Kano that created more controversy with both principals and civil servants than the selection of the students for the Science Schools. Under the standard procedure, students considered academically good in Form II in all secondary schools in Kano owned by the Ministry of Education were given a selection examination and those who passed taken to the Science Schools where they continued with Form III.

The selection examination papers were in integrated science, mathematics and English language. A student had to pass each at a level determined by the Science Board to be eligible for interviews, after which if successful they were placed in one of the Science Schools. Not all the principals of the conventional schools were happy with this selection. As the principal of a feeder school explained:

> Believe me, not me alone but many people, the teachers, you see are grumbling that the best students have been taken away and as such nobody should blame us for having very bad students. There is nothing we can do about this. This is a government project and they can do whatever they want.   (Interview 30/9/1986)

The possibility that the selection process could be influenced in favour of certain socio-politically powerful groups in Kano was raised with the officials of the Science Board. However, it was made clear that selection of students to the schools was based purely on merit and passing the examination. As the principal of one of the Science Schools explained:

> The criteria in selecting the students for this school is not based on any social class. Rather it is strictly based on merit, and therefore any averagely intelligent student, no matter his background, can be able to come here if he satisfies those criteria. And certainly, we have an aggregate of students from all sorts of backgrounds.
>   (Interview 8/10/1986)

After the initial selection exercise in 1977, the first set of 240 students was selected from 22 secondary schools in Kano. A total of 120 students were sent to (each of) the (then only) two Science Schools in existence in September 1977. Subsequently, however, some of the principals in the feeder schools responded to the situation by presenting for the selection examinations their poorer, instead of their above average students. But the Science Board discovered this quickly, as a principal of a conventional secondary school explained:

We cannot even substitute bad students for good students during the selection. These people come from the Science Board and they try to examine the files of my students and they may like to see my students physically. We have to be honest in this. The question of my opinion (as a principal) does not arise because nobody will ask for my opinion: do I like it or not? No, nobody will ask me ... Then there are many students who would like to go to these schools because they feel that the science secondary school is better than any school in which they are.   (Interview 30/9/1986)

The principals of the feeder schools argued against the Science Schools on the main point that they take away their best students. Further, if it is true the Science Schools are special in the sense of having better equipment and teachers and other facilities, then it makes more sense to select not the best students from the feeder schools who, if they are good anyway would succeed no matter where they are, but to take students who are less than average, but very likely with latent abilities in science and allow the good environment of the Science Schools to develop them. In this way, the conventional schools will develop their good students, and the Science Schools will enable students with latent abilities in science to manifest themselves to the benefit of everyone. But the Chairman of the MDC did not agree with these arguments and pointed out:

The system was not supposed to drain the schools of the best students. We are concerned with the students with a natural endowment in science. The teachers should not be feeling they have lost their best students unless you are saying only science students are the best. But of course that is not so.

(Interview 7/1/1987)

But all these issues reflect the various stages any education reform policy undergoes before it becomes part of accepted tradition, especially if it had unorthodox origins. And despite the uncertain start, the Science Schools Project gradually stabilised, and in 1980, the first Ordinary level examinations in the school were taken. In 1981, a Girls' Science School was eventually established, even though there was initial opposition to it from the Kano State Ministry of Education. In 1985, another boys' school at Kafin Hausa was also started, while in 1987 a second Girls' Science School was opened in Jahun, bringing to five the total number of Science Schools in Kano in 1987, with a combined student population of over 3000 science students – the highest number of such a category of students since the establishment of modern schools in Kano in 1927.

IMPLEMENTATION OF THE PROJECT: OBSERVATIONS OF CLASSROOM STRATEGIES IN THE SCIENCE SCHOOLS

To determine how aspects of the Science Schools Project were being implemented, I undertook a seven-month period of fieldwork which included studying two of the Science Schools (a boys' school and a girls' school) during which a substantial period of time was spent in structured classroom observations of biology and physics teachers. The observations were deemed necessary to the design of the main research because in the analysis of the antecedent factors that led to the development of the Science Schools, the specific academic emphasis of the Science Schools was one area where purposes and intentions were less clear than in the policy formulation of the entire project as described above.

For all the elaborate steps taken to ensure the survival of the project, neither opponents nor supporters based their arguments on a careful consideration of the science curriculum. And since no specific science curricular modules or packages were developed for the new Science Schools in 1977, they simply adopted the Nigerian science curriculum which, interestingly enough, was already under criticism as being inadequate to the aspirations of the contemporary Nigerian society (Ivowi 1982).

However, in September 1985 the federal government introduced a new science curriculum in all Senior Secondary Schools (NERC 1985) which contained similar themes to the predominant science curricular reforms in other countries, emphasising science as a process rather than content. With the implementation of the new science curriculum, the Science Schools assumed the unique property of combining two science education change strategies in one place.

My classroom observations therefore provided an opportunity to determine the extent to which carefully selected teachers (with high science qualifications), and equally carefully selected students (who had passed rigorous science aptitude examinations) interact with specialist provisions (given high priority by government policy) to create a medium for the successful interpretation of science learning objectives. Part of the results of these observations are summarised in Table 3.2.

TABLE 3.2 *Science teaching in Kano State science secondary schools*

Category	Freq.	Minutes	Percentage
1 Settling down	31	155	11.7
2 Teacher talks and			
introduces topic,	25	125	9.4
reviews topic,	21	105	7.9
expands explanation of topic	189	945	71.5
3 Students ask questions	1	5	0.3
4 Teacher asks questions	13	65	4.9
5 Teacher refers to text	0	0	0.0
6 Teacher writes on board			
for students to copy	37	185	14.0
7 Teacher demonstrates activity	5	25	1.8
8 Students carry out activity	5	25	1.8
9 Class discussion of activity	0	0	0.0

It is interesting to note the teachers' emphasis during science teaching in the Science Schools. This is because the new science curriculum clearly expects teachers to teach science using the 'process' approach which inspired its development. For instance, in the introduction to the biology curriculum, it was urged by its developers:

In accordance with the stated objectives, the contents and context of the syllabus places emphasis on field studies, guided discovery, laboratory techniques and skills, coupled with conceptual thinking. So teachers are strongly encouraged to employ the student-activity [method] based on an inquiry mode of teaching.

(NERC 1985 Biology:ii)

Yet an analysis of the distribution of the performance objectives in the three science subjects of the new Nigerian science curriculum reveals that 90 per cent of the performance objectives were stated so as to test the cognitive domain, with only 10 per cent aimed at testing the psychomotor domain. None were stated in the affective domain (Adamu 1988).

Thus with a predominant emphasis on the cognitive domain in the science curriculum, it is not surprising that, despite the curricular rhetoric, teachers spend over 85 per cent of biology and physics teaching in predominantly verbal exposition. Student involvement accounted for less than 2 per cent of the student-teacher interactions (as indicated in Table 3.2). This is similar to the findings by Lewin (1981, 1984) of science teaching in Malaysia and Sri Lanka who observed that:

Less than 16 per cent of the class time was spent with pupils actually undertaking experimentation as the main activity. Most class time – over 32 per cent – was spent with the teacher addressing the class as a whole ... Further analysis of the observation data indicated that the 'guided discovery' approach recommended in course materials was used by very few teachers. For example, on no occasion were pupils observed contributing to the design of experiments, and they were rarely asked to hypothesise, predict, interpret or infer.   (Lewin 1984:40)

From both the strategic emphases of the teachers during the lessons in the Science Schools, and the opinions expressed, it was clear that not all teachers shared the same pedagogical views of science teaching objectives as those of the developers of the new science curriculum. As one teacher expressed it:

They are not realistic, because if you follow the set down objectives, as far as the new science curriculum is concerned, you find that it is too demanding, too demanding. It is demanding on the teacher. You see so many demonstrations which you need to do, but when you look around you can't find what to demonstrate with.   (Interview 25/2/1987)

In any event, the Science Board, itself none too clear on the specifics of the pedagogic emphases of the Science Schools Project, was not convinced that recommending any teaching style to its teachers would have been useful. As an official of the Board argued, there would be problems:

... if you recommend a particular technique [of teaching science to the students]. It may not be known to the teachers. You have to realise that in Nigeria today, it is not all teachers who are in the classroom who are actually teachers. They don't even have the basic qualification for teaching. They just wear degrees, you know, up and down; but they are not professionally trained teachers. Now if you tell him to adopt a particular technique or strategy, how does he do it? Now this is something totally unknown to him.
                                      (Interview 23/9/1986)

Thus the development of educational policies in Nigeria is often characterised by a considerable lack of correlation between policy expectation and achievement. This has significant consequences for implementation, as well as attainment of outcomes, in the sense that major parts of the policy rationale behind such change strategies were not incorporated in the methods of the implementation or monitoring mechanisms.

The relatively few instances where students were actually involved in experiments could not have been enough to expose them to the full range of potentialities of practical work in science as implied by the ethos of the Science Schools Project. And even in the few cases where students were engaged in some form of practical activity, the feeling generated for the observer was that the exercise was more of a routine task than a deliberate process designed to enhance a specific mode of scientific thinking in the student. This is illustrated by one practical I observed in the boys' Science School:

Teacher comes to the laboratory about five minutes late. Spends another twenty-five giving a theoretical preview of the practical. The practical has two stated aims: to study the effect of heat and to see the difference between heat value and temperature. Since the experiment involved heating, one piece of equipment is a wire gauze.

The group to which I attach myself (four students, each with a different 'assignment' – their arrangement, not the teacher's – concerning observation and recording of the experiment) has a faulty wire gauze which actually catches fire in parts whenever it is placed over the bunsen burner, and the group leader reports this to the teacher. But no replacement can be found and the teacher tells the group to 'manage' with the one it has. This it does, and obtains a far different result from those obtained in other groups.

At the end of the practical students gathered their books and left. Interestingly, the teacher did not point to the significance of this situation to the students in our group as a background to scientific technique, and when I pointed out this potential source later, he replied there was no time to go into that.

(Observation Notes 26/1/1987)

From this, and other observed lessons, it would appear that the messages about, or the curricular emphases in, the new science curriculum, important as they are to the educational planner, do not emerge as points of particular emphasis during the teaching of biology and physics in the Science Schools.

The relatively little amount of student practical activity during teaching (1.8 per cent as suggested in Table 3.2) is, ironically, explained by the insufficiency of materials and equipment which necessitates some regulation in both the frequency of the practicals and mass student participation in them. One teacher summarised the comments made by his colleagues about the laboratory situation in the Science Schools by explaining that, due to insufficiency of laboratory materials:

> Last year [1986] we had to compel students to answer certain questions in the GCE physics practical, which was unfair. But this is because the apparatus for each question were not sufficient if it were to go around.   (Interview 25/2/1987)

The emergence of the lack of laboratory materials as a hindering factor to effective teaching in the Science Schools must come as a surprise considering the rationale of the entire Science Schools Project, and the investment of the Kano State Government in it.

When faced with the situation of a lack of sufficient materials and equipment for full practicals, or for involvement of students in an activity-based mode of learning, teachers resorted to largely theoretical expositions rather than organising practical events which might have involved the students, or at least the teacher, in some demonstration; this then became the established routine of teaching both biology and physics.

This had a burdening effect on both the teachers and students and was illustrated by several of the observed lessons in which, after a series of complicated explanations, the teacher promised a full practical at a later stage. A typical lesson with this characteristic which took place entirely in the classroom reflects this:

> The topic is 'Effect of Heat'. Teacher introduces topic by asking questions on the definition of heat.
> Teacher: What is heat?
> Student: It is a form of energy.
> Teacher: Correct, but can you explain further since there are many forms of energy? What about light?
> Student: (getting uncomfortable) It stimulates vision.
> Teacher: (to another student) What is the effect of heat?
> Student: Produces feeling of hotness or coldness.
> Teacher: What about substances like rubber. Do they increase or decrease with heating?
> Student: Decrease.
> Teacher: Actually it does not decrease in size, but changes shape. But we will consider that when we come to the side-effects of heat in the experiment. If you are vigilant you will see that the rubber

does not melt. But I am saying its size must increase before melting. If you do the experiment you will find an increase in volume so do not say it contracts. (Diary 30/10/86)

This lesson was conducted without any specific aid which would communicate the concept more clearly. The adopted style of teaching in the Science Schools is always rationalised by the teachers by reference to the inadequacy of laboratory materials and equipment. As a teacher observes:

The two labs are fairly equipped when compared to other [non-science] schools. But when it comes to the real consideration of whether a lab is equipped or not, I have to say that they are badly equipped, or perhaps poorly equipped. You find that if it is the day-to-day running of the teaching courses, then you can do with the few apparatus, and you can call the students around and you demonstrate something and you are okay. But when it comes to the GCE exams where you need every student to have an apparatus to himself, that is where you find the problems: that is when you find that the lab is so poor in terms of apparatus. (Interview 25/2/1987)

But disparity between what the curriculum developer (or administrator) aims at and what teachers do in the classroom is emerging as a standard feature of science education curriculum reform, in both developing countries (Lewin 1980, 1981, 1984, Maddock 1981b), and interestingly, in some developed countries such as Canada (Aikenshead 1984, Ste-Marie 1982). For instance the report of various case studies of observations of science teaching in many Canadian schools revealed:

Senior-year teachers view science as a precise method and as a system of exact numbers, highly organized bodies of information and specialized terminology. Their concern is to provide students with the notes and with the practice in solving problems that will result in high marks on examinations and allow the student to move through high school to university. Work in the lab is geared towards illustrating facts and theories presented in the classroom, confirming what is discussed in class, obtaining precise facts and getting the right answers to problems ... Alternative approaches, such as those emphasizing inquiry processes or the relationship of science to social issues or technology, are not seen as central activities for the science classroom, but as a means of encouraging interest. (Orpwood and Souque 1984:23)

It would seem therefore that science education reform strategies, especially if perceived as part of a developmental process, are characterised universally by a considerable lack of correlation between policy expectations and classroom realities.

THE OUTCOMES OF THE SCIENCE SCHOOLS PROJECT

A discussion of the outcomes of the Science Schools Project in Kano is not possible without some qualifier since 'outcome' has a different meaning for an analyst and a policy maker. In the policy maker's perspective, the term is used to emphasise the successes of the Science Schools Project, especially as there were two basic reasons for setting up the project. The first was to increase the number of qualified science students who graduated from secondary schools and who would continue their studies to higher institutions, as compared with the output of such students before the establishment of the Science Schools. The second was to increase the amount of scientific and technical manpower in Kano State through the Science Schools.

Examination Outcomes

The first question about outcomes therefore focuses on the extent to which the establishment of the Science Schools has made any difference to the number of GCE Ordinary level science graduates from Kano. This is difficult to answer without accurate information about the number of science graduates produced by secondary schools in Kano before the establishment of the Science Schools. But according to figures made available by the Science Board, 2447 science students from the Science Schools have graduated between 1980 and 1987. And from various discussions with policy initiators of the project, this alone justifies the project since this number far exceeds the number that all the conventional secondary schools have produced since the establishment of Kano State in 1968.

However, a more important measure of success of the project is provided by the Nigerian General Certificate of Education Ordinary Level examination results of these students. The results are in five core subjects and are shown in Table 3.3.

Table 3.3 indicates an average pass rate of 56 per cent in the five core subjects in the Science Schools – results with which the Science Board is quite happy, since they enable a lot of the students to gain

TABLE 3.3   *Science schools general GCE ordinary level examination passes,*
1980–1986

Subject	D/Tofa No.	Pass	D/Kudu No.	Pass	Taura No.	Pass	Totals No.	Pass	PCT
Chemistry	1053	690	1235	849	127	63	2415	1602	66
Maths	1054	610	1269	892	129	34	2452	1536	62
Biology	1053	504	1238	858	129	100	2420	1462	60
Physics	1053	473	1237	924	129	50	2419	1447	59
English	1053	368	1237	432	128	35	2418	835	34
Average	1052	529	1243	791	128	282	2424	1376	56

SOURCE   Science and Technical Schools documents. Figures exclude Taura
1986 results.

admission into higher institutions to study science and technological
disciplines. As the Executive Secretary of the Science Board
explained:

> Our achievements have been that we have produced the calibre of
> students envisaged in the programme. Obviously Kano State
> wanted to produce these kids who are rich in science background
> for their degree courses. Luckily enough, we have been able to
> produce these kids. I'll say on the average between 50–60 per cent
> of those students in the schools meet university admission require-
> ments. In the past Kano State has been lagging behind in the
> science-based areas. But with the maturity of the Science Schools
> we have been able to get our students in all areas where our quota
> (in admission to Nigerian universities) is earmarked. In fact in
> some cases we even fill up the quotas of other states.
>
> (Interview 23/10/1986)

Labour Market Implications

The second question about the outcomes analyses the extent to which
the project has provided a basis for specialised manpower production
in the areas required. As with the first focus, this also has its
problems, not the least of which is that follow-up services do not exist
within the Science Board which would enable a more accurate
investigation of the various careers of the former students to be
carried out. However, a population check on the distribution of the
former students in various degree courses in three universities in

Northern Nigeria, Ahmadu Bello University at Zaria (ABU), Bayero University, Kano (BUK) and Usman Danfodio University, Sokoto (UDU) provides an indication of the discipline specialisation of 308 of the former Science School students. This distribution is shown in Table 3.4.

TABLE 3.4   *Course distribution of Science School students in ABU, BUK and UNISOK, 1984–86*

| | | | | Graduation | |
Course	No	%	ABU	BUK	SOK
Science	87	28.2	1987	1989	1990
Engineering	40	12.9	1989	1988	–
Agriculture	39	12.6	1989	–	1990
Human medicine	22	7.1	1989	1991	1991
Pharmacy	13	4.2	1988	–	–
Environmental design	11	3.5	1988	–	–
Veterinary medicine	6	1.9	1989	–	–
SBS-science*	87	28.2	–	–	–
Non-science Library science	1	0.3	–	–	–
Education	1	0.3	–	–	–
Business administration	1	0.3	–	–	–
Total	308	100.0			

SOURCE   Science and Technical Schools documents.
*SBS – School of Basic Studies; preliminary and non-faculty.

The expected year of graduation of the most recent student in that course is also given. This means, for instance, by 1991 Kano State expects to have 22 medical doctors, since by then all of them will have graduated from their courses; 11 of the 22 potential doctors will graduate from ABU by 1989, and the rest from BUK and Sokoto by 1991. It should be emphasised the figures refer only to students in three universities. Other former Science School graduates from other institutions (Universities of Maiduguri, Ife and Nsukka where they are found) are not included. As such the figures in each course could be higher.

Similarly, by 1990, Kano State expects to have 87 scientists graduating in various disciplines ranging from biochemistry, micro-biology and physics, to computer science and chemistry. Engineering, like medicine, is a discipline for which the policy initiators of the Science Schools expected a high turnout. It is therefore significant to note that 40 engineers will be available to Kano State by 1988 from two of the universities in various sub-disciplines which included civil, mechanical, agricultural and chemical engineering.

The impact of the Science Schools, especially in the production of so many science students from Kano State in institutions of higher learning has not gone unnoticed, especially in Northern Nigeria. This was indicated during the 1985 Macroscope event in the Ahmadu Bello University, Zaria. Macroscope is an annual event organised by the Faculty of Science of the university, and features several scientific activities designed to promote the teaching, learning and use of science at all levels of formal education in the catchment areas of the university. Not only did the Dawakin Tofa Science School win the third best position during the events, but the Permanent Secretary, Kaduna State Ministry of Education, who was an observer at the events, remarked:

Having realised the fact that Kano State can now fill in its quota in the science disciplines in our higher institutions, as a result of the large number of scientifically sound students it graduates every year from its Science Secondary Schools, Kaduna State government has now completed plans to follow its footsteps. From the next academic year (1986/87), every Local Government Area in Kaduna State will have a fully-fledged Science Secondary School.

(Quoted in a speech delivered by the Principal, Dawakin Tofa Science Secondary School during the Parent Teacher Association General Meeting of the School, 23 November 1985)

The importance of this for Kano State is seen in an appreciation of the rationale of establishing the Science Schools by a former member of the Committee that proposed the establishment of the project who observed:

We had so many Uncle Toms, cold feet and the rest of it all along, but I think the end justifies the means. What we have produced with the Science Board has now cleared everything. Later on even those who were opposed to the idea saw that the salvation was in the Science Schools. We produced the best, we had the best. The next set of doctors we are going to have this year from the Ahmadu Bello University Teaching Hospital are going to be all 'yan Kano' (Kano indigenes), and Kano for the first time will have 20 doctors this year; all 'yan Kano', all 'Musulmi' (Muslims) and they were all from Science Secondary Schools. They will make impact because everybody will see doctors in Murtala Muhammad Hospital, very many of them 'suna *Assalamu Alaykum, sai an jima, wane*'.[2] And they are all from the Science Secondary Schools.

(Interview 22/2/1987)

Interestingly, none of the officials interviewed was willing to consider any unexpected outcomes of the Science Schools Project. However, the Executive Secretary was able to state:

Well, I anticipate the Science Schools will create positive and negative problems obviously. Now everybody is smiling; they are doing well, students are going into universities. They are being absorbed, they have started graduating and they are coming out. But certainly, within a space of ten years probably from today, there may be an over-production of science graduates in Kano State. In fact it won't be ten years. In the next seven to eight years there will be an over-production of science-based graduates from the Science Secondary Schools.   (Interview 23/9/1986)

But although the official response to the outcomes of the Science Schools Project indicates satisfaction with these outcomes from a policy perspective, the change analyst would wish to reflect on the extent to which the outcomes of the project can be considered satisfactory.

This is because the evidence presented indicates that the Science Schools have not succeeded in changing the teaching and learning styles of teachers and students in the schools – despite the special resources created for them. It would seem therefore that in considering projects such as the Science Schools as part of a large-scale national development drive, policy formulators need to clarify the range of expectations and outcomes of massive participation in science education if they intend it to become an agent of intellectual and social transformation. Unless such purposes and intentions are shared by all participants in the scheme, there is bound to be confusion about whether the outcomes of such projects can be attributed to the students, to teachers or to the expensive learning contexts created by such projects.

REFLECTIONS, CONCLUSIONS AND IMPLICATIONS

The purpose of this chapter has been to study the Science Secondary

Schools Project in Kano as a long-term scientific and technological manpower development strategy, to determine the rationale and mechanism of its initiation and to evaluate its outcomes.

Since completing the main work from which this chapter was adapted (Adamu 1988), the author has had a chance to go over the fieldwork strategies, and meet the central actors in the Science Schools drama again, but under less formal conditions than during the fieldwork (1986–87). These post-fieldwork encounters confirmed the usefulness of the analytical approach adopted for the entire research, which, in the main, was the illuminative framework (Parlett and Hamilton 1972).

Certainly, the wholeness of the picture of the project that emerged as a result of using this analytical approach would not have been possible if attempts had been made to use quantitative measures that involved, for instance, lengthy analysis of questionnaire responses from officials. The massive databank such analysis would yield would probably make the overall data presentation more impressive – but not much more useful than the naturalistic processes adopted under the illuminative framework. Further, there was absolutely no way by which the insights provided by the policy formulators connected with the project could have been extracted using any other method. Thus the subjective nature of the illuminative analytical framework does not seem to have hampered the data collection, analysis or interpretation of this particular project.

From the evidence presented, we have seen that the purpose of setting up the Science Schools Project in Kano State was to encourage a more effective understanding of science in social transformation, using specialised institutions of science teaching and learning. However, the intellectual advancement of the students of the Science Schools, which was a major part of the rationale of the science education reform movement, did not emerge as a primary concern of the project. This situation came about because, while there was extensive problem diagnosis in the process leading to the establishment of the project, there were no clear specifications of how the project could achieve those outcomes associated with the use of science in personal and social development.

This is because an analysis of how the science curriculum is applied in the Science Schools reveals a lack of correlation between the way the students are taught, and the emphasis in science teaching expected by the developers of the science curriculum. As the data suggests, science teaching in the Science Schools does not develop the students' abilities in terms of the acquisition of the intellectual characteristics envisaged by the new science curriculum. It merely identifies these abilities so that those who continue with education beyond the Science Schools and go to the University can do the sort of programmes expected of them by the progenitors of the Science Schools Project.

The development of the Science Schools also suggests that policy implementation in Nigeria is less reliant on the emergence of the policy as a rational strategy for social transformation than on the way socio-politically powerful individuals connected with the policy become committed to it.

Thus what emerges from the findings of this chapter is that a political rationale for educational change strategies in Nigeria provided a suitable basis for projecting beliefs about social progress, but little attention was paid to how these change strategies would be sustained, or how they fitted in with social realities. The issues facing any change strategist are not just those of needs, clarity, complexity or the quality of the materials used, but the constant production of personnel who identify with the rationale of the change strategy enough to see to its maintenance and to achieve a reasonable measure of its objectives. That is the essence of science education as a long-term service aimed at radical social transformation.

The findings in this chapter are significant in that most developing countries rely on administrative initiative for curricular reform. And if a practice is established whereby administrative priorities override academic considerations, then attainment of development goals through science education becomes susceptible to the instability of economic and political forces prevalent in developing countries. This will have a retarding effect on the achievement of national development goals.

NOTES

1. Transcript of a Kano Community Television (CTV) documentary programme, The Dawaki Experiment, broadcast Kano 22/2/86. I am grateful to Mallam Aminu Mahmood of CTV for making available the mastertapes of the interviews, film footage and script. The latter part of the interview was based on my own transcripts from the interview I held with the former Chairman of the Manpower Development Committee.

These two interview sources are subsequently identified either by a date to indicate my own interviews, or CTV to refer to the interviews given for the programme.

2. Literally: 'peace on you, see you later'. This linguistic lapse was used by the interviewee to convey the impressions of identification between the doctors and the patients in the hospitals since they are now the same, as opposed to previous years when expatriates and other Nigerians beside Kano indigenes dominated the medical field in Kano.

Part II
Teacher Development
Projects

Perhaps one of the answers to the problem of implementing curricular change in practice lies in the re-education of teachers. The next two studies present strongly contrasting models of professional development. Noor Azmi Ibrahim investigated the inservice programme designed by the Malaysian Ministry of Education to introduce all primary school teachers in the country to the new national primary school curriculum. This was done by a 'cascade' training model, in which key personnel attended a central induction course before training other trainers who would then pass on the information to classroom teachers. He charts the reactions of both the trainers and the teachers to the way this model worked in practice: despite their professional commitment many teachers felt the short courses they attended had not met their needs. Noor Azmi's classroom observations confirmed that, while teachers had taken on board some elements of the new curriculum such as schemes of work and materials, the teaching and learning approaches had not altered far in the directions laid down by the new curriculum. He concludes there was too much emphasis on content and too little on process in the way the courses were designed; they were too highly standardised, giving little latitude to trainers to respond to teachers' needs; there was too little time and no follow-up.

Janet Stuart's study was, by contrast, a small-scale grassroots initiative based on an action research model; this involved analysing the situation in which she and a group of teachers were acting as change agents. The study records her year in Lesotho working as 'consultant' to five development studies teachers who were trying to improve their own classroom practice. She describes how the teachers identified certain problems they encountered in their teaching and how they began experimenting with new methods, collecting data and analysing it as they went along. Each teacher conducted two or three action research cycles during the year; evidence is offered of how they had developed professionally in several ways by the end of the period. However, although this process was effective for the teachers concerned, it was time- and personnel-intensive and only a few ripples seem to have spread to other teachers or institutions.

The contrasts are obvious and striking: the Malaysian programme covered everyone but only superficially and ineffectively; the Lesotho project covered a handful effectively but was too expensive for many to take part in. Whether and how a middle way can be found remains to be explored.

Stuart's method can answer the criticism Noor Azmi makes of the centralised, didactic model: the action research was needs-led, teacher-centred, allowed time for change to take place, and produced classroom changes. But it is not practical to work with large numbers of teachers in such an intensive way, nor would it be appropriate for a Ministry wishing to impose a particular model on a country, since the action research model expects teachers to find their own answers, albeit within a framework of shared assumptions.

What lessons can be drawn for encouraging teacher change through inservice courses? Both studies emphasise the eagerness of teachers to attend courses to get help to improve their teaching; this enthusiasm can be tapped. Time is important – teachers need time to interact with trainers and to assimilate the new ideas, adapting their own practice. Some degree of central support and direction is probably necessary, coupled with rewards and recognition to teachers who commit themselves.

A central question is how far teachers' professional development can and should be directed from the centre in pursuit of governmental policy; is it more effective when undertaken in small peer groups, or school-based, in response to teachers' own felt needs?

4 Inservice Training in Malaysia for the New Primary Curriculum (KBSR)

Noor Azmi Ibrahim

INTRODUCTION

This chapter examines the dissemination and implementation of a new national curriculum (KBSR) in Malaysian primary schools. It describes and seeks to explain the nature and the effectiveness of inservice courses in the dissemination and implementation of the curriculum, and the factors influencing them; and the state of teachers' professionalism in the implementation of the curriculum. It looks at the implications of such factors for the dissemination and implementation of KBSR and other future curriculum innovations in Malaysia or elsewhere.

The Setting

The Malaysian school system consists of three types of primary and secondary schools. The primary schools, for six to eleven year-olds, are differentiated by the medium of instruction used in the schools: Bahasa Malaysia (Malay) for the national school, Chinese for the national type Chinese school, and Tamil for the national type Tamil school. The secondary schools, for 12 to 18 year-olds, are differentiated in terms of academic (including science), technical and vocational schools. The language of instruction in all secondary schools and at tertiary level is Bahasa Malaysia.

The administrative machinery exists at four hierarchical levels, namely the federal (central), state, district or divisional, and school. Formulation of policies and guidelines for planning and the co-ordination of the implementation of all programmes at federal level is done by the Ministry of Education. The policies and programmes are

Map of MALAYSIA

implemented in schools through the co-ordination and supervision of the State Education Departments and the District Education Offices.

The New Primary School Curriculum (KBSR)

The introduction and implementation of a new national primary school curriculum, better known as 'KBSR' (the acronym for the curriculum in the Malay language), from 1982, was seen as a major innovation, if not a total reform, in the field of primary education in the country.

The decision to develop and introduce the new primary school curriculum (KBSR) was mainly due to the general dissatisfaction with the curriculum taught in schools throughout the 1960s and 1970s. It was argued that a large proportion of the subject matter in the curriculum was not relevant to the pupils' immediate environment.

Besides that, the curriculum was also said to be 'overloaded in content', and 'too rigid and compartmentalised', thus reducing the effectiveness of the teaching and learning tasks. The structure of the new curriculum is shown in Table 4.1. The teaching and learning strategy recommended for KBSR went along the following lines:

an integrated approach in teaching and learning;
variety in teaching methods with group teaching for same ability or mixed ability groups, class teaching and individual instruction;
variety in learning activities;
'flexibility' in the choice of content and in the use of teaching methods and aids;
continuous evaluation that is incorporated into the teaching and learning process;
an 'informal' classroom atmosphere with spaces to allow varied activities.

The structure and the features of the new curriculum affected teachers in many ways. Since some of these features were not given

TABLE 4.1 *Structure of KBSR*

Area	Component	Subjects	
		Phase I (Grade I–III)	*Phase II (Grade IV–VI)*
Communication	Basic skills	Language of instruction B. Malaysia Eng. Lang. Mathematics	Language of instruction B. Malaysia Eng. Lang. Mathematics
Man and his environment	Sprituality, values, and attitudes	*Islamic religious ed. *Moral ed.	*Islamic religious ed. *Moral ed.
	Humanities and environment		Man & environment
Individual development	Art and recreation	Music Art ed. Physical ed.	Music Art. ed. Physical ed.

*Muslim pupils are taught Islamic religious education and the non-Muslims are taught moral education.
SOURCE Malaysian Ministry of Education, 1982, p. 4.

much emphasis in the old curriculum, teachers had to adjust their teaching behaviour to accommodate these features. They include:

(a) The emphasis on, and integration of, remediation and enrichment activities into normal teaching and learning situations: this requires teachers to give considerable attention to pupils' individual differences and the promotion of independent learning.

(b) The concept of continuous evaluation as an integral part of teaching and learning: this requires teachers to have a good understanding of both formative and summative evaluation and the skills to administer them. In the past evaluation had been taken to be almost synonymous with assessment in the form of monthly or termly paper-and-pencil tests.

(c) The integration of subject matter and skills: teachers have to apply a more integrated approach to teaching. This is in contrast to the old curriculum where teachers were used to a rather compartmentalised form of teaching based on separate disciplines.

(d) The concept of group and individual teaching: this requires teachers to change their normal teaching strategies of teaching the same skill or knowledge to all pupils in the same class. Teachers have to get used to teaching pupils in groups rather than in rows as they used to.

(e) The concept of 'flexibility': this requires teachers to be flexible in their choice of skills and knowledge to be taught, and materials to be used to suit changing situations and pupils' needs. This is in contrast to textbook-based teaching usually practised in the old curriculum.

(f) The introduction of new subjects: many teachers find themselves having to teach new subjects in which they were not trained before, for example, music, moral education and 'commercial practice'.

What has been listed suggests the extent of changes needed in the teaching situation and the emphases that needed to be given in the orientation of teachers to the curriculum innovation.

Infrastructure for Implementation

A number of working committees were set up to co-ordinate work to ensure that the dissemination and the implementation of KBSR ran smoothly. This was done through a hierarchical structure of committees at the federal, state, district and school level. Figure 4.1 shows this organisational structure.

The curriculum was conceptualised and planned by the committees at the first two levels as shown in Figure 4.1. Implementation of the curriculum began at the third level committee (the KBSR Implementation Committee). The committee, which consisted of directors and secretaries of a number of divisions in the Ministry of Education, was responsible for planning the strategies for the implementation and for co-ordinating implementation activities carried out by various divisions and levels in the whole Ministry.

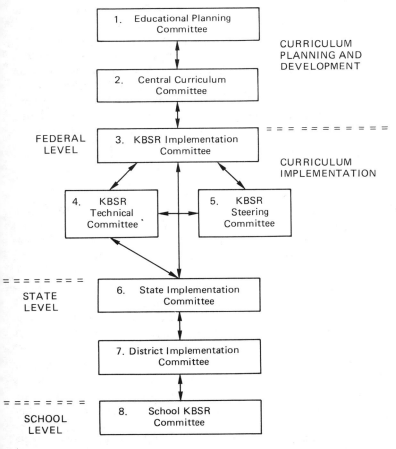

SOURCE   Adapted from Malaysian Ministry of Education, 1985.

FIGURE 4.1 *Organisation chart of KBSR implementation*

This committee was assisted by the KBSR Technical Committee and KBSR Steering Committee. The main task of the Technical Committee was to decide on details of steps to be taken for the implementation of the curriculum at state level, and to communicate feedback on the progress and problems on all aspects of KBSR to the above committee. The main function of the Steering Committee, on the other hand, was to settle problems that required immediate attention at the federal level. Members of the Technical Committee comprised all the State KBSR Co-ordinators and their counterparts at the Ministry of Education, while the Steering Committee had an *ad hoc* membership representing the divisions that were related to the problems posed to the committee from time to time.

To encourage full involvement and participation at the state, district and school level, an infrastructure consisting of committees was set up at various levels. Special personnel both at the state and district level were also identified to deal with KBSR for the same purpose (Asiah 1981, Malaysian Ministry of Education 1986). The infrastructure and the nature of communication between the different levels follow the centre-periphery model of innovation implementation.

Rationale for the Study

Ensuring the success of curriculum innovations is one of the prime concerns of every educational system. Much of the research in the late 1960s and 1970s documented how attempts to implement innovation frequently failed to produce actual changes in practice (Fullan 1982).

Implementation becomes more complicated the more the innovation is open to interpretation. Thus the basic problem for the KBSR innovators (the Ministry of Education) and the change agents was that of translating the ideas (KBSR) into action – of putting the ideas clearly to teachers and making sure that the teachers would accept, internalise and implement the ideas as far as possible. It is the teacher who has the final say about what is to be done when the innovation is implemented in the classrooms; the teachers, therefore, require the most sensitive handling and training in the introduction and implementation of curriculum innovation.

The Malaysian Ministry of Education had decided in 1982 (KBSR Implementation Committee, 1982) to adopt inservice courses as the main strategy for orientating teachers to the new curriculum. Each

year about 23 per cent ($M1160 of $M5000) of the total yearly grant
for the implementation of KBSR for every school was spent on inservice
courses[1] (Malaysian Ministry of Education 1983). Considering that the
grant was meant to cover all expenses related to the teaching and
learning of KBSR, including the cost of teaching and learning
materials such as stationery and readers in schools, the amount spent
on these orientation and training programmes was quite significant.

Although it has been said that most inservice efforts are not cost-
effective (for example, Corrigan 1979, cited in Eraut 1985), this
strategy was adopted firstly because it enabled the Ministry of
Education to ensure that every KBSR teacher received the required
exposure to the curriculum within the limited time available for the
implementation. Secondly, it was considered to be one of the best
ways to create opportunities through which teachers could interact
with each other and react to the new curriculum. However, since its
effectiveness had not been empirically established, it seemed important to look at how this aspect was being managed.

The need to look at the inservice courses in relation to the
implementation of KBSR was heightened by the fact that they would
play an important part in the implementation of a new national
secondary school to be introduced in the country from 1988.[2]

THE RESEARCH APPROACH AND DATA COLLECTION

Identification of concerns and understanding of issues related to the
inservice training programmes (courses) were sought through a case
study approach based on the 'illuminative evaluation' model. A case
study approach was adopted since it allows one to discern on-going
behaviour, which is central in determining the effectiveness of the
courses, as it occurs. The case study was conducted from June to
September 1986, and from December 1986 to February 1987 in the
district of Kuala Kangsar, Perak, Malaysia.

Issues related to the courses were gathered from different viewpoints, and assumptions held by a cross-section of the people
involved in the implementation of the curriculum were investigated.
Judgements were made based on documentary evidence and on data
obtained through interviews, observation and questionnaires; the
data came mainly from a group of sampled teachers, headteachers
and education officers.

The use of interviews, observation, and questionnaires at the same
time was employed in order to elicit as much information as possible

within the constraints of time and mobility of the researcher. The use of these methods proved to be very helpful since it facilitated triangulation of information from the different sources. This multi-method approach reduces the chances that any inconsistent findings are attributable to similarities of methods (Cohen and Manion 1980). It increases both the validity and the reliability of evaluation data (Patton 1980).

Interviews

The number of people interviewed is shown in Table 4.2.[3]

TABLE 4.2   *Interview respondents*

	Respondents	Number interviewed
1.	Primary school teachers	48*
2.	Primary school headteachers	9*
3.	Key personnel	20
4.	Course organisers	3
5.	Education Officers (District, State, Federal level)	22
6.	Teacher Union Officials	2

*See note 3. (p. 126)

Observation

Two typical training courses for teachers in the district were observed: KBSR Course for Year 4 and 5 Teachers (Course A), and KBSR Course for Year 5 Teachers (Course B). Details of the courses are given in Table 4.3.

TABLE 4.3   *Details of KBSR courses*

Course	Date and Duration	No. of participants	Course objective
1. Class Teachers year 4 & 5 (Course A)	3–13 Dec. 1986 (33 hrs)	170	To orientate trs to Year 4 & 5 KBSR curriculum specifications
2. Class Teachers Year 5 (Course B)	15–17 Dec. 1986	165	To orientate trs to Year 5 KBSR curriculum specifications

Teaching of the curriculum was also observed after the courses to see the extent to which teachers had applied in the classrooms what they had been exposed to in the courses. This observation lasted three weeks. Eleven teachers who attended the courses from nine schools were observed. A total of 25 lessons were observed, ranging from a single period of 30 minutes to three combined periods of 90 minutes.

Questionnaires

Two types of questionnaire were distributed:

(a) *Teacher questionnaire.* This contained questions and attitude statements to elicit both information about the teaching of KBSR in schools and teachers' attitudes towards the curriculum and the courses.

The questionnaires were distributed, by systematic sampling, to a total of 926 teachers in the three districts of Kuala Kangsar, Perak Tengah and Kinta. 835 (90.1 per cent) gave their responses. The sample comprised 37.5 per cent and 36.3 per cent of the teacher population in the first two districts (K. Kangsar and Perak Tengah) respectively, and 8.6 per cent of the teacher population in the third district (Kinta). The size of sample in Kinta was kept small in order to keep the number of questionnaires manageable.

(b) *Course questionnaire.* This questionnaire contained statements on different aspects of the course for which respondents were required to give their rating. The items were generated to elicit the respondents' feelings and impressions of the course and the extent of similarities or differences between the course and other previous KBSR courses they had attended.

The questionnaires were distributed to all course participants who were present on the last day of the two courses observed. The number of questionnaires distributed and collected was as follows: (a) KBSR Course for Year 4 and 5: 157, returned 152 (96.8 per cent); (b) KBSR Course for Year 5: 147, returned 143 (97.2 per cent).

Reflections on the Research Methods

By analysing both qualitative and quantitative data obtained through the multi-method approach this study provides an understanding of the issues related to the inservice training of teachers in the implementation of KBSR. Although the study is based on a sample group of teachers and on only two training programmes, the analysis and judgement on the actual state of the matter, based on relevant theoretical and conceptual frameworks, is fruitful and necessary not only to provide information for decision-making but also to dispel invalid assumptions and preconceptions on the matter. This will make decision-making on the matter more effective.

The experience of this study suggests the necessity of using the multi-method approach in undertaking research work in Malaysia. The use of this approach is necessary because of the possibility of respondents being too 'polite' and hiding their true feelings in interviews, or being 'uncommitted' in questionnaire responses, when giving opinions about 'policy' issues. There is also a possibility that the respondents may try to be guarded in their responses so that they might not appear to be too different from the prevailing trends of thought. Although these tendencies are not very significant in this study, one may still trace a few examples of them. As shall be shown later, the positive opinions given about courses in interviews which did not exactly match the behaviours displayed during courses, for instance, may be attributed to these tendencies.

THE KBSR INSERVICE COURSES

The Aims of the Inservice Courses

Short inservice courses, usually lasting two to six days, designed to expose teachers to new methods and techniques in classroom instruction, became an established phenomenon in teacher education in Malaysia from the early 1970s onwards. They formed an integral part of the curriculum development process carried out by the Ministry of Education (Malaysian Ministry of Education 1981).

The general aim of the inservice courses for teachers was to provide them with the necessary information and skills, and to promote a positive attitude towards the effective implementation of the curriculum. The specific objectives of most inservice courses were:

(a) to expose teachers to the concept of the curriculum;
(b) to provide guidance concerning the approaches and methods in the classroom;

(c) to expose teachers to the contents of the curriculum;
(d) to develop teachers' skills in various teaching techniques;
(e) to develop teachers' skills in evaluating pupils' performance.

The courses were usually held locally (at district level) during vacations or weekends. They were conducted by teacher 'key personnel' (a term used to refer to the state-level or district-level inservice course trainers) usually trained by the Curriculum Development Centre (CDC) – a division in the Ministry of Education responsible for the development of most school curricula in the country. It was this system of inservice course that was being adopted for the training of teachers in KBSR.

KBSR Dissemination and Training Model

The training of KBSR teachers through inservice courses under the 'key personnel system' is depicted in Figure 4.2.

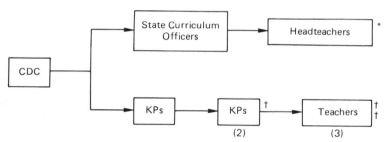

* State/District level courses for the headteachers and senior assistants – conducted by state curriculum officers with the help of key personnel.
† State level courses for 'second level' key personnel.
‡ District level courses for teachers.

FIGURE 4.2 *Dissemination and Training Model: KBSR*

Under this system, the curriculum officers who developed the curriculum at the CDC orientated a group of teacher key personnel from all the states in national-level key personnel courses at the CDC. The courses for each KBSR programme, which usually lasted a week, were held in the year preceding its implementation. For each subject in the curriculum, each state usually sent two key personnel to the course. The key personnel courses were also attended by officers from the State Education Departments and various divisions of the Ministry of Education.

Having attended the course at the CDC, the key personnel then conducted courses for other key personnel who were not selected to go to the CDC in their state. Information gained from the CDC was then conveyed to the 'second level' key personnel to enable them to conduct courses for teachers at district level on their own or together with the key personnel who were trained at the CDC. The appointment of 'second level' key personnel was necessary for two reasons. Firstly, the number of key personnel needed to train teachers in most of the states was usually large. In the state of Perak, where this study was focused, for instance, 225 key personnel were needed to conduct KBSR courses in 1986, but only 28 of them could be trained by the CDC. Secondly, with the presence of 'second level' key personnel the inservice course programmes would not be disrupted if for some reason a key person was indisposed or not available. This was important in the implementation of KBSR where time was of the essence. A disruption of a course might throw other inservice courses scheduled for a particular year into disarray and affect the preparation of KBSR teachers for the following year.

The figure above gives an indication of the importance of the key personnel as the link agents in the dissemination and implementation process of the curriculum. It shows the flow of information and its 'multiplying effect' in the dissemination and training process, and the levels of inservice courses through which KBSR was disseminated to the headteachers and teachers.

General Information on the Courses

Course planning

The two courses observed in this study were part of the KBSR courses designed by the KBSR Unit of the State Education Department, Perak, for all districts in the state. The course contents were decided by the KBSR Unit based on the contents of the key personnel course conducted by the CDC.

Although the actual timetables for each district centre were drawn up by the district course organisers with the help of the key personnel, the time allocation for each subject in all district centres throughout the state was fixed by the KBSR Unit of the State Education Department. The State Education Department considered it necessary to standardise the amount of time for each subject in all the districts in order to avoid over-emphasis or under-emphasis of some subjects in some districts, and to facilitate administrative work, especially in terms of calculating and paying allowances to the key personnel and participants.

A one-day meeting-cum-workshop for all key personnel in the state was held in April 1986 to discuss the contents and methods of these two courses. In the meeting, all the key personnel were briefed by the senior key personnel of each subject, who had attended the one-week key personnel course at the CDC, on what they had been shown at the CDC. All handouts received at the CDC were reduplicated and distributed. The contents were discussed in subject groups and outlines were drawn up of what needed to be delivered and how it should be delivered to the course participants in the districts. It should be noted that this was the only training received by the 'second-level' key personnel before they were sent out to train the teachers.

Course participants
Participants of both the observed courses consisted of teachers from all the primary schools in the district. The participants were nominated by their headteachers based on a guideline given by the State Department of Education.

The key personnel
The courses were conducted by 14 key personnel. They were appointed by the District Education Office from among teachers in the district on the basis of their 'performance' in schools, and the interest and willingness they had displayed in carrying out extracurricular programmes organised by the District Education Office or the State Education Department.

Course contents
Table 4.4 gives the course contents according to subjects and the main topics or areas covered in the subjects in the two courses.

Main Observations and Issues

Conduct of courses
Almost all sessions in both courses were conducted using the lecture method. 70.6 per cent (836 minutes) of the total time for sessions observed in Course A (for Year 4 and 5 teachers), and 65.7 per cent (580 minutes) of the total time for all sessions observed in Course B

TABLE 4.4 *KBSR course contents*

Subject	Topics/Areas*	
1. Language of instruction (B. Malaysia) (Chinese lang.) (Tamil lang.)	a.	Learning objectives
	b.	Learning units/skills – grouping of skills
	c.	Scheme of work
	d.	Evaluation and items bank
	e.	Citizenship education in language
	f.	Co-curriculum in language
2. Mathematics	a.	Learning objectives
	b.	Learning units
	c.	Scheme of work
	d.	Teaching techniques
	e.	Commercial practice
3. Art Education (A.E.)	a.	Activities and learning skills
	b.	Teaching techniques
	c.	Scheme of work
	d.	Citizenship education in A. E.
4. Moral Education (M.E.)	a.	Activities in Moral Education
	b.	Development of teaching materials
	c.	Evaluation and record keeping
	d.	Citizenship education in M.E.
5. Man and Environment (M & E)	a.	Learning objectives
	b.	Subject contents
	c.	Scheme of work
	d.	Teaching/learning strategies
	e.	Evaluation and items bank
	f.	Teaching materials
	g.	Citizenship education in M & E
6. Co-curriculum	a.	Learning objectives
	b.	Teaching strategies
	c.	Scheme of work
7. Physical Ed.	a.	Scheme of work
	b.	Gymnastics (demonstration)

*The same topics and areas were covered in both courses, except that in Course A, the topics/areas were dealt in relation to the contents of Year 4 and Year 5, whereas in course B, they were dealt in relation to Year 5 only.

(Year 5 teachers) was used to convey information regarding the curriculum and other matters. There seemed to be very little time given to the development of teachers' skills in teaching techniques or in evaluating pupils' performance. Evidently, not all the aspects listed in the specific objectives of inservice courses spelt out earlier were given due emphasis.

The time spent on the different categories of activities carried out in the courses is shown in Table 4.5.

TABLE 4.5   *Time spent on different course activities*

Categories of Activities	Course A Time spent	% of time	Course B Time spent	% of time
1. Administration	22 mins	1.9%	20 mins	2.3%
2. Giving information on:				
objectives	34 mins	2.9%	18 mins	2.0%
cur. contents	316 mins	26.7%	110 mins	12.5%
pedagogy	166 mins	14.0%	162 mins	18.4%
material	30 mins	2.5%	18 mins	2.0%
evaluation	134 mins	11.3%	134 mins	15.2%
others	156 mins	13.2%	138 mins	15.6%
3. Asking questions	36 mins	3.0%	40 mins	4.5%
4. Clarification	128 mins	10.8%	32 mins	9.3%
5. Giving opinions	68 mins	5.7%	34 mins	3.9%
6. Demonstrating, performing tasks, reading, writing, viewing	42 mins	3.6%	82 mins	9.3%
7. Sundry	52 mins	4.4%	44 mins	5.0%
Total	1184 mins	100.0%	832 mins	100.0%

In the above table the amount of time shown for each category is the total amount of time spent on the particular category of activity in all the sessions and subjects observed throughout the courses. The table shows that different amounts of time were spent on the same category of activities in the two courses. The most significant difference is in terms of giving information on curriculum content. This difference is not unexpected. With so many factors that could affect the conduct of a course session, no two sessions, let alone two courses, could be exactly the same.

This difference could be interpreted as a shift, planned or unplanned, in the course emphasis. It was perhaps the result of attempts by the key personnel to make their sessions flexible in order to accommodate the needs of the participants during the courses. Indeed, one could observe conscious efforts by all the key personnel to do so when they were conducting the courses. These efforts show an attempt by the key personnel to meet the criterion of 'relevance' which Stufflebeam *et al* (1971) identify as one of the practical criteria in assessing the effectiveness of educational programmes.

Degree of involvement
This study assumes that the degree of involvement of the participants in the courses is an important indication of the extent to which the courses affect the teachers. The question of 'degree of involvement' is, however, an abstract one. While it is easy to see how 'involved' the participants and the key personnel are by what they do out-wardly, it is impossible to assess how involved they are in the courses mentally.

As this concept is abstract in nature, it was not possible to quantify the degree of involvement in the form of indices or measurement. Because of this, attempts to assess the degree of involvement were made by looking at how much of the course time was dominated by the participants on the one hand and the key personnel on the other, and how much of the time was spent in active interaction between the two. Subjective judgements based on their apparent involvement were made to assess this. It was observed that in all sessions, except in two workshop sessions in Course A, the greater part of the time was dominated by the key personnel. This pattern is illustrated in Table 4.6.

The trend observed is not peculiar to these two courses only. Interviews with teachers brought responses that suggested all the courses they had attended were similar in nature. Some comments

TABLE 4.6   *Use of course time by key personnel and participants*

Use of course time	Course A		Course B	
	Time in minutes	%	*Time in minutes*	%
1. Dominated by KPs	704 mins	59.5%	594 mins	67.4%
2. Active interactions	300 mins	25.3%	182 mins	20.6%
3. Dominated by participants	180 mins	15.2%	106 mins	12.0%
Total	1184 mins	100.0%	882 mins	100.00%

were: 'Most of the time the KPs gave us lectures', and 'there has not been much change in the style of the course'. Besides this, a study done by the Ministry of Education in 1981 on 86 inservice courses throughout the country (though they were not KBSR courses) also showed that the trend was prevalent everywhere. Fifty-eight of the courses (67.4 per cent) listed lectures, talks, briefings and discussions as the main method of delivery, while only fifteen (17.4 per cent) made extensive use of plenary sessions and workshops, with the others using other methods such as demonstrations and practical work (Malaysian Ministry of Education 1981).

This observation, however, cannot be used as conclusive evidence to establish whether the courses were conducted by the key personnel and absorbed by the participants in the way they should be. Firstly, how the courses 'should be' was never explicitly spelt out. Secondly, the review of the literature has not revealed any analysis of similar courses that provides statistics with which these findings could be compared. Probably domination of courses by the key personnel is a common phenomenon, especially in short courses where the key personnel believe that they have so much information to convey in a limited time. Even in longer courses such as B.Ed. and PGCE courses in the UK, there is a marked tendency for tutors to dominate proceedings and a dearth of practical work (DES 1987).

Teachers' views on their nomination for courses
This study also assumes that the extent the courses affect the teachers depends to a large extent on their interest and willingness to attend them.

Three-quarters of the teachers interviewed in this study said that even if they had not been nominated to attend the courses, given the option they would still have liked to attend. The expectation that the courses would help them get new ideas and make their work easier the following year was quoted as the main reason. This is similar to Lewin's finding in his study of science teaching in Malaysia where 189 (75 per cent of) science teachers responding to his questionnaires expressed the desire for more inservice training and only 44 (17 per cent) judged inservice programmes as being of little or no value (Lewin 1981).

Responses from other teachers through the questionnaires in which more than two-thirds of the respondents (68.9 per cent) indicated their willingness and interest in attending courses also reflect this general trend.

Four of the teachers interviewed (8.3 per cent), however, admitted that they were reluctantly forced to attend. They felt that they would not be able to gain anything much from the KBSR courses. They also expressed the view that it was difficult for them to take in so much information in the limited time usually given for such courses. Considering that three of them were over 50 and the other was in his 40s, the difficulty expressed could be, firstly, due to the fact that older people tend to take more time to learn something because, as has been observed in real situations and in experiments, the older people are, the more information they like before making a response (Rogers 1971). Secondly, teachers usually learn things through experience the hard way. Once they have developed a teaching style that works for them, the commitment to stick to it is very high (Flanders 1980). The older the teachers, the more committed they are to the style they are comfortable with, making it difficult to accept something new. Thirdly, there seemed to be a general feeling among these teachers and a number of others that there was nothing new they needed to learn from the KBSR courses. To them, what KBSR was advocating was what they had been teaching all these years.

In order to find out whether other older teachers shared the same view as those interviewed, the responses to a statement, 'I would prefer not to be chosen for KBSR courses' were cross-tabulated with variable 'age' in the teacher questionnaire. The finding is shown in Table 4.7.

TABLE 4.7   *Teachers' responses to Statement 'I would prefer not to be chosen for KBSR courses', according to age groups*

Age		Agree	Cannot decide	Disagree
Less than 30	Frequency	37	29	203
	Row %	13.8%	10.8%	75.5%
30–39	Frequency	38	33	163
	Row %	16.2%	14.1%	69.7%
40–9	Frequency	48	35	163
	Row %	19.5%	14.2%	66.3%
50 and above	Frequency	26	8	38
	Row %	36.1%	11.1%	52.8%

Missing cases: 14
Chi Square:22.757 (D.F.6)   Significance = 0.0009
Kendall's Tau B: −0.117   Significance = 0.0001

Based on Kendall's Tau B's level of significance test the responses show that there is a correlation between teachers' age and their willingness to attend courses. The figures suggest that the older the teachers, regardless of sex, the less interested they seem to be in attending courses.

Teachers' attitudes towards the course
About three-quarters of the teachers interviewed considered the courses as 'interesting' and 'worth their time', while findings from the teacher questionnaires show that only 29.9 per cent of the teachers considered the courses they had attended as 'boring'. If this can be taken as an indication of their attitude, it means that more teachers had 'positive' attitudes towards the courses compared to those who did not.

However, the observed behaviour of the course participants as a whole did not seem to reflect an adequately positive attitude. The findings on the degree of participants' involvement have shown that 'active interactions' and time 'dominated by the participants' constitute only 40.5 per cent (480 minutes) of the observed time in Course A, and 32.6 per cent (288 minutes) of the observed time in Course B (see Table 4.6). There is no way to establish firmly whether these figures reflect a high or low degree of involvement. On the assumption that teachers with positive attitudes would participate a lot in the course, especially when they were given the opportunity to do so,[4] these figures probably give one reason to doubt that the majority of the teachers had such positive attitudes as suggested by the teachers and some officials interviewed.

Assuming that the general attitude of the participants could also be gauged by the number of participants who asked questions or gave opinions in the sessions, attempts were also made during the observation to note down the number of people who did so. The number of questions and opinions offered were also noted. Although participants' willingness to ask questions and to give opinions is influenced by many factors, having noted that it was the same four male participants in Course A, and three male participants in Course B, who were asking most of the questions or offering opinions, it can be said on this count that the general attitude shown, as judged by participation in commenting and in asking questions, was not up to reasonable expectations.

The other factor that could be used to make inferences about the attitude of the teachers towards the courses was their punctuality.

The lack of punctuality in coming to the course sessions was quite evident. It was observed that the start of most sessions was delayed between three to twelve minutes before the key person decided he or she had a reasonable number of participants in the room to start the session.[5] Although the observation seems to be relevant and helps to indicate the unfavourable attitude of the participants, one has to be guarded in making any conclusive inferences on this matter. One could argue that their lack of punctuality was more of an indication of their attitude towards management of time as a whole rather than their attitudes towards the course.

Other behaviour suggestive of a lack of positive attitude of some of the participants includes reading newspapers and chatting during course sessions. Although the number of participants who engaged in these was small, it still reflects the attitudes of some participants towards the courses. These observations make one reserve judgement about the attitudes of teachers towards the courses in spite of the favourable findings gained from the interviews and the questionnaires.

Through the interviews it was possible to extract some of the reasons why some teachers did not find the courses interesting. The reasons were related to a number of aspects including the techniques of presentation, the contents of the courses, the personality and credibility of some key personnel and the facilities available at the course centre. Teachers who considered the courses to be boring were those who felt that they were already familiar with the contents of the courses. The interviews revealed that there was a strong correlation between the two variables. This correlation was also found in the responses to the questionnaires. Table 4.8 gives the degree of the correlation when the two variables were cross-tabulated.

The negative attitude of some teachers towards the courses may be attributed to the fact that more than one-third of the participants in the two courses felt that they were not able to learn much from the courses. 37.4 per cent of the course participants 'strongly agreed' or 'agreed' with the statement which says 'I learnt very little from this course' in the course questionnaire. Again, 41.3 per cent of the participants felt that the content of the course was difficult to implement in schools.

Issues on key personnel
A number of issues related to the key personnel are worth highlighting since they also influenced the effectiveness of the courses.

TABLE 4.8 *Cross-tabulation of variables 'Bored' (I always find courses boring) and 'Alknow' (I already know the contents of KBSR courses)*

Variable 'Bored'		Variable: 'Alknow'		
		Agree	Cannot decide	Disagree
Agree	Frequency	125	63	59
	Row %	51.2%	24.6%	24.2%
Cannot decide	Frequency	50	92	80
	Row %	22.5%	41.4%	36.0%
Disagree	Frequency	72	65	213
	Row %	20.6%	18.6%	60.9%

Total: 835

Missing cases variable 'bored': 17
Missing cases variable 'Alknow': 16

Chi Square: 126.330 (D.F. 4)   Sig. level: <0.001
Kendall's Tau B: Value: 0.303   Sig. level: <0.001

(a) *Roles of key personnel.* The key personnel formed an important linkage between the primary change agent (CDC) and the teachers. The type and the amount of information teachers received on the new curriculum and the degree of understanding they acquired depended greatly on this link. As the State Director of Education put it:

The key personnel are very important in the whole machinery. Their roles are to transmit information to the teachers and provide guidance and assistance to fellow teachers in their own school and other teachers in the districts. They are the ones who get to the grassroots level, with bigger audiences than we have.

The course participants had similar but more specific expectations. To them the key personnel should 'show us how to teach some of the skills in each subject especially to different ability groups'; 'provide us with sample lesson plans and test instruments', and 'see whether what we do in school is right'.

Based on these expectations, the roles were clearly many and varied. Besides disseminating information through the courses, they were also expected to provide guidance and to help other teachers in schools. However, due to administrative constraints the key personnel had no opportunity to visit other schools to provide guidance and help to teachers. Thus, whatever roles they were expected to perform, whether as a 'solution giver' or as a 'process helper', these could only be carried out within the context of the courses and their own schools. The key personnel themselves perceived their role very much in relation to the simplistic linker concept as a 'conveyor' (Havelock 1973) of information between the 'experts' and the teachers, since their main concern in the courses was to convey information to the participants.

The differences in expectations resulted in a degree of role ambiguity. This role ambiguity was heightened by the existence of a number of documents containing varied job descriptions of the key personnel given to them at different times.[6] The fact that the duties of key personnel seemed to differ between states (KBSR Technical Committee 1984) might also have contributed to role ambiguity among the key personnel. While role ambiguity could lead to role stress (Handy 1985) for the key personnel, role ambiguity could also cause insecurity, lack of confidence, irritation and even anger among the course participants, teachers in schools and officers in the District Education Office and the State Department of Education. The mismatch between expectations and reality in this respect was evident.

(b) *Credibility of key personnel.* The extent to which the key personnel could play their role effectively also depended on their credibility. As one of the practical criteria in the evaluation of an educational programme, Stufflebeam *et al* (1971) describe credibility as the quality of trust in the sources of information. In this case it was the trust the participants had in, and their opinions towards, the key personnel. Teachers interviewed used a range of criteria to assess the credibility of the key personnel. Below are three of the main criteria with the number of teachers quoting them:

> (i) Key personnel's understanding of teachers' problems (30 teachers).
> (ii) Key personnel's ability to conduct sessions in an 'interesting manner' (28 teachers).
> (iii) Key personnel's knowledge of the subject they handle (28 teachers).
> Note: about 75 per cent of the teachers quoted more than one criterion.

Although the teachers generally considered the key personnel to be good, they had a lot to say about the weaknesses of some of them.

The main weaknesses of the key personnel, as perceived by the teachers, (with a rough indication of the number with whom the weaknesses are associated) are given below:

(i) Not able to give satisfactory answers to questions raised by participants during sessions (about 30 per cent of the key personnel).

(ii) Not able to give enough examples in aspects covered during the course, especially in relation to teaching methods, preparation of teaching material and test items (about 30 per cent of the key personnel).

(iii) Having the tendency to talk about irrelevant matters, and giving what was considered as unnecessary information during course sessions (about 25 per cent of the key personnel).

(iv) Using the same method of course presentation all the time (almost all the key personnel).

(v) Very little use of audiovisual aids to make delivery clearer and more interesting (almost all the key personnel).

The key personnel themselves acknowledged these weaknesses, citing a number of reasons why some of them were unavoidable.

Firstly, teachers seemed to require a 'yes-no answer' to most of their questions in the courses. The key personnel felt that they were not in a position to give authoritative answers to questions regarding policy matters without consulting the district course organiser or other officers. Even if the questions were not on policies, the key personnel still felt that they should not give such answers since the teaching of KBSR was supposed to be based on 'flexibility' that required teachers to exercise their own judgement in ways suitable to their own situation.

Secondly, to equip the key personnel for their tasks they were only given a one-day state-level exposure to the Year 4 and Year 5 curriculum, as described above. None of them had been chosen to attend the one-week national level key personnel course at the CDC early in 1986. Except for two of the 'senior' key personnel who had had the opportunity to attend courses at the CDC in previous years, the key personnel felt that the state-level exposure was not enough to enable them to know everything they felt they needed to know.

Thirdly, only four of the 14 key personnel involved in the courses had had any form of training in course management and presentation. These four had attended a one-week course organised by the National Institute of Educational Management of the Ministry of

Education in October 1986. The others had only their classroom and on-the-job experience to fall back on. Thus they had limited knowledge and skill in using a variety of course techniques or audiovisual equipment.

Fourthly, the key personnel attributed some of their weaknesses to the lack of facilities at the course centre. As an example, they said that there were only two overhead projectors available for the courses. Apart from these overhead projectors there were no other audiovisual aids that the key personnel could use to make course presentation more effective.

Finally, the key personnel felt that the time they had was too limited to attempt to use other methods of course presentation, considering the amount of information they had to convey.

Besides these factors, the lack of credibility of some of the key personnel could also be attributed to the way the key personnel were appointed. The appointment of the key personnel was based on the qualitative criteria of 'being a good and experienced teacher'. But being 'a good teacher with sufficient experience' would not necessarily make a teacher a good key person. Each has a different role with a different type of client. While one deals with children, the other deals with adults. The difference between pedagogy and andragogy is clear.

Effects on teachers

It is difficult to establish the extent to which these two courses affected the teachers since any change displayed after the course could not be attributed merely to the two courses. They could be due to a number of factors such as the accumulation of knowledge and experience the teachers obtained from a number of courses. Nevertheless, an attempt was made to find evidence of the effect through the interviews, observations in schools and the questionnaires.

Findings from the interviews and the course questionnaire show that the majority of teachers found KBSR courses 'useful'. About 80 per cent of those interviewed, and 76.3 per cent of the course participants considered them so. To them the courses were useful because they gave them 'new ideas' and examples of teaching methods they could use in the classrooms. Responses from the teacher questionnaire also suggest that the teachers generally felt that the courses had had some effects on them. Only 26.9 per cent of the respondents agreed with the statement that the courses they had attended made no difference to their teaching.

It was, however, rather clear from the interviews and the observations that the changes the teachers were referring to were more in terms of the contents and the skills they were teaching and the materials they were using, than in the teaching methods or approaches they were employing. Quoting an example of the change, a teacher said that she was now using more worksheets instead of textbooks. Another teacher said that he was using a lot more teaching aids now than he used to. Other changes expected in the teaching of the new curriculum, especially in terms of teaching methods, though apparent in the first three years of the KBSR implementation, according to the headteachers and KBSR officers in the District Education Office and the State Department of Education, seemed not to be lasting.

The observations done in the classrooms also gave an indication of the actual nature of the effects the courses had on the teachers. The observations revealed that in terms of contents and skills to be taught, teachers tended to adhere to everything that was given in the courses almost to the letter. Their record books showed that sample schemes of work for each subject given during the courses were adopted by all the teachers observed without any alteration. In the teaching of Bahasa Malaysia, for example, the 'grouping of skills' according to learning areas suggested by the key personnel in the courses were followed by all Bahasa Malaysia teachers in all the sample schools despite the differences in the abilities of the pupils. Table 4.9 illustrates this. The table shows the grouping of skills (represented by the numbers that denote the language skills listed in the syllabus) as they were suggested in a course handout, and the skills taught in Grade 5 classes that were observed in the same week.

The table shows the extent to which the teachers adhered to the suggestions given in the handouts. In the 11 classes observed in six schools over a period of three weeks it was evident that there was only one teacher in a school (School D) who taught a skill (skill no. 22.8) that was outside the grouping suggested for the week.

While suggestions about contents and skills were faithfully followed, many suggestions on teaching strategies were not given the same treatment by the teachers. Group and individual teaching, provision of opportunity for the pupils to learn by discovery, or provision for varied activities to cater for different ability groups were very seldom seen.

TABLE 4.9   *Comparison between grouping of skills suggested and skills taught. Subject B. Malaysia, Grade 5*

Week	Grouping of skills suggested in the handout.	Skills taught in schools
Week 1	22.1*; 22.5; 22.12 22.17; 22.23; 22.26.	School A: (on 6 and 7 January 1987): 22.1; 22.5; 22.12
		School B: (on 8 and 9 January 1987): 22.17; 22.23; 22.26.
Week 2	22.1; 22.6; 22.9 22.17; 22.21; 22.27.	School C: (on 12 and 13 January 1987): 22.1; 22.26; 22.17.
		School D: (on 14 and 15 January 1987) 22.9; 22.17; 22.8; 22.1.
Week 3	22.6; 22.8; 22.9 22.14; 22.27; 22.3	School E: (on 19 and 20 January 1987) 22.27; 22.14; 22.9; 22.8.
		School F: (on 21 January 1987): 22.6; 22.14; 22.8

*The numbers represent the learning skills as listed in the syllabus.

MAIN FINDINGS

Course Planning and Key Personnel's Autonomy

An important aspect of change seemed not to have been given due emphasis in the course planning. One has to remember that one of the main barriers to the implementation of curriculum innovation is the unwillingness of teachers to change. Their willingness to adopt the innovation varies. The attitudes of teachers in this study showed that there were teachers who were keen on inservice courses and there were others who were not. This suggests that there is a need, in the design and conduct of courses aimed at training teachers on a new curriculum, to use different approaches or techniques for different groups of teachers at different times and at different phases of the implementation.

The course design also reflected the degree of autonomy given to the key personnel and how much, or how little, the key personnel were able to use it in selecting and defining the course contents and the way they should be delivered. While the key personnel were always encouraged by the authorities to use their own discretion in selecting the topics or areas to be covered, the ability and the freedom to do this seemed to be restricted. A number of reasons may have contributed to this.

Firstly, despite constant reminders that key personnel had to be selective in choosing the contents for the state or district level courses, the whole body of knowledge given by the CDC on the new curriculum seemed to be considered as new information that must be disseminated to all teachers. Indeed in a letter outlining the course preparation sent by the State Department of Education to course organisers it was explicitly stated that the key personnel should 'ensure all information on KBSR Phase II are conveyed to all participants' (Perak Department of Education, 1986). Failure to do so seemed to be taken as an indication of weakness in the running of the courses.

Secondly, there seemed to be a great concern on the part of the course designers for 'uniformity' in almost every aspect of the course for all districts in the state. The need to systematise and to standardise the courses was assumed by some quarters to be a good thing in itself. According to the State KBSR Coordinator, standard course contents for all districts were stressed in order to reduce the possibility of some information not being conveyed to the teachers. 'Uniformity' was also emphasised in order to facilitate course administration at the state level.

Thirdly, whatever was given by the CDC was assumed to meet the needs of the participants. Since there was no assessment of needs done for the courses, the key personnel had no reason to alter the course contents and preferred not to. Indeed, about half of the key personnel felt that altering the course contents was an unnecessary risk to take.

Finally, the time allocation for each subject also tended to restrict the freedom of the key personnel in their selection of contents. The limited time allotted in the courses was an obstacle for the key personnel who wished to have extensive coverage of topics they considered relevant. All these constraints undermined the effectiveness of the courses.

Needs Analysis

The courses were conducted along the lines of a 'content model', where the emphasis was much on information-giving, rather than on 'process model' lines. The basis of communication seemed to be on what the key personnel and the authorities wanted to say rather than what the participants wanted to hear. This apparently contradicts the general communication theory which assumes that the effectiveness of communication is based on what is received rather than the message or information that is given. Here the actual needs of the participants did not seem to have been adequately taken into account.

The importance given to the transmission of information is understandable in view of the fact that information was the basis for any action in the implementation of the curriculum. But, while the need to convey information was of primary importance to the course organiser and the key personnel, the neglect in taking the needs of the participants into account before the course affected its usefulness. Attempts were made by the key personnel to accommodate the expressed needs of the participants during the courses, but at best they could only provide relevant information rather than the relevant experience needed to enhance the effectiveness of the courses.

The findings have indicated that whatever is the prime concern of the course organiser and the key personnel, the needs of the participants should be assessed and be taken into account in the planning and the conduct of such courses. Research does suggest that the question of perceived needs makes a difference in terms of the impact of a programme (Fullan 1985a). The needs have to be identified before the courses so that courses can be designed to address these needs. To be effective the identification of needs should be done through interviews with a reasonable number of teachers and headmasters, observation of classroom teaching and school activities, administration of questionnaires to teachers and headmasters, feedback from supervisors and school inspectors and other 'experts'. Presently the identification of the needs by course organisers at the state and district level seems to be based only on the perceptions of officers and a few key personnel. The course organisers cannot be totally blamed for this. They neither have the skills nor the time to do proper identifications of needs.

Adult Learning Theory

The relatively little time spent on discussion during the courses implies that there was a neglect of one of the most important factors in the course situation, that is the experience of the participants. Indeed there seemed to be little emphasis placed on techniques which could provide maximum opportunities for participation and which could tap the experience of the participants, such as group discussions, demonstrations, case studies and the like.

The importance of giving more thought to adult learning theories in the design and conduct of teachers' inservice courses cannot be over-emphasised. To be effective inservice courses need to be conducted by using techniques that provide maximum opportunities for participation in order to tap the experience of the participants. The concern of inservice courses should not only be in the transmission of information but also in helping participants to acquire the understanding, skills, attitudes and values necessary to support and sustain the implementation of the curriculum in schools. Courses need to be designed and conducted more in line with the process model rather than the content model. It is worth remembering that the course participants, being experienced teachers, often have as much to contribute as to receive. In relation to this, appointing key personnel on the basis of their pedagogical ability might not be a good way to achieve the desired result.

Adults are usually sensitive to the surroundings, the reception and the treatment they get in any situation. This does not only mean that course organisers and key personnel should be friendly and helpful to the participants, but it also suggests that the physical facilities at the course centre should be such as to make the course participants comfortable and at ease (Knowles 1970).

Role Ambiguity and Credibility of Key Personnel

The study has also shown that the effectiveness of the inservice courses was partly affected by the lack of credibility of some of the key personnel. Though the lack of credibility could be attributed to a number of factors, the main reasons seemed to be role ambiguity and the key personnel's lack of training in course management. As Katz and Kahn (1966) say, role ambiguity can be 'troublesome'. It may cause role stress (Handy 1985) and loss of confidence among the key personnel. These would affect the effectiveness of the inservice courses. The need to make the roles and duties of the key personnel clear to the teachers, the key personnel, the headteachers and officers, as well as to the key personnel themselves, should be emphasised.

Once the roles of the key personnel are clear and the same perceptions and expectations of the roles are shared by different people, the task of enhancing their credibility will likely be made effective. Comprehensive and systematic programmes to provide the key personnel with the skills and knowledge necessary for performing the roles can be designed and conducted effectively.

The importance of improving the credibility of the key personnel is highlighted by the fact that the most popular suggestion given by the respondents in the teacher questionnaire in order to improve the effectiveness of future courses was for the course organiser to 'provide better key personnel'.

Follow-up Activities

The ultimate goal of inservice courses for the dissemination of a new curriculum is the improvement of pupils' learning through improvement of teacher performance. Thus the linkages between inservice courses and actual classroom practice is very important. This implies that follow-up activities in the form of 'meetings' and 'supervision' should be made integral parts of training strategies. Unless there is an integration between the inservice course activities and teachers' classroom practice, the course will serve little purpose in terms of curriculum dissemination and implementation.

In-service courses organised and conducted in the way exemplified by the two courses, with no follow-up activities and limited post-course guidance for the teachers, will not be very effective, especially when the curriculum introduced is no longer a novelty.

Theory of Motivation

The effectiveness of inservice courses must also be seen in relation to the theories of motivation and learning. The amount of learning taking place through a course can be attributed to the degree of motivation the participants have. This is an area that seems to have been ignored in the planning and conduct of the KBSR courses. For future courses, organisers and key personnel have to encourage teachers' intrinsic motivation by providing course contents that are directly relevant to classroom tasks to help teachers solve their teaching problems. There is also a need for the relevant authorities to provide extrinsic motivation by, for example, paying course participants an attractive rate of inservice course allowance, awarding certificates for course attendance, and ensuring that attendance and participation in courses are taken into account in teachers' promotions.

CONCLUDING REMARKS

The evidence suggests that the courses had a surface effect but not the impact that could bring deep assimilation of all the KBSR features. One could attribute this to the weaknesses in the courses, which were informative rather than experiential, or in terms of other factors such as the course techniques, the limited time allotted for the courses, the credibility of some key personnel and the poor facilities. However the situation could also be seen as a reflection of the teachers' sense of professionalism, for besides these external factors, it is the teachers' sense of professionalism that goes a long way in determining how much they are ready to change after the course.

One has to be realistic in one's expectations of the change such short courses can bring. A lot of changes cannot take place merely through the transmission of information and within such a short time. A course is only one of the many factors that can make teachers change. As an exogenous factor its effectiveness in bringing change depends on a number of variables: situational, environmental and inherent. What needs to be achieved has to be seen in the light of all these variables.

NOTES

1. From 1982–1987, the Malaysian Government provided a yearly grant of about $M36 million for the implementation of KBSR in all states. Each state was allocated an amount based on the number of schools it had. The money was not, however, granted direct to schools because the amount was meant to cover all KBSR costs in the state. This included the purchase of materials, cost of conducting inservice courses,

supervision, and other KBSR activities at state, district and school level. Allocation to schools was made after all these costs had been taken into consideration. The actual cost of conducting inservice courses for teachers varied from state to state depending on a number of factors such as the number of teachers to be trained, the number of key personnel, the distance the state of Perak, where this study was undertaken, the amount spent on KBSR inservice courses was $M748940.00 (total KBSR grant was $M3.65 million) in 1982, rising to $M813092.00 (total KBSR grant was $M3.715 million) in 1984. The number of teachers trained were 6601 in 1982 and 6792 in 1984.

2.   A new secondary school curriculum was, at the time of writing, being developed by the Ministry of Education. The curriculum was to be introduced in stages in all secondary schools throughout the country from 1988.

3.   A total of 48 teachers (21 males and 27 females) and nine headteachers from nine primary schools in the district of Kuala Kangsar were interviewed. The choice of the schools was made by stratified random sampling. The number of schools chosen (11.4 per cent of the total number of primary schools in the district) was based on what was thought to be a manageable number to cover within the time available for the fieldwork. Supplemented by information from questionnaires distributed to another 30 per cent of the schools in the district, the percentage does represent a large enough number to allow some degree of confidence in making any interpretation about all the schools and teachers in the district. There was no apparent reason to suggest that these schools, and the teachers interviewed, were not typical of the populations from which they were drawn. The total number of teachers interviewed represents 38.1 per cent of the total number of teachers in the sample schools.

4.   It was observed that, with the exception of one, all the key personnel often tried to invite participation by asking for opinions and comments from the participants although they (key personnel) always considered themselves to be hard-pressed for time in conducting their sessions.

5.   Most of the key personnel waited until almost all the participants had entered the room before starting their sessions.

6.   Besides the roles spelt out by the CDC there were two other documents spelling out the duties of the key personnel found in the state and district level.

5 Classroom Action Research in Africa: a Lesotho Case Study of Curriculum and Professional Development

Janet S. Stuart

CONTEXT AND RATIONALE

Introduction

This is an account of a small-scale project carried out with teachers of Development Studies in Lesotho at post-primary level. I worked intensively with five teachers over a year, to help them firstly to reflect on the teaching and learning processes in the classroom and then to change these as they thought appropriate.

The project sprang from an individual initiative and was the only one of its kind; the Ministry of Education sanctioned it but was not involved in any way. The findings, however, are capable of wider application; they indicate some of the possibilities for change when teachers are encouraged to study their own practice and given some support in experimenting with and evaluating alternatives. The project produced results at the levels of both curriculum development for the subject and professional development for the teachers involved.

Origins of the Study

The starting point was the problem of how best to teach Development Studies in secondary schools. Development Studies had been introduced some ten years previously; it comprised elements of history, geography, economics, political science and sociology, and was intended to involve students in practical work as well as academic

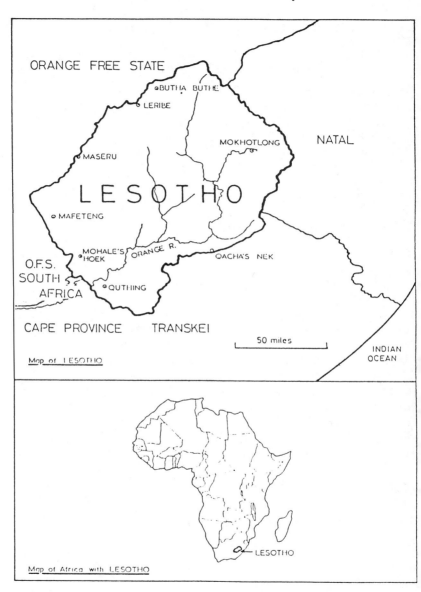

Map of LESOTHO

Map of Africa with LESOTHO

studies. Its early proponents stressed its integrated nature, its importance for nation-building, and its relevance to students' own lives (Taylor 1982, Van Rensburg 1974). Curriculum documents advocated student-centred activity-based teaching methods that would encourage participation, intellectual debate and problem-solving. But teacher educators, teachers and students alike seemed unclear about the feasibility and effectiveness of such methods.

I had been teaching curriculum studies courses in Development Studies at the National University of Lesotho (NUL); the project grew out of my own uncertainty about the most appropriate and effective pedagogy for the subject in Lesotho school conditions. I wished to discover what 'good' Development Studies teachers considered 'good practice'; whether they actually used these methods in class; what problems and constraints they found and how they could be encouraged and supported to try out more of their ideas in practice.

Collaborative action research seemed to offer scope for grounding the enquiry in the concerns and practices of Lesotho teachers, rather than starting with models developed in other countries which might prove inappropriate; the flexible and cyclical format would allow for shifts of focus in response to feedback; the findings would be immediately useful; and it would train the participating teachers in research skills. All this was borne out in practice; what I had not altogether foreseen was its powerful effect on the professional development of the teachers. What began essentially as a curriculum development project turned into a study of teacher change.

Action Research

The action research tradition goes back over 40 years in the United States to Kurt Lewin (1946) who used the term to describe his approach to solving social problems, and to Stephen Corey (1953) who first used it with teachers. Later, in Britain, Lawrence Stenhouse (1975) developed the ideas of the 'teacher as researcher' and in the last two decades a 'Classroom Action Research' movement has spread in the UK (for example, Elliott 1976, Nixon 1981, CARN 1980, 1984, 1986, 1987) and in Australia (Kemmis and McTaggart 1988, Carr and Kemmis 1983) as well as in Europe (Letiche 1987). It has not yet been often applied in less industrialised countries, though some of the 'popular and participatory research' movements in Latin America share many of its characteristics (Avalos 1986), and in Africa Wright (1988) has pioneered a similar approach.

Essentially, action research is a process in which the actors in a social situation, such as a group, a community or a classroom, take deliberate steps to study their situation and to improve it concurrently; systematic enquiry and change are both built into the process. It usually proceeds through several cycles of planning, acting, monitoring, analysing and reflecting. It is categorised by Chin and Benne (1969) as one of the 'normative-reeducative' strategies for change. The basic process is shown in Fig. 5.1.

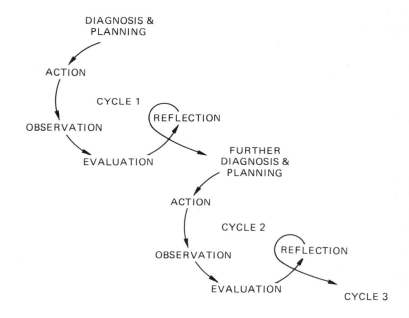

FIGURE 5.1   *Basic action research cycles*

It seemed to me that the framework was potentially very appropriate for the Third World; it is a grassroots, development-oriented approach, dialogic rather than didactic (Freire 1972), which might encourage the growth of endogenous models rather than uncritical acceptance of imported ones (Wright 1988); it can be cheap, flexible and practicable. Further, it could empower the teachers to continue the process of change and development in their own classrooms.

The Baseline Schools

While the action research project was going on, I carried out observations and tape-recordings of Development Studies lessons in 12 other schools in order to give some background to the case study classes. When I observed these lessons and analysed the transcripts I used as a framework the categories and concepts that were being developed by the project team, so as to draw comparisons between the 'case study' and 'baseline' classes. I also interviewed the teachers who gave the lessons, using a semi-structured format to elicit some of their perceptions.

The data confirmed that most Development Studies teaching in Lesotho was formal and didactic. The most common methods seen were what I termed 'QUANEX' (question, answer and teacher's exposition) or lecture. The main resource was the textbook, which was used as a guide for lesson planning and a source of assignments. Activity-based learning was rare. Teachers were aware of other methods but said they rarely used them.

Classroom interaction was dominated by the teacher who, on average, contributed 85 per cent of the talk. Most teachers stressed their desire for pupils to participate, hold 'hot discussions' and to ask questions, yet the pupils' 15 per cent of the dialogue typically consisted of responding to teachers' questions, either singly or 'in chorus'. Very seldom did they ask questions or initiate an exchange.[1]

Analysis of the questions and answers confirmed that most interchanges were pitched at recall or comprehension levels; teachers rarely demanded such skills as comparing, inferring, reasoning or evaluating. Nor did they model such skills in their lectures.

The implied view of knowledge was that it is fixed and closed, ready to be handed over to pupils, rather than open to question and debate, or to be constructed by pupils through problem-solving. However, teachers did give pupils some freedom to draw on their own experience when providing examples, and occasionally they encouraged personal opinions.

Few teachers interviewed saw Development Studies as a radical curricular change and many were unclear about the syllabus aims or the suggested pedagogy. Most teachers appeared to follow a 'transmission' model of teaching. Here is a typical answer to a question about learning aims: 'To know facts. They should answer questions in class, write essays, and express themselves well. They should participate by raising their hands to show they've understood.' I came to the conclusion that teachers were not pushed into this mode of teaching by pressures from the school, community or even exams – though these were important – but by lack of role models and lack of opportunity to see or experiment with alternatives in a supportive atmosphere. Other factors were lack of confidence in the subject matter, and lack of time or opportunity to think through what they were doing, reflect on their practice and articulate values and theories.

Much of the value of the action research project lay in the way it was able to meet such needs, and help the project teachers – whose first taped lessons were usually quite similar to the baseline ones – to extend their skills and overcome some of the barriers.

THE ACTION RESEARCH PROJECT

Overview and Methods

The project was carried out in 1984–85 with a team of five selected Basotho teachers of Development Studies: they volunteered or were invited to take part. Four taught in secondary schools and one lectured at the local Teacher Training College. We chose three Form B classes (second year of secondary school, average age 16), one Form D (fourth year), and a group of student primary teachers as case study classes for the research. All the members of the team had taken my courses at NUL at one time or another, so there was a certain shared background of interests and assumptions.

Two things seemed important at the start: that the teachers should select what aspects of their teaching they wished to focus on, and that we should move out of our former roles of tutor and students to become collaborators. The first meeting was therefore carefully planned: I asked the teachers first to write down some successful aspects of their teaching and then to note some problems they found in class. These were shared and discussed; the third stage was to suggest possible solutions. After that I circulated some short articles and case studies on action research, asked them to elect their own chairperson, and to plan what they wanted to try out in their classes during the year. By the end of the weekend, with minimal guidance from me, they had come up with six research themes, which became known as the Guiding Propositions. Here are the four that proved most fruitful:

(a)   Students are passive in class; they do not participate actively in learning and they expect teachers to feed them with information. They can be helped through discussion, especially in small groups, and role-play/simulation.

(b)   Students show a lack of higher-order skills such as comprehension, application, analysis and synthesis. They can be helped through more discussion, debate, relevant literature and role-play/simulation.

(c)   Students believe that knowledge is 'closed' or 'fixed'; it is a 'thing' which they 'are given', rather than explorations in which they take part. This can be changed by a consistently open-ended teaching approach.

(d)   Students find it difficult to pose questions for enquiry. They can be helped by fieldtrips, by interviewing guest speakers, through role-play.

At the end of the meeting one remarked: 'I thought you were going to give us all hypotheses to test. I've learnt a lot about research today.' The process of becoming teacher-researchers had begun.

Over the year I worked with each teacher individually in their own classroom, helping them to plan and carry out three cycles of action and reflection. Typically each cycle contained a week-long sequence of lessons: for example, some learning activity followed by group discussion and reporting. We collected data by tape-recording lessons and making notes of what went on in the classroom; we elicited pupils' views through questionnaires and interviews, and analysed some of their written work.

After each lesson the teacher and I had a short discussion; then I transcribed the tapes and sent them to her. After we had both studied them we had a longer review session to analyse the data and plan the next cycle. The team met between cycles to share findings, review conclusions and give each other support and encouragement; this was a very important element. From the start the team became involved in producing progress reports for local and international meetings, which encouraged them to write up their experiences in the form of case studies at the end of the year; these were published for local use (Stuart *et al* 1985). Fig. 5.2 shows the project in diagram form.

I called myself the 'consultant'. I defined my role primarily as 'process-helper' (Eraut 1977, Day 1984) which included being both a

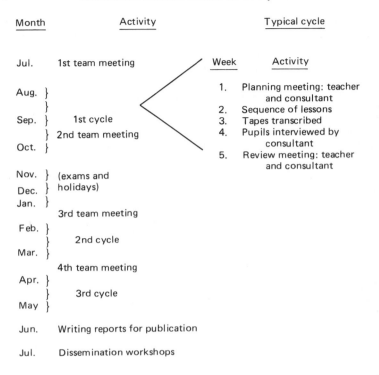

Month	Activity	Typical cycle	
		Week	Activity
Jul.	1st team meeting		
Aug. }		1.	Planning meeting: teacher and consultant
Sep. }	1st cycle	2.	Sequence of lessons
}	2nd team meeting	3.	Tapes transcribed
Oct. }		4.	Pupils interviewed by consultant
		5.	Review meeting: teacher and consultant
Nov. }	(exams and		
Dec. }	holidays)		
Jan. }			
	3rd team meeting		
Feb. }			
}	2nd cycle		
Mar. }			
	4th team meeting		
Apr. }			
}	3rd cycle		
May }			
Jun.	Writing reports for publication		
Jul.	Dissemination workshops		

FIGURE 5.2 *Outline of project and action research cycles*

facilitator (Rogers 1969) and a commentator. Thus I would try to elicit the teachers' ideas, reflect them back, summarise and sometimes offer alternatives or mention points they had overlooked, acting as a 'critical friend' (Elliott 1976). Sometimes I took on a 'coaching' role (Schön 1987), especially where research methods were involved. I explicitly eschewed a directive or tutorial role, although at first some of the team wanted me to tell them what to do. There is evidence that all became more independent through the year and in two cases this was very marked.

Examples of Action Research Cycles

All the team members carried out interesting and successful research cycles. I will choose here just two contrasting ones: Puleng's work with B1, a bright and co-operative class at Fora School, and

Mathato's efforts with the slow and apathetic B2 at City School. This will also illustrate the kinds of qualitative data we collected. (More details of the team's work can be found in Stuart *et al* 1985.)[2]

Puleng at Fora School

Puleng's main focus was on Propositions 2 and 3 (using higher order skills and encouraging an open-ended approach). Here is an extract from her first lesson, on population:

Teacher: Why do you think population increases? What reasons make population to increase so fast? Because this is what is happening in the world today . . . Yes?
Boy 1: I think that medicine has improved.
Teacher: He says that medicine has improved. What does he mean? Will someone try to expand on that? What has medicine got to do with people? Yes?
Girl 1: Prevents them from germs.
Teacher: From germs? So if there are no germs?
Girl 1: They live better, live longer [unclear].
Teacher: Yes, they live better, they are healthy, they live longer. So that is one reason why the population is increasing so fast. Any other reason? Would you like to give me any, another reason? Do you want to try?
Boy 2: Medicine protects you against diseases.

After listening to the tape, she concluded:

It was more of a question-and-answer session than a discussion . . . participation was too low (only 11 out of 38 spoke) . . . they are looking for a consensus . . . yet they have some potential for thinking. I want to get them using higher order skills without my prompting.   (Review meeting)

During the first cycle she monitored class reactions to a fieldtrip and a guest speaker, and taped small group discussions on both. She decided she accepted students' answers too easily and needed to challenge them more. In the second cycle she focused both on challenging the class to raise the level of thinking and on making them look at several sides of a question, to see that there could be more than one answer. To help herself she devised a regular sequence of activities for each topic: introduction – brainstorm – activity – discussion – written work. She tested this out and modified it to include a summary lecture to help weaker students.

Evidence from lessons, more group discussion tapes and students' work all showed an increasing ability to be 'open' to alternatives and to use higher level skills, so in the third cycle she developed these ideas further, introducing new methods (a simulation game and guided reading), and monitoring the results. The students continued to respond to the teacher's challenges and to improve. Here is an extract from a class report-back on 'Should Basotho farmers use improved technology?' (Lesson 10).

Girl 1: It will be better if Basotho farmers can continue on using simple technology, until they get rich, so that they will afford to use improved technology. Improved technology may be used in project that produces more goods. Reasons: Lesotho, because Lesotho is not yet a rich country, to use complex technology. Another thing is that it is useless to buy complex technology because the country is too small. That's all.

[Laughter from some pupils.]

Boy 1: I don't understand because . . . to use complex [unclear] to improve our production. So what do you mean when you say our country is small?

Girl 1: If we use machines we have to . . . er . . . we have to . . .

[Pause.]

Teacher: Yes, other group members can help.

Girl 2: What she means is that it is useless to buy improved technology, because there is not enough land, we only have small land which is for ploughing ourselves, our labour . . . .

Pupils: No/Yes/Not quite [Discussion.]

Boy 2: Do you say that if you use simple technology, can it, can you produce more for our people?

Girl 1: Even if you can use that complex technology, you see that Lesotho is mostly a mountainous country, so where are you going to use that, those machines?

[Vigorous discussion among pupils.]

Boy 3: We'll use them on the lowlands, not the mountains . . .

Girl 1: The lowlands are too small . . .

[Confusion.]

Girl 1: Madam, they don't want to understand, these people! They don't want to understand.

[Discussion among pupils.]

Teacher: What she means by that, is that the arable land, the land that is suitable, is too small. Yes?

Boy 3: Even if the land is small, I think we have to use complex machines, so that, er, even if in one land we can use [unclear] so much, enough land, so that our people can get enough, even if suitable land ... but, ach, I don't understand why people are saying it's useless. So what they say is, otherwise you mean that, er, it's better to die for hunger?

This shows how participation, discussion techniques and levels of thought had all improved over the previous nine months. To take one quantitative measure, the ratio of teacher's talk to student's talk (calculated as percentages of the total dialogue) was 29:71, compared with 73:27 in the previous lesson.[3] The difference in the two lessons can be depicted graphically as in Fig. 5.3.

Mathato at City School
Mathato's original problem concerned the passivity in B2, a low-stream class seen by the school as 'difficult'. She began by monitoring the low student participation rate, in accordance with Proposition 1. They seemed very reluctant to respond to her questions in class, so she split them into small groups with questions to discuss. Our observations, confirmed by tapes, showed that the students did not know how to 'discuss': they simply wrote down the first answer suggested. One result of analysing and reflecting on this lesson was that Mathato played the tapes back to the class and explained exactly what she wanted them to do in 'discussion'.

But she also concluded that the topics – conservation and population – had been presented in too abstract a way and she formulated a new proposition:

less able students are passive when they have to learn abstract things from books, of which they have no direct knowledge; learning from first-hand experience will enable them to take a more active part in learning, and find out knowledge for themselves.

(Planning meeting)

In the second cycle, taking the topic 'production', she organised a fieldtrip to a local industrial estate of small workshops, giving the students a questionnaire to help them take notes. The class appeared eager, and asked many questions, in Sesotho, during the visit. Back in class she divided them into groups to prepare reports. While I was taping two groups she circulated among the others and seeing several had collected very little information, decided 'to arrange the report-

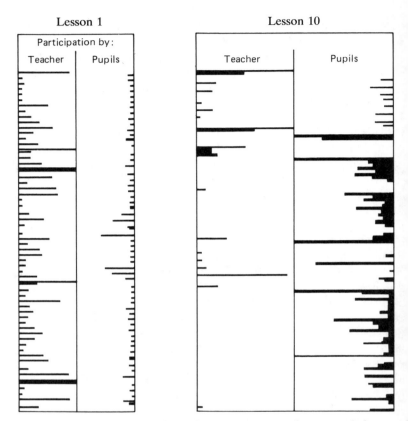

FIGURE 5.3 *Comparisons of pupil participation in classroom dialogue at beginning and end of project*

back session in such a way that the groups which had not achieved much could be helped to understand through my probing questions' (case study report). However, the report-back lesson proved unsatisfactory. In asking the 'probing questions' to try to add information to the group reports, she found she interrupted them so frequently that the class relapsed into silence. Disappointed, she sought more data.

Firstly, she asked a Sesotho-speaking consultant to give the students a short questionnaire and then to interview the class. This revealed that the students found problems in reporting in English the information they had collected in Sesotho, and that they lacked the skills of taking notes and writing reports. Secondly, she listened to the tapes of the two other groups. These shed a new light on the pupils; she was impressed by the information they had gathered and the points they raised. In a later meeting she said:

> I realised if I had listened to the tapes before holding the class discussion, I might have asked them to present differently; I would have asked the secretary of the group to stand up and read out what they had compiled, so that all this information and creativity would have been shared, instead of my leading them all the time. They were reporting within a structure which did not allow for this new information to be brought in.　　　(Report to team meeting)

In the third cycle she organised a second fieldtrip and made several changes. Instead of giving the pupils a prepared questionnaire, she spent a class period helping them to write down their own questions. After the visit, she simply told the groups to discuss what they had seen and to write a report, organising their information themselves. The results pleased her; the pupils produced reports between 100 and 200 words long, which they read out in class and then displayed on the classroom wall.

She had not only experimented successfully with new ways of presenting information and concepts and of organising learning activities, she had also learnt to reflect on her own practice. As a result, she was able to trust the students more and give them more responsibility for their own learning. A significant result of the research was that rapport between the teacher and this 'difficult' class improved considerably.

ASPECTS OF CURRICULUM DEVELOPMENT ARISING FROM THE STUDY

General Findings

At the end of these cycles certain common findings had emerged. Although the team was working at three different educational levels – Form B, Form D and teacher training – the problems they encountered and the conclusions they reached were broadly similar; consequently they felt that these findings were potentially generalisable to other teachers, other classrooms, and probably to other subjects.

Appropriate teaching methods
The team had experimented with a number of student-centred activity-based teaching methods and found that in spite of crowded classrooms and lack of resources most of them were feasible and effective. Once the class was familiar with the procedures they did not take up too much time and the learning appeared to last longer. *Fieldtrips* produced good results in terms of motivation, participation and open-ended learning, but needed careful preparation, such as setting questions which would challenge the students to analyse and evaluate rather than just to collect facts.

Small group discussions proved extremely valuable on several levels: they increased participation and helped students assimilate new ideas, as well as providing language practice (cf. Barnes and Todd 1977). However, students needed to be shown how to use discussion for weighing up alternatives. *Role-play* and *simulations* were not investigated to the same extent, though both worked well when tried out.

Two teachers used *stimulus pictures* in the form of large coloured photographs of people in both developed and developing countries. These were particularly productive for opening up discussion, as they forced pupils to infer and speculate, constructing knowledge for themselves rather than relying on the teacher.

Only *guest speakers* proved unsatisfactory, as the visitors were seldom able to adjust the level and length of their talk to student needs.

Teaching learning skills
One important general conclusion was that teachers should pay more attention to teaching their students appropriate strategies for learning. Small group discussion only became effective after students understood what was expected of them: Dineo taught the Primary Teachers' class through demonstrating a model discussion, and Mathato played their own tapes back to her groups, explaining what was wrong. Equally, before fieldtrips the students had to be taught how to take notes and to organise information into a report. With Form D, Sechaba found he needed to spend several lessons teaching the skills of planning and writing essays. To help students to gather information from books, Puleng invented a guided reading formula: students were given short questions to answer from a chapter and if something was not clear they were to put '???' in the margin so that the teacher could clear up confusion at the next lesson. Tumelo

helped his students to pose research questions (Proposition 4) by demonstrating a questionnaire on the first fieldtrip, and then getting the class to write the questions for the next one.

Role of language
It was clear that lack of competence in English was a major reason for students' silence in class, and that it also militated against the effective use of higher cognitive skills. This remained a major unsolved problem, though we had some evidence that the training in study skills also helped improve both oral and written language skills.

Student strategies for dealing with confusion
I collected much evidence from both baseline and case study classes that students frequently sat through lessons in a mist of incomprehension. When I enquired why they so seldom asked questions, they would usually mention language, embarrassment, or lack of time, but the most revealing comment came from a bright Form D lad, who said:

> If I understand the main gist of what he is teaching about, but there's just something that isn't clear, I put up my hand, but if I don't understand anything, I don't raise up my hand, because he would have to start from the beginning.

We felt that the next step would be to involve students more explicitly in the action research and help them to study their own learning strategies in order to improve them.

New Propositions

When the project ended the teachers realised they had not arrived at precise or easy answers to their problems. It is, I think, significant that their original plan, to write a definitive Teachers' Handbook for Development Studies, was dropped in favour of writing about their own experience in the form of case study reports to encourage other teachers to involve themselves in a similar process of action research. In these reports they showed how they had neither 'proved' nor 'refuted' their guiding propositions, but rather that they had refined them through the process of the research. From their reflections emerged new propositions, which they offered to local teachers to test out and develop further. Here are some examples, which will serve as a summary of the team's main findings:

(a) Students have the potential ability for using higher order cognitive skills; this can be developed by setting higher level questions that challenge and stretch them, and by teaching them ways of tackling such questions.

(b) Students will adopt a critical and open view of knowledge if a teacher uses a consistently open-ended teaching approach, such as accepting alternative views, leaving issues open, and encouraging independent enquiry.

(c) Teaching by student-centred activities, like discussion, research, reading and reporting, provides an environment conducive to open and independent learning.

(d) Experiential learning – fieldtrips, role-play, simulations – facilitates recall and understanding and lays a foundation for thinking.

(e) If students lack the necessary skills for active and independent learning, teachers need to provide training in such skills as discussing, taking notes, formulating research questions, or planning and writing essays.

(f) The combination of varied methods into a stable pattern provides a good framework for teaching and learning.

(g) Students frequently have inadequate strategies for dealing with incomprehension; teachers have to provide opportunities for checking comprehension and answering students' questions.

(h) Involving students in action research in their own classroom will help them to improve their own learning strategies.

Evaluation of Student Learning during the Project

The results of action research, because of its flexible and process oriented approach, are not amenable to formal evaluation. We cannot measure the effects the project had on student outcomes; all we can say is that it did not detract from student learning, and probably enhanced it. Students were positive about the new methods singling out fieldtrips, groupwork and discussion as particularly helpful. Some written tests involving certain 'thinking skills' were administered to the three Form B classes and to three comparison classes at the beginning and end of the year; the results showed the case study pupils did somewhat better at the end of the project than their peers, though the data was not susceptible to statistical analysis. In the national Junior Certificate exam, taken six months later Puleng's Fora class did much better in Development Studies than in other subjects, which suggests her policy of consistently challenging and setting high level questions bore fruit.[4]

ASPECTS OF PROFESSIONAL DEVELOPMENT

In discussing the professional development of the teachers, I have drawn extensively on the concept of the 'Reflective Practitioner' (Schön 1983). Schön encourages us, in studying 'how professionals think in action' to move away from the 'technical rationality model', which presupposes that professional problems can be solved by the application of scientific principles. Rather, the professional – manager, doctor, engineer or teacher – is faced with unique situations which are full of 'complexity, uncertainty, instability and value conflicts' (op. cit. p. 14), and needs the skills of the artist as well as those of the scientist. In particular, she needs to be able to 'reflect-in-action', a process which combines framing the problem, drawing on a repertoire of skills and experience, hypothesising and experimenting as she goes along, getting feedback from the situation and creating a solution which, while not perfect nor definitive, works in that particular case and is in keeping with professional goals and values.

In analysing the effects of the action research project on the teachers, using not only the data from lessons but also tapes of my planning and review meetings with them, my journal notes and the teachers' own reflections as presented in their case study reports, I found Schön's model fitted our data well. Adapting his framework slightly, I could distinguish at least seven different ways in which the teachers had become better and more reflective practitioners.

Developing the Ability to Frame Problems

Firstly, the team developed their ability to break out of a situation where they felt 'stuck' or confused, and to reframe the problem so as to make it more amenable to action.

This happened both on a collective and an individual level. For example, there was a general and striking shift from defining their problems in deficit terms, such as 'pupils lack . . . pupils are not . . .' to focusing on ways of developing pupils' potentials: 'we need to teach skills . . . teachers should . . .' This happened with all the teachers. As Tumelo put it in his report:

I have been all along thinking that if the teacher 'teaches' students and exposes them to new knowledge they would be able to 'learn'. But my exposure to action research has refuted this belief that I previously had. I would like, in the future, to concentrate much of my time in trying to cultivate these skills in students.

(Stuart *et al.*, 1985 p. 88)

The examples given above of Puleng and Mathato also show how teachers individually reframed their problems as they went along.

Enlarging their Repertoires of Teaching Skills

All members of the team extended their repertoires in several ways, by sharing ideas and by being stimulated to try out new approaches. Everyone organised discussion groups, and some experimented with different types of grouping, or different types of discussion guidelines. Some of the team tried out teaching methods which they had been taught about in college but had never practised themselves. For example, Dineo wanted to do role-play with her trainee teachers and asked me to observe and tape one session; she then repeated it with other groups, inventing new techniques as she went along.

Tumelo had always wanted to do research with a class, but felt unsure of how to organise it. He used the research project to plan and carry out this activity; he demonstrated to his class how to prepare a list of questions and then made them do it for themselves. In the process, he experimented with a number of new ways of structuring lessons and organising fieldtrips. He used the consultants as sources of support and advice, but in the event carried out all the steps on his own.

Experimenting-in-Action

They carried out a number of experiments-in-action and received enhanced feedback through the use of various forms of data collection.

In Mathato's case, described above, the second cycle shows this process particularly clearly. She deliberately planned the fieldtrip as a method of encouraging participation and conceptual learning. Halfway through, she decided that the class needed more information from her, so she structured the report-back lesson to provide this. However, this discouraged the pupils from participating; the results were unsatisfactory. Using a consultant to collect independent feedback from the pupils and listening to tapes provided her with enough information to realise what had happened and to try out a different format which proved more successful.

Evaluating their own Teaching

They looked critically at their own practice, again using feedback of different kinds, and became increasingly able to evaluate themselves. All the teachers said they had become much more aware of how they taught and more able to evaluate their own practice critically. Sechaba said at the beginning: 'I feel challenged to think very carefully about my teaching for the first time . . . how effective am I being?' and undertook to research the impact on students – both cognitive and affective – of his teaching. In the first cycle he told his Form D students to do library research into some fairly complex questions, and to report their findings to the class. After discussing the experience with me he decided they needed more preliminary information and for the next topic he gave an introductory lecture. Afterwards he wrote in his own notes:

> It was obvious I should not attempt to squeeze so much into a short time . . . People were attentive, but one could tell they were getting bored . . . There were few questions . . . For the next topic maybe the introduction should be done in 3 stages, so the teacher could throw questions at the students after every bit . . .

The interviews I held with the students at the teacher's request confirmed these insights and revealed further problems with new terminology; a useful dialogue was set up between the teacher and his class over different teaching and learning strategies. This 'triangulation' (Elliott 1981) enhanced the feedback Sechaba was already picking up, correcting and deepening his perceptions. There was 'double-loop' learning going on (Argyris and Schön 1974): he was also improving his own ability to reflect and to monitor the effects of his teaching.

Strategic Organisation of Teaching

Using their increased awareness, new insights and extended repertoires, some designed new personal patterns of teaching, exemplifying the 'teacher as artist'.

Working as a team often produced useful cross-fertilisation of ideas. Sechaba had outlined in June a new 'stable pattern of teaching: introduction – research – group discussion – visual display – teacher summary – written evaluation'. As described above, Puleng adapted this idea for her own use. She explained the rationale to me as follows:

> After [the fieldtrip] I felt it had failed, to some extent. I felt I didn't know whether the failure came from the visit, or because they could not discuss, or what was it they lacked ... I couldn't really tell what they had failed to do, so I said this new pattern will help me focus ...
>
> I introduce the topic – sometimes it takes the whole lesson. Then I can tell if we are still together or not. The next one, maybe they are discussing in groups. I know this is the second stage of my plan ... in this way, up to the last stage when they are writing, I know whether they are still coming on all right; that here is where the obstacles come.

This goes, I think, beyond reflection-in-action. It can be seen as a personal theory of practice, firmly grounded in her own experience, offering an experimental framework which she then proceeded to test out and modify in the second cycle. In the third cycle she commented: 'I'm not sure yet if it's working, but it helps me to organise my teaching' and she decided to continue with it.

Clarification of Educational Values

In focused reflection and discussion, they elaborated aspects of their value systems, clarifying what they understood as good practice. An example of this process was the way the team developed and refined the two ideas of 'an open conception of knowledge' and 'independent learning' throughout the course of the project.

These concepts were very closely related in the minds of the teacher-researchers. The central image seemed to be that of pupils or students who do not wait for the teacher to hand out correct answers, because they have understood that knowledge is not a finite bundle of facts, that there are many possible alternative views, and that one can never 'know everything'. This concept held some fascination for the team; they commented that they themselves had not grasped this broader view of knowledge until their own high school or college years. The project gave them an opportunity to work out their ideas further, and the concepts became embodied in the 'Further Propositions' (see above).

Theorising about their own Practice

They began to develop new concepts and to build theory grounded on their own findings; these were shared, critiqued, refined and made available to the local professional community. This happened partly through the team meetings, partly in dialogue with the consultant, and partly as a result of individual reflection and writing. For example, Dineo articulated a new theory which referred to Basotho students' learning problems in general. On the basis of the data she collected from monitoring small group discussions and setting various kinds of test questions, she rejected the original proposition that students were incapable of higher order cognitive skills, and set up a new theory. She postulated a cause-effect link: that their previous schooling experience had failed to develop the required skills or to give them confidence to learn on their own, and she set up a new proposition, that 'a learning environment conducive to open-ended and independent learning should be created'.

Challenged to operationalise her ideas about this 'conducive learning environment', she elaborated five working hypotheses about student-centred and active learning methods, and over the next three months proceeded to experiment-in-action with this new theoretical structure. While continuing to give lectures to present ideas and content, she also organised a number of activities designed to involve students in their own learning, and to challenge them to think for themselves. These included group discussions, role-play, analysis of written material, translating relationships into diagram form, the use of open-ended stimuli to provoke ideas, and a Bulletin Board for current events. In her case study report she outlined both the successes and the problems she encountered.

As she commented 'as you go along, some other problem comes out', and by May 1985 she had come across a new contradiction. She phrased it as a 'dichotomy between teaching for understanding and teaching for exams' and devoted two pages of her report to wrestling with the theoretical implications of this position.

Evaluation

To try to get more independent feedback, I asked a colleague to

interview the team for me towards the end of the project. This confirmed my impression that while their own teaching had improved,
they had not yet reached the stage of becoming fully fledged teacher-
researchers. Tumelo summed it up by saying: 'It has increased my
awareness . . . I am able to look at my teaching critically and that way
I think it has improved my classroom teaching'. Puleng felt she had
become more organised and more self-critical:

I have changed a bit . . . I have to sit back and assess the whole
situation and say, maybe here I am going wrong, or here I am
responsible for this poor teaching. So I have had time to assess my
teaching in general.

They seemed to have internalised the process. Talking about the
consultant's role, Dineo said:

I think I have become so accustomed to it that even when the
facilitator will not be there in class, it's like she is there, because I
know I have to sort of evaluate or criticise my work, so may be in
that case I'm my own consultant.

However, they said they did not feel that they had reached the stage
where they could facilitate the process for others, nor carry out
independent research on their own.

Two years later, when I revisited Lesotho, the evidence was consistent with these comments. Sechaba and Dineo had left to do
masters' degrees overseas. When I interviewed two others, they said
that though they had not done any more formal action research, they
still used the new methods in their classrooms. Puleng was applying
similar principles to teaching English, and occasionally carried out
mutual observation with another teacher, and Mathato had become
an informal consultant to a colleague who was doing a part-time
B.Ed.

The project had not been designed with dissemination in mind.
However, there were some spin-off results from personal contacts
and publication of the reports. A related project concerned with
monitoring teaching – learning strategies in primary schools called in
the project team to help plan observation schedules. Interestingly,
some of the primary teachers involved began asking the observers for
feedback and assistance in improving their practice; as a result of our
conclusions about the usefulness and feasibility of action research,
the last phase of the project was replanned to include the setting-up

of self-evaluation groups in ten primary schools (Lefoka and Chabane 1987). Simultaneously a colleague began incorporating action research techniques into Business Studies curriculum courses at National University.

In sum, the action research project had helped the teachers to be more aware of what was going on in their classrooms, more able to analyse what they were doing and to change their actions appropriately. There was some evidence that this process did not end with the project; they had developed the capacity for self-sustaining professional growth, and the results were encouraging others to follow the same path.

USING THE ACTION RESEARCH MODEL IN PRACTICE

This project was small-scale and resource- and personnel-intensive. Does it have lessons for more wide-scale implementation of educational action research in developing countries? I believe it does.

One of the strengths of action research is that it is a process which is not very far removed from normal practice; well-intentioned teachers often look at their classrooms and reflect about what goes on, even if this is only shared at an anecdotal level in the staffroom. Rather than being seen as an alien process imposed from outside, action research is, I think, best presented as a systematic deepening and extending of professional 'reflection-in-action'. Through action research, teachers are helped to make the process more conscious, more explicit and more rigorous, to the point where, if made available for public critique and discussion, it can be called research.

At the same time, one should also be aware that the actual processes of reflective research are extremely complex. I realised in the middle of the project that far more was going on with the teachers than our framework suggested: at the very least, there seemed to be a number of mini-cycles nesting inside the formal cycles, in which teachers were perceiving, reflecting, acting and evaluating within a lesson, or between cycles; once aware of something, they did not always wait to collect all the data; they acted and if the results felt right they went on, if not they changed tack. Often they were working on more than one proposition simultaneously.

In part, this is simply the experience that real research is messy, fragmented and sometimes obscure. But it also, I think, proves Schön's point that teaching cannot be described in terms of 'technical rationality'; it is a process more akin to artistry, where the practitioner interacts creatively with the situation, changing and being changed by it. Teaching is holistic: while other research methods try to study it by cutting it up into little bits, action research tries to keep it together. This makes it difficult to evaluate, particularly when the researcher is also part of the situation; it also makes it more useful, and that for me is an important criterion.

In spite of, or perhaps because of, these problems of complexity, I think the action research framework is useful as a heuristic device; it provides a disciplined and systematic method to help teachers to start studying the teaching-learning in their classroom, even if the real process remains elusive.

From this experience I think it best to start with a simple model of the basic action research cycle. I gave the team a flowchart (Elliott 1981) which details 11 possible steps: they found this mystifying and I would now use that shown above (see also Kemmis and McTaggart 1988, Hopkins 1985). I would in future also negotiate with the teachers some time for a brief but formal training in methods of collecting and analysing classroom data. I expected them to pick these up from me as we went along; they might have become independent sooner if we had spent a little time on induction.

Crucial aspects of action research are ownership of the plans and control of the pace and direction of change. In this project, it was the team of teacher-researchers who identified the changes needed and chose what innovations to try out; each stage was negotiated, with the teachers having the deciding word. I am convinced, *pace* Havelock and Huberman (1977) that a prerequisite for effective curricular and pedagogic change is the full involvement, as partners, of the teaching force; the speed may be less but change is more sure. On the other hand it is clearly hard to sustain impetus and motivation against pressure – of exams, traditions, peers – if the whole system is unsympathetic, and for teacher-centred research to be successful, some degree of support and incentive from the Ministry is probably necessary.

There are also big problems of time and energy. To reflect by occasionally listening to a tape is quite easy and intrinsically rewarding; to carry out a systematic evaluation of oneself and one's class requires considerably more effort, and to undertake rigorous research suitable for public critique demands massive commitment as well as skill; few will do this without the promise of some reward. Full time teachers anywhere have little time and there are many other pressures at home and school which take up their energy. In less-industrialised countries schools are often geographically and socially isolated from each other and from higher education institutions; the professional milieu is often underdeveloped and little support is forthcoming in the schools.

One way of overcoming this would be to incorporate action research into teacher training. It would be particularly appropriate for part-time inservice courses where the teachers could be carrying out reflective research in their classrooms and receiving support and training during study periods, with the motive to analyse and write up the results to gain an award. The basic ideas could also be taught in preservice courses. If students have a long teaching practice or internship period, this could be partly assessed on their ability to reflect on their own practice along the lines suggested above.

Another possibility would be to make it part of a school-based improvement programme. Clusters of teachers within schools could give each other support in similar ways to the project team. Certain teachers could be given training in the rationale and methods at residential workshops and pass these on to interested teachers in their schools. This would, I think, require a peripatetic consultant to visit such schools regularly, both to act as a resource person and to boost morale.

In conclusion, the collaborative action research model proved very potent. Not only did it enable a team of teachers to test out some appropriate pedagogy for a new subject, but at the same time it helped them to develop their own skills as teachers in ways that seemed relatively long-lasting. The method worked well in practice and proved capable of adaptation to local conditions. This project was, however, small-scale and made intensive use of a consultant's time. Ways of making the method available to a larger number of teachers and of creating school-based support systems for them remain to be worked out.

NOTES

1. Similar patterns are reported from elsewhere in Africa: for example, my data closely parallels that found by Namuddu in Kenyan biology lessons (Namuddu 1984).
2. Names of teachers and schools used here are pseudonyms.

3. This was measured by counting words from the transcript.
4. In three of the baseline schools, matched as closely as possible to the case study schools in terms of type, location, management and academic standing, I administered questionnaires and tests to Form B classes to see whether the students in our Form B case study classes were in any way atypical. Analysis of this data confirmed that taken as a group our case study pupils were not significantly different in background, achievement or attitude from others. However, one of our Form B classes was in an élite boarding school; here the children were younger and came from wealthier homes than the average. In practice, this factor did not appear to make much difference to the teaching and learning in that class.

Part III
Institutional Contexts

Innovations and initiatives for change are often inhibited by factors that lie hidden within the cultural contexts and climates of institutions. The following two studies look at some of these problems by studying closely the perceptions and feelings of the actors within such contexts.

Fiona Leach's study concerns the perception gaps between expatriate and local staff working on aid projects in Northern Sudan. Her data, collected through interviews, reveal how differently people involved in these projects perceive certain important issues. For example, expatriate staff saw the success of the project to lie in institution-building, while local staff tended to stress the material benefits – funds, equipment and scholarships. There were considerable cultural differences in their conceptions of the appropriate roles and duties of professionals employed in the public sector, and often the Sudanese appeared to be working to different sets of organisational objectives from those of the expatriates. They differed too in their views of how consultation was being carried out, and on how knowledge and skills could best be transferred.

Although the projects she studied were not exclusively educational ones, Leach's research is relevant to educational innovation, particularly where there are social or cultural gaps between different groups of actors. It may be noted that she found perception gaps not only between expatriate – mostly West European – staff and Sudanese, but also between Sudanese management and their technical staff and between men and women. She argues that such differences in perception, which neither side are aware of, can substantially affect the success of the projects.

Baboucarr Sarr's study focuses on two Gambian secondary schools – a high school and a technical school – and compares some aspects of the teaching and learning climates as perceived by teachers and students.

After outlining how the Gambian two-track schooling system developed, he illuminates the contradictions that exist between the aims of the policy and its practice, and then turns to examine the reality and thus to gain a deeper understanding of the possibilities for

153

change. Sarr looks in turn at school aims, teachers' roles as perceived by teachers and students, obstacles to effective teaching, students' subject preferences and the effects of exams. He compares the two types of schools on each of these aspects, collecting data from a wide range of sources.

The study shows how important it is that policy-makers should examine curriculum reality in the schools for which they are planning, so that policies for change can be grounded in a real understanding of the processes at work rather than on rhetoric and wishful thinking.

These studies use various methods to explore and tease out some of the social and social-psychological factors that hinder or facilitate the innovation process. Neither researcher became an actual participant observer, for various reasons, but both had previously been actors within their respective contexts and had therefore 'insider' knowledge and understanding of the situation and of the likely perceptions of other actors, which contributed to the way the research was organised. Leach gathered all her data through long semi-structured interviews which allowed the concerns and perceptions of the actors to emerge. Sarr also mainly employed interviews, while using a more focused approach, and supplementing these with questionnaires, observations of teaching and documentary sources. This enabled him to cross-check and to compare official views with those of teachers and students.

Such studies as these complement research on curriculum, teacher education or educational systems by looking at how people's motivation and attitudes – and therefore their actions which further or impede innovation – are subtly shaped by the contexts in which they operate. The interaction of the personal with the cultural, social and political dimensions is a crucial area for the study of the process of change.

6 Perception Gaps in Technical Assistance Projects: the Sudanese Case

Fiona Leach

INTRODUCTION

The aim of the research described in this chapter is to explore the working relationships that develop between expatriates and Sudanese during the implementation phase of technical assistance projects.[1] All the projects studied were based in the public sector in Northern Sudan and all but one (a rural development project) in institutions. The technical assistance being examined is therefore categorised as 'institutional' rather than 'engineering',[2] the former being generally recognised by aid practitioners as having a lower success rate than the latter. This is due to the fact that complex human interactions are involved in the 'institutional' type of project where the aim is to build up intangible assets such as human resources and institutional infrastructure. This often demands radical behavioural changes of the recipients (Cassen 1986, Lethem and Cooper 1983).

The Context

The Sudan is now the most heavily aided country in Africa, receiving over 1.1 billion $US in 1985 (Economist Intelligence Unit 1987). Most project aid is concentrated in the Northern Region, largely as a result of the civil war in the South. The government is in a precarious state, with dwindling sources of revenue and trained manpower resulting in poor institutional infrastructure and lack of absorptive capacity for externally generated activities. Government employees are extremely demoralised, having seen their once enviable position as civil servants with high salaries and prestige eroded very rapidly to a place now at the bottom of the professional ladder. There is

155

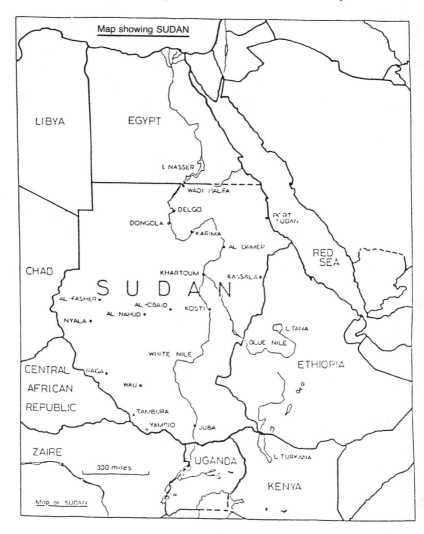

growing disparity in earning levels between the public and the private sectors (a typical ratio in income disparity for middle-level professionals being 1:4). Moreover the enormous brain drain to Saudi Arabia and the Gulf since the mid-1970s has resulted in an estimated one million Sudanese working in the rich Arab states, among whom are Sudan's best qualified and most competent former civil servants. This availability of lucrative employment for Sudanese professionals arouses dissatisfaction and envy in those who have not yet found their way abroad or into the private sector.

The findings of the research analysed below must therefore be seen in this context: most of the Sudanese staff who took part in the fieldwork suffer from low morale and find in their daily work a lack of professional support and meaningful goals. They see themselves working with expatriates whose salaries may be as much as 15 times their own, and whose living standards reflect this disparity. There has also been a rapid deterioration in educational standards over the past 15 years, with the result that those counterparts who have only recently graduated have been poorly educated. For the expatriates, they find themselves working in a difficult economic and institutional environment, frequently with demoralised and unresponsive colleagues, a situation which nevertheless presents a challenge to many.

The Data

For the fieldwork I held one-to-one interviews with 98 people, of whom 60 were Sudanese and 38 were expatriates. Of the 98 all but one of the expatriates and the majority of the Sudanese were currently working in the aid sector, mostly as project team members, while the remainder had been involved in project aid in the Sudan in some previous capacity. The material specifically used for this chapter is drawn from three institution-based projects studied in depth through lengthy interviews conducted with 26 Sudanese and 12 expatriates at several intervals during 1986–87. Supporting evidence is also provided by interviews with 29 individuals working on another five projects which were studied less extensively. Some of these latter informants were familiar with the three case study projects.

These case study projects were funded bilaterally by western donors. Of the three, one was based in an agricultural training institute, another in a university postgraduate institute and the third in a government department responsible for renewable energy (primarily forestry). All three are still in operation; at the time I started the fieldwork the longest had been running for seven years, the shortest for two.[3] Of the five other projects, two were funded by UN organisations, one by the World Bank, and the others by bilateral donors. Three were in education, one in agriculture and one in rural development.

Interviews were held with those most closely involved with implementing the projects: expatriates (project managers and technical specialists) and local staff, most of whom were counterparts to the expatriates. Apart from the project co-managers, very few Sudanese at the management level were interviewed extensively as they were not responsible for carrying out tasks within the project framework.

The data revealed high levels of criticism on both the expatriate and the Sudanese side as to the way in which the projects had been set up and were being implemented. It also revealed the existence of very wide perception gaps between individuals on a variety of project-related issues. In this chapter I examine the nature and causes of these perception gaps and the ways in which they fostered attitudes towards the project and towards colleagues which might adversely affect performance within the three case study projects. Predictably the wider the perception gaps, the less successful the project was in reaching its objectives, and the greater the potential for resentment and conflict.

I found that perception gaps existed between several groups of individuals, primarily between expatriates and Sudanese but also between local management and staff, and on one project between male and female staff members. (For the purpose of this analysis, I have drawn a distinction between local management and local staff, with the latter being regarded as the implementers of the project.) While I was already aware that perception gaps between expatriates and Sudanese existed and suspected that they might be a major cause of poor co-operation on projects, it was a surprise to discover that they also existed between local staff and management on project-related issues. I found that this also contributed significantly to implementation problems.

The majority of those interviewed on both sides had many adverse comments to make about the projects and their colleagues' performance, with broad consensus on the issues which formed the basis of their criticism. However the Sudanese on all eight projects were on the whole more critical than the expatriates. Given a cultural reticence to criticise others, especially foreigners, their frankness was unexpected.

At the same time very few of the expatriates interviewed seemed aware of the full extent of the local staff's feelings about the project, although many knew that there was considerable resentment of aid and technical assistance personnel among the Sudanese in general. It is likely that the local staff's resentment frequently led to their active non-cooperation, which was interpreted by the expatriates as conservatism, indifference or laziness. This lack of understanding of the breadth and intensity of the local staff's feelings can be attributed partly to the expatriates' insularity and partly perhaps to the reticence of Sudanese to criticise others to their face. In contrast the Sudanese interviewed were much more aware that the expatriates had a low opinion of their capabilities and their performance. This may have been because the expatriates were more ready to criticise individuals openly. This awareness among the local staff of the expatriates' opinion of them further aggravated their resentment and placed them on the defensive because they felt it was unjustified: they believed they were capable of doing well if given the opportunity and the resources. The existence of such resentment can go far in explaining why implementation of externally-funded projects is often so unsatisfactory. Yet such an explanation has been largely ignored by writers on the subject.

A comparative analysis of the three case study projects is difficult because the circumstances surrounding the university project were different. At the time of the fieldwork its donor input was being scaled down both in personnel and scope after running for a considerable number of years. While tension and conflict had certainly existed (see 4 below), this was now largely a thing of the past, so that informants on both sides were able to minimise its importance and to view the project achievements, which were considerable, in better perspective. In contrast the other two projects were at a peak of donor input, with as yet few successes to speak of and were more susceptible to stressful relationships. The university project was also different in that it was based in a much smaller institution with fewer communication problems, its objectives were strictly academic and demanded less radical change of individuals than the other two (being more ambitious development projects) and it offered clearly recognisable benefits to individuals on both sides.

Rationale for the Research

Most project analyses and evaluations see problems of implementation in terms of structural constraints such as weak government infrastructure, poor project design, over-ambitious objectives and unrealistic time schedules. These are undoubtedly important factors; however there is another set of constraints which are just as crucial for project success but which are rarely taken into consideration. These relate to the human dimension of aid work. It is neglect of the importance of human interaction and ignorance of the kinds of roles and relationships that develop during project implementation that has inspired this study. There is almost no published literature on aid which takes an anthropological approach to the analysis of projects, viewing them from the inside as a network of human relationships; in most works the local implementers (usually the staff of the institution concerned) are almost totally ignored. The thesis of this research is that project success depends largely upon them. If they choose to withhold their co-operation, implementation cannot be satisfactorily achieved, even if the donor exerts great effort.

PERCEPTION GAPS

The fieldwork often revealed a disparity in the accounts of events provided by the two sides. Given the difference in cultural background, language, education, work experience, personal goals and ambitions *vis-à-vis* the project, all of which produced a great deal of tension, this was not surprising. Cross-cultural situations are prone to tension and conflict and in conflict situations human beings may rewrite events in their own minds to suit their personal logic and beliefs and to rationalise their own inconsistent behaviour.

Disparity in factual information can be either deliberate or spontaneous. If deliberate it is in effect information distortion, if spontaneous it is the result of an unconscious selective perception or interpretation of reality. In this research the disparity was more likely to be spontaneous as both sides held very ethnocentric views of the project. This selective perception can be termed 'perceptual bias', leading to the concept of 'perception gap', being a state in which a gulf separates two or more parties in their perspective on a certain issue. This concept of perceptual bias has been explored to some extent in the literature on change and development as a cross-cultural phenomenon, though only minimally with regard to aid projects and then only in connection with rural development projects (Chambers 1980, 1983, Richards 1979).

Given this constraint it was impossible to establish a single truth behind the varying accounts presented and to reach an objective assessment of individuals and events. Objectivity and veracity in the accounts offered may however, in this context, be less important than the nature and causes of the underlying tensions so evident in the relationships observed. Indeed the focus of this study is on investigating such disparities and the consequences of their existence rather than simply attempting an objective account of events.

The most important perception gaps were obviously between expatriates and Sudanese. On two of the case study projects these were very significant, while on the third, the university project, perceptions converged to a greater degree and, although there had been conflict, implementation was more satisfactory. Of the other five projects, at least three showed serious divergence in perception which affected implementation.

There were also important perception gaps between local management and staff over project matters, with the greatest differences on the same two case study projects. The existence of such perception gaps was not surprising since it was normal practice that only the most senior management (dean/director) should be involved in formal negotiations with the donor. Staff usually had little opportunity to express an opinion at this stage and did not have access to the project document. Lack of information led to misunderstandings and resentment about the motives of senior management in agreeing to the terms of the project. During the interviews staff on these two projects accused their superiors of working only in their own interests, even of looking to make financial gain for themselves, and of accepting the donor's terms because they wanted funding at any price. To some extent therefore it was more likely that convergent perceptions would exist between donor personnel and local management on the project framework rather than between local management and staff, although this did not always occur.

On one project there was a further dimension to the staff-management divide. This was between male and female staff, with the latter sharing their perception of events with the project management and siding with them against the male staff. This alignment was to a certain extent predictable as one of the main objectives of the project was to promote the role of women in development; while the female staff were strongly in favour of this, the male staff saw it as an irrelevant issue for their institute.

On the university project perceptions were less divergent and there was greater consensus on objectives and benefits, thus creating reasonable cohesion between the different groups (expatriates, local staff and local management), which in turn led to more effective implementation. In contrast the other two case study projects were characterised by polarisation and fragmentation resulting from discord over objectives and benefits. Since it is generally agreed that successful innovation depends on consensus and cohesion, their chances of sustainable impact were much lower.

The fact that there is a lack of consensus and shared perception intra-culturally, between local management and staff (and sometimes between male and female), as well as cross-culturally, between expatriate and local colleagues, seems not to have been noticed by those assessing project performance; yet it would appear to be an important factor in explaining the frequently poor level of implementation since the responsibility for this lies ultimately with the staff who carry out the necessary tasks. It is surprising that this aspect has been overlooked, especially as existing organisation and management theory frequently analyses the management/staff dichotomy at length, albeit in the context of organisational theory developed in industrialised countries.

The potential for internal division may be greater in aid projects than in projects where aid is not involved, at least for those based in institutions, because the divisions inherent in most large organisations are complicated by cross-cultural differences in perception over roles, time horizons, needs and benefits. Thus, instead of the usual dichotomy of personnel found in monocultural organisations, there is a trichotomy − expatriate management/local management/local staff.

It would be too simple to assume that differentiation only existed between the groups identified and not also within them. No doubt there were differences of opinion, even conflict, between individuals on certain aspects of their project, but on the broad issues identified as important to implementation, there appeared to be a high level of consensus (while on the details there may have been disagreement). It does not therefore jeopardise the validity of the data to present each group largely as a cohesive unit.

The greater part of this chapter is used to exemplify the concept of perception gaps as they appeared in the three case study projects, with supporting evidence from the other five projects, in regard to certain important project-related issues. I have identified six areas of significance for project success. These are: (1) project benefits; (2) project sustainability; (3) the consultation process; (4) institutional roles and duties; (5) organisational objectives; (6) the transfer of knowledge and skills. The chapter concludes with a section detailing the methods used to carry out the fieldwork.

1. Project Benefits

The potential benefits of the project were perceived very differently by the two sides, expatriate and local. Almost all the informants on the three case study projects agreed that the project had resulted in positive achievements but these were seen by the local staff primarily as material benefits: funding to help with the institution's recurrent costs, equipment, books, and scholarships or short visits abroad, with the latter being most eagerly sought after. In the two educational institutions the new curricula and syllabuses were seen as major gains. Psychological benefits were also named but were given less importance: enhanced status to the individual (through postgraduate qualifications and trips abroad), prestige for the institution and moral support for the job in hand.

In contrast the expatriates saw material benefits as ancillary to the main task of institution-building; human resources were more important than material resources and were to be developed less by sending counterparts for training abroad than by working closely with them within the institutional context and by this means creating appropriate professional attitudes and behaviour. Most of the local informants did not see this; to them lack of funding, and especially lack of an adequate incentive system for all the staff, was the main reason why their institution did not function properly, and they saw no need for radical changes either to its existing structures or to their own attitudes and behaviour. However on all the projects there was some recognition of organisational improvements brought about by the expatriates.

This finding was the same on all the projects studied. It was not surprising that local staff saw mainly material benefits since these are immediate and tangible and hence more readily appreciated. Intangible benefits relating to institution-building are less welcome because they require structural changes, which may not be perceived as necessary.

The local staff's preoccupation with material benefits, in particular trips abroad, was one of the most common sources of conflict on all three projects. On two projects the selection of individuals for trips abroad had led to accusations of favouritism and patronage and a souring of relations between the two sides. The expatriates often accused their local colleagues of being materialistic and greedy, of seeking to extract the maximum from the donor, and of only being ready to work if they were paid extra for the effort; they were also reproached with not being interested in learning for its own sake. On the Sudanese side there were complaints that the expatriates failed to understand their difficult financial and family circumstances and expected them to work long hours for very little pay when they had extensive obligations elsewhere (see Havelock and Huberman 1977: chap. 8, Heaver 1982).

The high levels of performance reputedly achieved by Sudanese working in the oil-rich Arab states, and to a certain extent in the indigenous private sector, is an indicator that, if provided with suitable financial incentives, and preferably a supportive and well-structured work environment, they are capable of performing extremely well. None of the expatriate informants saw lack of inherent ability as the prime cause of poor performance; they blamed pervading socio-cultural traditions, in particular inappropriate attitudes towards work and a lack of intrinsic interest in learning. However, lack of incentive, and in particular financial incentive, must also be considered a major factor.

2. Project Sustainability

The same perception gap was apparent in the assessment made by the two sides of the sustainability of activities initiated by the project once the external support was withdrawn. Predictably the Sudanese tended to see this as determined largely by the availability of funds, although some also saw their local management as problematic in that it was apathetic or else acted out of self-interest. The expatriates saw sustainability as dependent primarily on human resources, in particular appropriate work attitudes and increased commitment on the part of the staff, and on improved infrastructure.

On the university project the local staff were optimistic that the institute would continue to function well once the project was terminated because it was generating its own income and the new curricula were already well established. On the other two projects the local staff were more pessimistic: the institution's main problem was funding and, as the Sudan government would be unable to match the heavy external support, they feared that it would soon return to its previous state.

The expatriates on the university project were also reasonably optimistic about the institute's future. The local academic staff would remain motivated for as long as there were financial benefits to be gained personally from the fee-paying courses that had been set up by the project, and the institute had the potential to be financially self-sufficient; however some doubt was expressed as to the institute's administrative capabilities.

The expatriates on the other two projects were not very optimistic: the heavy external input in implementation, the weak institutional infrastructure and the low levels of commitment on the Sudanese side precluded the long-term viability of the project activities. One project manager admitted frankly that his project represented a completely artificial injection, with all funding, administration and expertise being provided from outside; in such circumstances there was little hope for the future. With few exceptions the expatriates on all eight projects thought that with their withdrawal there would be a noticeable decline in administrative efficiency, largely resulting from lack of competent administrative staff, lack of commitment and a poor appreciation of the complexity of organisational structures on the part of the professional staff.

3. Consultation

Perceptions as to what constitutes genuine consultation during project implementation differed between the two sides. For the purpose of this analysis, consultation is only discussed with reference to the implementation stage, since this is the focus of research. However consultation during the planning stage of a project is also of great importance as the quality of the planning process seriously affects implementation. There was, in fact, strong evidence on two of the projects that many of the problems of implementation stemmed from poor planning and both project managers provided specific examples of this.

At all institutional levels the most common and the most strongly felt complaint lodged by the Sudanese against the expatriates during the interviews was the lack of consultation, whether at the planning or the implementation stage. (On the university project the local staff did not mention this as an issue but two of the expatriate informants implied that it had been.)

While a few informants were fully satisfied with the level of consultation, the majority were very critical. This was particularly evident among the staff of the two non-university case study projects and many informants working on other projects voiced the same complaint in very strong terms. Their main grievance was that they were not consulted about important issues affecting their participation in the project and that, even if they were consulted, this was just a token gesture since the decisions had already been taken by the expatriates sitting together (with or without reference to local management).

One example provided was: circulating a memo among the staff to pass on information or to present some proposal for comment did not in their eyes constitute proper consultation, as they had not been involved in the earlier discussions. Hence their criticism concerned procedures as much as the subject matter for consultation.

On these two case study projects, although some of those in managerial positions also complained of a lack of consultation, the staff saw the situation differently. To them the expatriate and local managements seemed to be working closely together, especially as the project managers insisted on going through official channels as much as possible (even if in reality this only meant the formality of keeping local management informed). The staff felt excluded because their own relations with local management were not good and therefore they were resentful; in particular they criticised the latter for not passing on information and not delegating responsibility.

On the project where the male and female staff were polarised, most of the male staff members who were interviewed adopted a more radical position: they thought that the implementing body should be consulted not only during implementation but also during the project planning stage, and even invited to participate in the negotiations. The inclusion of what they saw as a highly inappropriate objective on women in development, resulting in much wasted expenditure, was blamed on the narrow range of these earlier consultations. They held senior government officials as well as the donor responsible for what they saw as defective planning: the former for being eager to secure funding at whatever price, the latter for wanting to impose its own priorities. On the other two projects this was less of an issue, probably because the objectives were less controversial.

In contrast the expatriates on all three projects regarded their approach as highly consultative and, where possible, participative. There was strong indignation expressed by the project managers at the suggestion that they did not consult the local staff. They said they kept them informed of all developments in connection with the project, either through regular project meetings or in writing, and there was ample opportunity for feedback through either of these media. Moreover their office doors were always open for staff to come and discuss issues. At the same time they were critical of the staff for complaining that they were being ignored, whereas they did not bother to read what documents they were given or to respond to persistent requests for suggestions and comments, and they would often deny having received information in the past.

To the outside observer it did indeed appear that expatriates, especially those working in large institutions, under-utilised opportunities to consult local staff and considered it unnecessary to discuss important issues with anyone but those in managerial positions. They appeared to take decisions among themselves, with or without the knowledge of local management, on matters that were to affect their immediate counterparts. They also tended to talk of the management as representative of the whole institution and to assume that, because the staff did not often approach them, they were satisfied with the way the project was progressing; it was not perceived that they may be reluctant for various reasons to come forward (see below). It is difficult to assess to what extent the staff's own lack of interest and initiative were responsible for this state of affairs since the expatriates said that they frequently tried to involve them in dialogue but met with little response. The project managers would clearly have preferred implementation through full consensus and participation but in their opinion the local staff's indifference, their inappropriate attitudes and the lack of institutional support often obliged them to act alone and even to resort to coercion. At the same time it must be recognised that some of the staff in relatively junior positions were unrealistic in that they were of the opinion that they should be involved in discussions and decision-making at senior management level.

In spite of the overwhelming criticism from local informants, on all three projects there were a few members of staff who expressed satisfaction with the consultation process, at least during implementation, and found their expatriate colleagues flexible and approachable. As a result they co-operated fully. This is significant because it indicates that effective consultation in this context is not an impossibility, although it may be due more to empathy between certain individuals arising from a fortunate mix of personalities and shared perceptions on important issues than to a consistent policy of consulting colleagues. Positive examples were also cited by informants working on other projects but they were a very small minority.

To explain this perception gap over consultation, one must look at the working environment. The expatriate's perception of the consultation process is influenced by the constraints of the project framework within which he must work and which is defined in terms of tasks and goals (see 5 below). While he does his best to involve the local staff, he is aware of the fact that consultation and participation take time, time which the project's operational structure does not always allow; the individual is under pressure to produce positive results quickly, as he is accountable to the donor for the funds being disbursed. This he must do in an institutional environment characterised by weak infrastructure and inadequate resources. If he is highly energetic and motivated and finds that he is not getting much support from local staff and management, who may be frequently absent when they are needed, he will be tempted to act alone and to ignore them more and more. Moreover the low calibre and lack of experience of some Sudanese working in the public sector may mean that the expatriate finds it easier to do the work himself in the first place.[4]

The Sudanese perspective on the lack of consultation is somewhat different. He sees the expatriate wanting to produce positive results quickly, not only because he is constrained by the project's time frame but also because he wants to impress his employer, the donor, and in this way to promote his own career. His preoccupation with implementing the objectives at all costs and his preconceived ideas about what needs to be done make him intransigent and unwilling to listen to suggestions for more flexibility.[5] Some informants were of the opinion that this could be attributed to a patronising or arrogant attitude: as an 'expert' and a 'resource-provider', the expatriate feels superior and always thinks that he knows best, especially if he has already worked in other developing countries. Some Sudanese also feel that expatriates consider them as inferior in ability and experience because they come from an 'underdeveloped' country; therefore they are not entitled to a high degree of consultation or participation in decision-making and have nothing to contribute to the innovation process.

Almost all the expatriates on these projects had developed very good personal relationships both within and outside the workplace with many of their local colleagues, which masked in the majority of cases a largely unsatisfactory professional relationship. While the expatriate's superior position makes it easier for him to voice his dissatisfaction with his colleagues' performance and attitudes, the Sudanese is obliged to be more restrained. The strict traditions concerning hospitality and politeness towards foreigners and the awareness that, as a poor country, Sudan needs all the aid it can get, makes him reticent to criticise openly.[6] Moreover the fact that he may get on well with the expatriates makes it difficult for him to be frank. He therefore withdraws into silence and non-cooperation as a form of protest; at best he will carry out his duties slowly and without enthusiasm. A vicious circle is then set in motion because the expatriate, misled by the apparent harmony on the personal level, will interpret this silence as either tacit approval or disinterest, and so will increasingly go his own way. At the same time there were examples on most projects of Sudanese resorting to the use of what Handy (1985) calls 'negative power', for example delaying tactics, distortion of information, non-cooperation, and even, in extreme instances, sabotage.

4. Institutional Roles and Duties

One of the areas of greatest perceptual difference, with serious consequences for project success, concerned institutional roles. This was largely due to differing cultural concepts as to the appropriate roles for professionals employed in the public sector. However the tension caused by this was further heightened by the effective division of responsibilities which took place during implementation both on the project and within the institution: there was considerable role distortion, whereby the actual roles taken on by individuals differed from those laid down on paper.

In practice the expatriate input on all eight projects was much more organisational than technical both for the project manager and the support team, even though the latter were recruited as 'technical specialists'. To a certain extent this was recognised in the project documents and job descriptions and was seen by the expatriates as appropriate. However, given the limited initiative and activity on the Sudanese side, this organisational role tended to become a predominantly directive and 'performer' role, in which the expatriate supervises his counterpart(s) and at the same time carries out many of the implementation tasks himself.

On one project in particular, where the counterpart staff were mostly young and inexperienced, they were usually given the role of implementing tasks assigned them by the expatriates, a role which they resented because they considered it to be professionally beneath them, such as being used as an assistant, which often meant translating, carrying messages or doing clerical work. On the other two projects roles were defined more in partnership, with tasks assigned on a collaborative basis, but with the expatriates still taking an initiating and supervisory role. In practice, however, because of the lack of local support the expatriates on all three projects also carried out many of their counterparts' tasks themselves, leading to what Handy calls 'role overload' and 'role underload', that is, too many roles being taken on by the expatriate and too few by the counterpart. Handy refers to role underload as 'the most insidious, but most ignored, perverter of organisational efficiency' (Handy 1985:65). 'Role overload' in turn leads to 'work overload' and this was evident in the very long hours worked by most of the expatriates on these projects, in sharp contrast to many of their local colleagues, some of whom put in only one or two hours a day. This division of responsibilities did not conform with the roles prescribed for expatriates in the project documents, where the emphasis was on 'assisting' and 'participating' rather than on 'directing' and 'performing'.

The imbalance in roles was aggravated by the fact that the expatriates also took on certain unofficial roles, which were largely determined by themselves in the face of practical constraints. These operated not only at the level of project management, but in some cases extended outwards, beyond the strict confines of the project into supervision of the institution's administration, as well as downwards beyond their professional roles into the execution of minor administrative and clerical tasks which would normally be the responsibility of the ancillary staff.

Where there was involvement of the project manager in the administration of the institution, this came about because the local management was apathetic or not very competent in administration. Most Sudanese in senior management positions have been promoted on seniority rather than on ability and experience and are often close to retirement; they may be content to let the expatriates supervise routine administration, in which they themselves may be relatively inexperienced. This then results in an imbalance of managerial authority in favour of the project managers, which may extend beyond the project to the whole institution.

Expatriate involvement in carrying out routine office tasks came about as a result of the shortage of competent ancillary staff, who were always poorly trained and underpaid and who could not cope with the increased and complex demands made by the project, compounded by the refusal of the professional staff to carry out such tasks, which they considered to be beneath their status and outside their sphere of responsibility. If there was any urgency over paper work, the expatriates often had to do it themselves.

Expatriate involvement in supervising general administration brought about conflict on the university project in particular (a contributory factor in the phasing down and temporary withdrawal of the external commitment at one stage), while involvement in non-professional tasks led to friction with the staff on this and on one other project. These two case studies revealed a serious perception gap as to the duties required of each post, and, since the local staff refused to join the expatriates in executing duties which they did not see as part of their brief, this jeopardised the future sustainability of the project once it was no longer externally aided. Although the expatriates were aware of the implications of this involvement, they considered that progress on implementation would not be made at an acceptable rate without some backup to the inadequate local administration.

There are numerous reasons for this perception gap over what constitutes valid professional roles and duties. On the Sudanese side there is a strong sense of what duties are appropriate to an individual's status, so, for example, an engineer will never do what he sees to be a technician's work, nor will an academic take on a clerk's duties. The highly privileged social status that education bestows on the individual (in the past, providing exclusive access to well-paid white-collar jobs) in a society which values social conformity means that he is expected to act in a manner befitting his status; if he is seen doing clerical or manual tasks, he will lose face and will be deemed unworthy of the education given him. Manual work is also associated with slavery and is therefore considered particularly demeaning.

In addition most Sudanese perceive their jobs as temporary: they are looking for better employment, preferably outside the Sudan, and in the meantime many supplement their government salaries through moonlighting. They are therefore unwilling to become too involved in their official work. At the same time, there is little sense of loyalty to a government which has allowed the status and incomes of civil servants to decline rapidly over the past 15 years or so, and has abandoned the concept of a career structure within the public sector. Local staff sometimes also claim that their posts carry no clear terms of reference, so they tend to define their duties according to their own narrow criteria. They are then reluctant to step beyond these narrow confines, partly for fear of being accused of undermining someone else's position.

To the Sudanese, the expatriate has different professional terms of reference and also does not risk losing face because the same social norms do not apply to him. He is ready to take on extra tasks because he is highly paid and wants to 'facilitate' his work and complete the project successfully in as short a time as possible. One informant queried whether an expatriate would be ready to do so much back in his own country, such as type letters, make photocopies or send out telexes just because his secretary was too inefficient or too lazy.

On the expatriate side, there is high motivation, the challenge of doing a job well in difficult circumstances, relatively good career prospects, a comfortable standard of living, adequate remuneration and the need to justify to his employer the high costs involved in his appointment. All of these may contribute to his willingness to take on additional duties. The operational time frame of the project further demands this. Moreover his work load is increased by the gradual building up within the project environment of a sophisticated system, which operates more and more autonomously of the regular institutional structure (as a kind of unofficial project implementation unit) and which requires greater administrative inputs and more supervision as it develops.[7]

Within this scenario the more the local staff insist on keeping rigidly to their own terms of reference, the more they find themselves in a marginal position, a situation which obliges the expatriate to try to implement the project alone and which ultimately fosters dependence.

Attitude and behaviour change

This subject of status and appropriate duties was the most vexed issue on the projects studied and in some cases had led to considerable tension and resentment on both sides and to serious problems of implementation. On all three case study projects the Sudanese staff were very conscious of their status as university graduates and had a very clear idea of what their legitimate duties should be. True to the academic bias of their university education, they resisted all attempts by the expatriates to make their work more technical or practical. The expatriates believed that, for the local institutions to function effectively, the staff had to be more flexible over the duties they were ready to take on and the barrier between what were traditionally accepted as the academic's and the practitioner's respective duties had to be broken down. For example, on the renewable energy project they considered that forestry and other related activities could not be run by academics from behind a desk, while on the agricultural training project they were of the opinion that technical teachers should not only teach theory in the classroom but should get out into the workshop and the fields to do practical demonstrations. On the university project the lecturers were expected to carry out certain administrative (and even clerical) tasks which would ensure a consistently high standard of teaching and research.

The local staff did not see any need for change (as they saw the institution's main need in terms of material resources). They perceived that, rather than bring them benefits, such a change in their terms of reference would only bring more work and, more importantly, would result in an effective downgrading of their professional and social status. The expatriates' insistence on the application of knowledge through practical tasks (which could include clerical and manual as well as technical tasks) was therefore seen as violating existing norms covering the academic's role in the workplace. In one case where a member of staff had shown himself ready to take on clerical (though not manual) duties he was highly praised by the expatriates but severely condemned by his compatriots for acting improperly, as a clerk or a messenger rather than as a university graduate.

Given these perception gaps combined with the fact that the projects were largely drawn up by donor personnel and conformed to western organisational criteria, it was inevitable that a significant change of attitude and behaviour would be required of the local staff if the projects were to be fully implemented according to their original design. The greater the perception gap on project-related issues, the greater the required change in attitude and behaviour and the more difficult implementation would be. However the literature on innovation and planned change in a developing country context shows that attitude and behaviour change seldom occur unless there is a clear perception of the benefits to individuals and the institution; techniques of persuasion and awareness-building may also meet with limited success (see for example Havelock and Huberman 1977, Rogers 1971, Foster 1973). There was little evidence on these projects that the local staff were persuaded of the benefits of any such change.

The literature also shows that the desired attitude and behaviour change in an institutional setting is frequently not limited to professional matters but tends to affect social norms and values and as a result meets with considerable resistance. There was ample evidence on all eight projects that where demands were made for changes which upset existing value systems, the staff either rejected the proposals outright or showed strong resistance to them, thus impeding progress in implementation.

One reason why the university project was better able to achieve its objectives was that it required fewer changes in attitude and behaviour of a social and ideological nature than the other two case study projects. These objectives were limited to academic matters so that any changes required were of a professional nature and hence minimal. As they did not threaten the local staff's status and offered clear benefits, they were largely accepted.

On the other two projects, the required changes were more radical because they affected social value systems, in particular status networks, and as a result were less acceptable. On one project an important objective involved promoting the role of women in development and this was strongly resisted by many of the male staff (while applauded by the female staff) because it required a fundamental rethinking of the role of women in Sudanese society which was perceived as a threat to the status quo both within the institute and in the wider society.

From the data gathered during the interviews it would appear that very few individuals had shown significant changes in work-related attitudes and behaviour, especially where these touched on social issues. In the majority this was minimal. Change is a very slow process and these projects had operated for far too short a time to realistically allow significant results in this respect. The project managers were of the opinion that positive and lasting change would only be achieved if the projects were funded over a lengthy period; one cited 12 years as preferable in the case of his project. In the meantime, given the project time frame and the resistance to change over roles and duties, the project managers were obliged to seek implementation through directive rather than consensual acts, though much against their will. This was particularly the case on the two non-university projects.

5. Organisational Objectives

The conflict over roles and duties has so far been attributed to cultural differences in the way society views the individual's professional image, at least in the public sector, and to situational differences in personal circumstances and lifestyle. However the individual's view of the organisational objectives he is working towards also contributes to this perception gap: expatriates and Sudanese were working to different sets of objectives and in different types of organisation.

Handy (1985) talks of organisations conforming to four basic ideologies or 'cultures': the 'power culture', the 'role culture', the 'task culture' and the 'person culture'. Each organisational 'culture' has a different set of objectives and roles for its members to follow. Within this paradigm one can see that the Sudanese institutions described in these case studies are in essence (though not necessarily in practice) 'role cultures', that is bureaucratic pyramid-like organisations, with well-established rules and procedures and well-defined roles for individual employees, who are not expected to perform over and above what are clearly laid down as their duties. (In some respects they are also 'power cultures' as those in senior positions exercise authority through patronage and the trading of favours.) The organisation in a 'role culture' is engaged primarily in systems maintenance, so that it is slow either to acknowledge the need for change or to carry it out. Within the present context it is usually poor in resources and this also militates against change. Into this 'role culture' is introduced a 'task culture', that is the project, which is of a fundamentally different nature. The project is task- and goal-oriented, not role-oriented; it is comparatively rich in resources, and individuals (expatriates) are selected as team members on the basis of their expertise and their ability to perform predetermined tasks quickly and competently. The individual is considered more important than the role he is given, as roles may have to be adapted to fit new circumstances; the individual must be flexible if he is to achieve his objectives within the specified time limit. Nothing is static or unchangeable; the 'task culture' is essentially a short-term injection of intense activity designed to generate rapid and significant changes in the system.

The local staff who had been temporarily placed within the project environment still defined their roles in terms of their employing institution and kept rigidly to the duties which conformed with these roles. These were largely concerned with the long-term perspective of systems maintenance. They saw no particular reason why they should change their terms of reference, and indeed these were not officially redefined when they were made members of a project team. On the other hand the expatriates conformed to a different organisation 'culture' and acted as trouble-shooters eager to get on to the next assignment. As a result there was a conflict of aims and strategies: the 'task culture' with specific short-term goals against the 'role culture' with the long-term aim of preservation of the existing system. Individuals paid allegiance to one or the other culture and their view of their responsibilities was coloured accordingly.

6. Knowledge and Skills Transfer

All three case study projects specified staff development as an objective. On two projects this was seen as counterpart training for those working with the technical specialists, such as the transfer of knowledge and/or skills by the expatriate to the local counterpart through informal on-the-job training. As for the Sudanese project co-managers and the lecturers on the university project, staff development was not envisaged in strict counterparting terms (judged inappropriate by senior personnel), but rather as a continual broadening of experience by close association on an equal basis with professionals from outside the Sudan, and in some cases by visits to similar institutions overseas. In all cases staff development was to cover both technical and organisational skills.[8]

However it was apparent that, although some learning had taken place, counterpart training had had limited success. One factor which posed a barrier to effective counterparting was a perception gap over training needs. This concerned, firstly, what knowledge and/or skills were considered relevant for the job in hand and, secondly, the means by which such knowledge and/or skills should be acquired. Furthermore a directive or 'performer' role such as the expatriates were obliged to adopt is not easily equated with counterparting since this role emphasises the end product (the achievement of objectives) while counterparting emphasises the process (the development of local capabilities to achieve the objectives).

There was general consensus from both the expatriates and the local staff that there had been little transfer of a technical nature and that many of the local staff had adequate knowledge in their particular specialisation to carry out their work reasonably well. However the two sides differed over the need for organisational skills.

Expatriates on most of the projects studied saw lack of organisational ability and/or experience amongst the Sudanese as a greater problem to the successful implementation of the project than any lack of theoretical knowledge or technical skills. The real need was for practical application of the knowledge already possessed by their local colleagues and the acquisition of organisational or managerial skills. In fact the project managers considered that it was in this latter area that the most significant transfer had taken place, at least among those counterparts who had worked closely with them. For example, they had learnt how to assess needs, to plan and present their work professionally, and, where applicable, to put together proposals for funding; the younger ones in particular had learnt from the experience of working in a well-disciplined environment so that, when they themselves reached senior positions, they would have a better idea of how to run the institution. In the two educational institutions the staff had learnt organisational skills from participating in the development of their own curriculum.

On the Sudanese side, while many local staff acknowledged that the expatriates had made a positive contribution to the institution, only a few saw this in terms of a transfer of knowledge and/or skills. Those who did see such a transfer, whether technical or organisational, had built up a good working relationship with their expatriate colleagues in an equal partnership where it was felt that they had learnt from each other. Most Sudanese, however, did not see the need for counterparting in either technical or organisational terms and either denied that any learning had taken place or played down its significance. There were various reasons for this.

Firstly, the majority of local informants drawn from all the projects studied were very self-confident, not only in their ability to carry out their own duties competently but also those of their expatriate colleagues when the time came for the latter to leave. It was difficult not to judge this self-confidence as being often quite unwarranted, at least if one used a western yardstick of the ability required to perform project-related tasks satisfactorily. The Sudanese defined competence in terms of academic qualifications, and not in terms of proven ability or practical experience. Since all the counterparts were university graduates, often with postgraduate qualifications, they tended to believe that they had nothing to learn from the expatriates and would not acknowledge that the latter carried out tasks that they themselves could not do (two informants expressed the opinion that any Sudanese accountant could do a project manager's job adequately). The local staff were also very dismissive of short-term international consultants and claimed that there were plenty of competent Sudanese available to undertake such assignments. Their observation that a university education made them an élite in society aggravated this attitude. To the majority, the only need in their institution was for material resources and expatriates were seen mainly as watchdogs for project funds. However, it was clear that their lack of familiarity with the management of organisations led them to underestimate the complexity of institutional structures and the importance of managing them efficiently, and therefore to downgrade the expatriates achievements in that area.

Secondly, where local staff did concede the validity of the expatriate input in organisation, and possibly their own deficiency in that area, they usually did not perceive that organisational responsibilities were part of their own professional terms of reference; if they did accept this, they still judged many of the tasks as falling into an administrative or clerical (or even manual) category which they were not ready to become involved in. They would only consider organisational tasks as valid if they related strictly to professional or academic aspects of their work (for example producing a well-written report collecting and analysing statistical information, preparing lesson plans). Hence the narrow definition of their responsibilities undermined the potential for a transfer of organisational skills.

Furthermore the short-term goal-focused nature of the project usually denied the local staff the opportunity to acquire these general skills, even where they did see them as valid and relevant, since the project climate was not conducive to extensive experience-based training in which tasks would be carried out more slowly and possibly less efficiently by inexperienced local staff. Instead the tendency was for the expatriates to make use of counterparts as assistants or 'gofors'. As a result they were not exposed to precisely the kind of training that they needed and had little opportunity to try out new skills, even if they were willing to acquire them.

Thirdly, the local staff were mostly unfamiliar with the concept of counterparting, and in particular of on-the-job-training, and hence they failed to recognise it for what it was. Furthermore they did not see the practical workshops and seminars which were held for staff development in their institutions as constituting real training; to them further training was academic and theoretical, and was preferably undertaken overseas. Even the short courses and study tours to neighbouring countries which many of the staff participated in were considered more as a holiday than as training, or at most as a general broadening of experience.

The expatriates perceived that the need was primarily for on-the-job training; courses and visits overseas were more a 'perk' than an essential training requirement. If there had been little transfer of knowledge and skills through on-the-job training, this was seen to be largely due to the local staff's inappropriate attitudes and lack of interest which had prevented them from working closely together on a daily basis. Such work attitudes were seen as having been more detrimental to successful implementation of the project than any lack of theoretical knowledge or technical skills.

Therefore the perception gap over the roles, responsibilities and competence of the local staff served to lower the potential for learning in these areas identified by the expatriates as necessary for the success of the project and the improved functioning of the institution.

FIELD METHODS

The fieldwork was undertaken during three visits in 1986 and 1987. All the interviews were conducted by myself individually and were in English, which did not appear to present a problem as all the Sudanese informants were university graduates with an adequate command of English for the current purpose.

Given that the fieldwork was aimed at gathering information on perceptions and attitudes, the only suitable approach to the collection and analysis of field data seemed to be qualitative and interpretive. Hence the interviews were semi-structured, or at most loosely guided, so as to allow the informants to focus attention freely on their own particular preoccupations concerning the project rather than on preselected issues. No questionnaires were used. As a result a genuine picture of individual concerns was built up; this made the frequent similarities in opinions and attitudes on each side all the more striking.

The gathering of such personal data in a difficult cross-cultural situation presented many problems, in particular obtaining access to the projects and gaining the confidence and co-operation of informants. To gain access I made use of personal contacts already established during the four years I had previously spent in the Sudan as an aid worker, so that on four out of the eight projects I knew one or more individuals personally and on the other four I obtained introductions through third parties known to the project managers. To gain the informants' confidence I adopted a very cautious low-profile approach by trying to make my presence as unobtrusive as possible and keeping the interviews informal and relaxed. With such a sensitive topic it would have been unacceptable to adopt the anthropologist's traditional method of observation and live with the project team day by day, so I did not visit the project every day or spend an undue amount of time there. I also guaranteed confidential ity to all the informants, and, after some initial trials, decided not to use a cassette recorder but asked permission to take notes. I avoided asking about personalities and waited until the informants offered their own comments on colleagues (the Sudanese being on the whole reluctant to speak in personal terms).

Understanding the attitudes expressed by the expatriate infor mants was not difficult since I shared the same broad mainstream culture with most of the expatriate project team members, that is that of western white middle-class professionals,[9] as well as the same sub culture, that of expatriate aid personnel working in the Sudan. For the much more difficult task of the outsider trying to come to an understanding of the point of view of people from another culture, obtained invaluable assistance from certain expatriate friends and acquaintances who were long-term residents in the Sudan (married to nationals) and who were asked to comment on the general attitude expressed by the Sudanese. Their unique perspective as participant of two cultures proved invaluable.

On the question of whether an outsider to the culture being studied is at a disadvantage when it comes to seeking co-operation from potential informants, I did not find this to be the case. It is possible that people confide more willingly in such a situation to a stranger, or at least an outsider, rather than to someone from their own environ ment or peer group, because they have little if anything to lose by doing so.

CONCLUSIONS

The purpose of the analysis presented in this chapter has not been to offer an objective evaluation of certain technical assistance projects Nor has it been to make judgements about the competence of individuals working on these projects; neither side is seen as being exclusively in the right. Rather the purpose has been to reveal the nature and causes of a number of perception gaps on project-related issues and the ways in which these might have an adverse effect on implementation. Those issues selected for analysis in this chapter do not present an exclusive list but they are all central to the implementation process. It is hoped that the findings will offer a new and useful insight to those involved in project aid.

There are many pitfalls in interpreting the findings of this fieldwork since they are drawn largely from subjective opinions expressed at varying times and in varying circumstances about a loosely defined topic. Moreover the findings relate only to the projects studied and generalisations are dangerous. This does not mean however that similar data would not emerge from research on projects in other environments. While there is minimal documented evidence about perception gaps and their effect on project success, there is no reason to believe that this is an exclusively Sudanese phenomenon.

Notwithstanding these limitations, the analysis revealed that both expatriates and nationals hold very ethnocentric views of their projects (West European or Sudanese), coloured by their own cultural and institutional environment. Hence they do not share the same perception of project reality. It is impossible to quantify the effect that such perception gaps have on implementation but there is no doubt that they have contributed to the low levels of commitment and co-operation on the Sudanese side, excessive control on the expatriate side, and to a frequently poor rate of project success. Other factors such as language difficulties, and the inadequate communication flows which existed on most of the projects as well as within the hierarchical host institutions (both expatriate – national and management – staff communication is predominantly one-way and top-down with a marked reluctance on the Sudanese side to delegate or to pass on information) serve to increase the perception gaps between the two sides.

Given that aid projects incorporate objectives, strategies and performance criteria that are largely the product of western cultures, these differing perceptions present an impediment to maximum utilisation of local potential and hence to long-term project gains. For the local staff to operate effectively alongside the expatriates within this cross-cultural framework, significant changes in attitude and behaviour are required. On the whole these are not forthcoming, and where the project demands radical change, it is unlikely to realise its objectives, at least in the short term. Furthermore the time constraints, the task and goal orientation of the project and the directive role played by expatriates in the face of local indifference all militate against the development of local expertise by stifling rather than stimulating potential energies, limited though these sometimes are.

As a result, long-term development goals, in particular those of self-reliance and self-sufficiency in human resources, are being sacrificed to short-term project success defined as the achievement of immediate objectives, the terms of which are largely dictated by the donor's priorities and the temporary nature of its commitment. This situation only serves to build up a relationship of dependence in which the Sudanese rely more and more on outsiders not just for material resources but also for the management of those resources. This is the direct opposite of the professed aim of most project aid, and particularly of the counterpart concept, and in terms of national development quite counter-productive.

The fieldwork revealed that resentment exists among both expatriates and Sudanese working on aid projects. The resentment on the Sudanese side was unexpectedly vehement. The existence of such feelings among local implementers has gone largely unrecognised because most aid literature is written by westerners, who through their published work are able to articulate not only their own theories and practical suggestions on the subject, but also, if they wish, their own opinions about the recipients of aid. The recipients have virtually no access to any kind of international forum; as a result aid theorists and practitioners have little idea of how aid activities are perceived at the receiving end, and moreover seem to attach little importance to this. The value of this research lies in the attempt to rectify the situation by drawing attention to this shortcoming. Furthermore donor–recipient contacts usually take place at a very senior level (on the recipient side, not lower than director of the institution seeking assistance) and, while this may be necessary, it is dangerous to assume that the views of senior officials are representative of a whole institution. This is clearly not so, and, as implementers of the project, the local staff are a powerful force which can exert negative control through non-cooperation or poorly executed tasks if they so wish. Their importance has usually been underestimated or ignored, both in the published literature and in project evaluations.[10]

It is difficult to ascertain to what extent the local staff's poor performance resulted from their general apathy towards public sector employment, the incompatibility of their attitude towards work with the demands of a western-style project, or from a genuine lack of expertise and experience, either in the technical or the organisational/managerial field. The reputation of Sudanese working in other Arab states would appear to testify that performance can be of a high standard, as it can also be in the Sudanese private sector and in aid

ɪgency field offices (where greater flexibility is demanded of local
ɛmployees in return for higher rewards). This would suggest that
ɪndifference caused by a lack of professional support, opportunity
ɪnd financial motivation is in large part responsible. Given the right
ɛnvironment and incentives, attitudes judged as inappropriate will
ɔhange; they will not change if there is no incentive to do so.
If this is the case, then no amount of technical assistance will help.
Ƒhis has worrying long-term implications, in that one can predict a
ɔontinuing neocolonialist-style presence of technical assistance per-
ɪonnel based on an assumption of a lack of technical and organ-
sational expertise when the deficiencies may lie elsewhere.

NOTES

1. The term 'technical assistance project' is used here to refer to
    externally-funded projects which employ at least one resident expatri-
    ate expert.
2. Lethem and Cooper (1983) define engineering TA as consisting of
    'professional architectural or engineering services for civil works and
    other hardware investments' and institutional TA as consisting of '(a)
    diagnostic and prescriptive assistance such as advice on institutional or
    policy matters and studies for national economic management and
    planning, public administration, or the management and operation of
    a particular sector or entity; and (b) managerial, technical, or other
    direct operational support as well as staff training' (p. 1).
3. The precise identity of the projects has been left deliberately vague for
    reasons of confidentiality.
4. For the sake of convenience and brevity I use the pronoun 'he' and its
    associate forms throughout this chapter as generic terms to cover both
    male and female. No offence is intended towards the many female
    informants who contributed so readily to this research.
5. The opposite can also be true; the expatriate wants to prolong his stay
    in a well-paid job and is less compelled to reach his objectives at the
    earliest possible date. This is perhaps not so common in the Sudan,
    which is generally considered to be a 'hardship post'.
6. This extends to general social relationships between Sudanese; in what
    is a strictly non-confrontational society overt criticism of individuals is
    avoided as much as possible.
7. On all three projects a minimum of administrative/clerical support,
    whether in the form of secretaries, clerks or administrative assistants,
    was paid for out of the project budget, and this allowed the project to
    function as a fairly autonomous body headed by the project manager.

8. The term 'technical' is used here to denote subject-related disciplines (in contrast to 'organisational') and should not be confused with its earlier use to define the work undertaken by technicians (as opposed to that of academics).

9. Of the 12 expatriate informants working on the three case study projects, one came from North Africa and one from Eastern Europe; the others were all from Western Europe.

10. However, in the literature on rural development the importance of seeking the opinion of beneficiaries is being increasingly recognised. Beneficiaries are often implementers, although in rural development projects not usually based in institutions.

7 School Climates in The Gambia

Baboucarr Sarr with Keith Lewin

INTRODUCTION

This paper is based on two case studies of Gambian secondary schools. Secondary education in The Gambia is double-track, comprising secondary high schools and secondary technical schools. The former are modelled on British grammar schools, and the latter were introduced to meet the needs of those who would enter the middle levels of the labour market.

This chapter describes the establishment of the two forms of secondary education and reviews official evaluative statements made of each. It then explains the rationale for the case study research undertaken and the methods used to explore features of both types of school. The data are used to portray the formal characteristics of the schools and provide an insight into the differences between them as experienced by staff and students. This offers some new perspectives on the realities of Gambian secondary schooling which illustrates some of the workings and consequences of the double-track policy that has been adopted.

Two Forms of Secondary Schooling

At independence in 1965 a survey was carried out by a UNESCO expert, Dr Sleight, to make recommendations about formal educational provision in The Gambia. At the time there were three forms of second-level institutions: high schools, secondary modern schools, and post-primary schools. The Sleight Report advocated the replacement of this structure by one which provided for two types of school only, secondary high and secondary technical (Sleight 1965).

High schools were to be schools which would retain their mainly academic curricula orientated to arts and humanities with some pure science. Provision was made for a stream in these schools which would emphasise technical and scientific education. Its aim was to provide a form of 'basic education for technicians at the intermediate

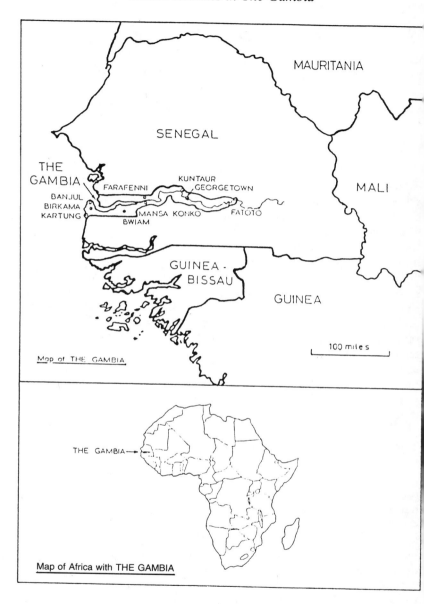

Map of THE GAMBIA

Map of Africa with THE GAMBIA

level'. But the high schools were seen predominantly as the institutions that would facilitate entry to overseas universities. The need for the schools and their curricula to 'conform to the entry requirements of other countries' was pointed out as inevitable in the absence of a national university. Thus significant changes in the colonially inherited curricula were not seen as a real possibility, nor were they thought desirable. The prestige enjoyed by the grammar school system which had historically provided most of the Gambian bureaucratic élite, together with the urge to retain the standards of excellence it was thought to represent, created strong barriers to changes in form and purpose. In contrast, the Sleight Report found a lot that was wanting in secondary modern schools and post-primary schools. Poor academic performance, and a quality of practical training that was insufficient to get school leavers jobs were the main problems identified. The schools were categorised as 'cooling out' students with educational aspirations that could not be satisfied, without offering worthwhile educational experiences. The report therefore recommended that their purposes be clarified and they be reorganised to reflect this. Thus the schools:

> are intended to develop a 'practical' bias and if this very sound policy is to succeed much more emphasis must be placed on practical training which should be related to employment opportunity. A more realistic and descriptive title would be Junior Technical School, which properly could include also domestic science, commercial and general education ... and each should specialise in, say, three skills plus a course in general studies. The course should lead to an approved qualification such as the West African Examination Council's proposed local modification of the 'City and Guilds'. The total range of skills covered by all the schools [together] should be as broad as possible to spread employment opportunity, and minimise the risk of over-training in any one field.... For most of the students the Junior Technical School would be a finishing school, but provision might be made for the transfer of exceptionally gifted students to a further course of study; ... students in technical courses might go on to the Senior Technical School and students following the general education course might transfer to a grammar school to complete Form 5.
> (Sleight Report 1965)

There was nothing in the nature of the recommendations that was likely to provoke serious opposition from those with power since these proposals would not affect the children of the indigenous civil servants, most of whom were to be found in the grammar school system. Equally, it was not clear that they would be widely supported or resourced, since demand for this type of education had not developed strongly amongst the small numbers enrolled at the secondary level.

Subsequent educational policy has not modified the substance of the Sleight Report and indicates that the original problems identified remain. Recent plan statements illustrate this:

> There is a national need for people with high school education who can be trained for the purpose of middle-level technical jobs. The present system produces school leavers with recognised qualifications in traditional academic subjects, and school leavers who are skillful with their hands but virtually illiterate [a reference to secondary technical school leavers]. It is vital that technical and commercial subjects be introduced into the high schools, and that school leavers with O Level qualifications in these technical subjects become available for further training.
>
> (Gambian Ministry of Education 1975)

> The function of high schools is mostly one of continued general education as a basis for post-secondary and higher education. Emphasis should, therefore, be on subjects which improve or reflect the student's intellectual ability to cope with higher studies, such as Mathematics and the three basic sciences; Physics, Chemistry and Biology, complemented by subjects like History, Geography and Economics. In addition to this field of academic subjects, the high schools will continue to teach more practical, pre-vocational subjects in non-technical fields of Agricultural Science, Commerce, Business Methods, Principles of Accounts and Home Management. Pre-vocational education in the technical fields will be done by Secondary Technical schools.
>
> (Gambian Ministry of Education 1982)

It seems that the high schools have retained their character with its emphasis on traditional subjects. The subjects that continue to dominate the curriculum are the academic subjects; the basic sciences first, then followed by the 'general subjects' (humanities and social sciences). They are the subjects that are able to reflect 'students' intellectual ability to cope with higher studies'. The other subjects are categorised as 'practical, pre-vocational subjects in non-technical fields' and almost appear as an afterthought. The view seems to be that academic subjects are more important for what performance in them can indicate about a student's ability, rather than any relationship that may exist between them and useful skills in the labour market. Practical and pre-vocational subjects in the high schools are justified with reference to useful job skills but it seems clear both in justification and in practice that these are of most importance for those who cannot achieve highly in the academic subjects. Subject choice is critical to subsequent career opportunities since the most attractive jobs are linked to entry conditions that require achievement in conventional academic subjects. For most students high school education is more important for the access it provides to formal educational qualifications of value in the labour market than for the vocational skills it might provide.

The various pronouncements that have been made about secondary technical schools since the Sleight Report have been very long on defining functions for them, but largely silent on taking the appropriate steps to allow these functions to become a reality. Many factors have been responsible for this. Much greater attention has been given to the development of the high schools; the cost implications of making secondary technical schools more than nominally technical appeared too great; the schools have maintained a reputation for poor general educational quality; and their graduates have a low status in the eyes of public and employers.

The vicious circle that this has created has been at the root of what is still considered by many to be one of the toughest problems facing the education authorities. Contradictions remain. Vocational and technical subjects are justified in high schools because the higher ability students they attract were assumed to have the academic attainment and potential required for 'further training' in these areas. Secondary technical schools offer 'pre-vocational education in the technical fields' for students who have much lower academic attainment (since otherwise they would have been selected for the high schools), with the unrealistic expectation that they will compete effectively with their more fortunate colleagues from the high schools in the labour market.

The most recent response to the dilemma of identity that has been created is to propose that high schools change their 'role and function' and become exclusively O level preparatory schools selecting their intake from middle schools, most of which would be redesignated secondary technical schools. The reason given for this is that it would offer more students the 'opportunity to do the O Level examination'. Selecting only the best students for entry into these new high schools might improve pass rates and allow teachers to concentrate single mindedly on O level teaching. It could offer staff 'greater chances of intensifying and improving the teaching of their subjects' but only at the expense of narrowing the curriculum as a whole. It is not clear how it could actually expand opportunity in aggregate.

It is suggested that:

> To give Secondary Technical Education the importance and priority it deserves it is proposed that there be a move away from the two-pronged second-level education that is Secondary Technical and Secondary High school education. In view of the fact that resources are not available to effectively equip these schools it is proposed that the schools be redesignated Middle Schools. After three years of middle school an exam would be taken to select a cohort for a two-year O Level course at high school. The middle school would also be a terminal stage for those not selected for the high schools. It is also proposed that the middle schools would offer 'a common core of subjects ... which must be compulsory for every child to do'.   (Gambian Ministry of Education 1982)

But none of these new proposals is grounded in any empirical evaluation of the ways in which the existing schools work. This research attempts to unravel characteristics of the high schools and secondary technical schools to illuminate and understand their problems. This seems a necessary first step before leaping into a set of reforms which may not result in the improvements hoped for. If this is not undertaken the result may suffer from the same kind of problems that have beset the system created by the Sleight report.

The Research

This research was designed to explore features of both types of school in action to gain some grounded understanding of the differences between them. It sought to get behind the level of the rhetoric in reports and official statements about what the schools were supposed to be doing to find out what was actually happening. An important element in this was to try to establish from different points of view perceptions of staff and students in five areas that preliminary enquiry had indicated were central to the identity and workings of the schools. These were concerned with:

(a) school aims;
(b) teachers' and students' expectations of teachers' roles;
(c) teachers' perceptions of obstacles to effective teaching;
(d) students' preferences in selecting subjects;
(e) the effects of external examinations.

Several considerations were behind the choice of research strategy. First, the study was responding to a need identified by others for more studies at the 'problem-specific' level (Lewin 1985, Psacharopoulos 1986). It tries, through case study methods, to begin to develop a qualitative understanding of school 'climates' that impinge on the implementation of policy.

Second, the choice of two secondary schools, one of each type, was made on practical grounds since the time available precluded a larger number. Clearly one of each type had to be chosen to contrast their features though in the nature of case study research there were limits to the generalisability of comparisons that could be made to other schools' of similar types.

Third, the sample chosen within the two case study schools comprised final-year students and their teachers. Final-year students have most experience of the institutions and more maturity to express their views. Their teachers, in the Gambian context, are those with the highest status, longest experience and highest qualifications. Their views were therefore identified as central to the understanding of the schools functioning.

Fourth, the research methods chosen gave emphasis to teachers' perspectives. Whilst both interviews and questionnaires were used for teachers, information from students was obtained mainly through questionnaires. Data was collected from a wide range of other sources (for example, documents, observation, examination results, policy documents, school records) and cross-related wherever possible.

Lastly, a kind of progressive focusing was used to identify issues in the case studies. This involved preliminary open exploration of issues significant to informants within a broadly defined number of areas of interest. Those that emerged from this process were then focused on more purposefully and some are presented here.

Previous experience as both client and practitioner in the schooling system of The Gambia was both a benefit and a handicap. It allowed the researcher to draw on insights from experience; on the other hand there had to be safeguards against these prefiguring the research too strongly and against blindness to perspectives that were not antici- pated.

As a result emphasis was placed on the way staff conceived of the issues raised, and on the meanings they gave to aspects of the school they worked in. Selected as key informants, their views about the school, their own teaching, and the final-year students they taught, were partly subjective. This could be mediated by cross-checking, using standard techniques to see whether interpretations given were corroborated by other evidence. Thus information on the role of the administration, students' perspectives, teaching methods and attitudes of teachers was 'triangulated' (Elliot and Adelman 1975). The questionnaire data provided many opportunities to check teacher interview data.

Gambian teachers have to work in a context where there are no hard and fast theoretical positions on pedagogy and professionality. This means that it was useful to devote attention to how staff view what they are doing rather than examine their practice against some kind of orthodox checklist. Where there are idealised perspectives these tended to be personal rather than institutionally grounded allowing some confidence that key informants were not repeating a 'conventional wisdom' in their recounting of events and their inter- pretation.

The student questionnaire was designed to collect the following range of information: primary school and family background; sub- jects offered; reasons for offering them; other subject preferences; post-school training and employment hopes. Students' patterns of motivation were also examined by inviting them to express degrees of agreement/disagreement with selected statements. These related to student-teacher dependence, student motivational type, attitude to homework, syllabus coverage, and to forms of student control. This information complemented that obtained from teachers.

The Two Case Study Schools

The High School
This school is officially classified as a secondary high school. It has been modelled on the British grammar school; and its traditional function has always been the preparation of students for higher education.

Area of enquiry	Data-gathering methods	Target
Intra-school context High School	7-week period of school visits;	
	Interviews	Principal, deputy 15 staff
	Observations	7 double periods
	Questionnaires	Given to 105 final-year students Got 76 back
	Reference to recent external exam results; Reference to record of punishable offences	
Secondary Technical	7-week period of school visits;	
	Interviews	Headmaster, deputy 13 staff
	Observations	7 double periods
	Questionnaires	Given to 82 final-year students Got 82 back
	Reference to recent external exam results; Reference to minutes of end of term department meetings; Attended end of term Head and Department Heads meeting Observations of school-based projects;	
Secondary school policy perceptions	Reference to educational policy documents; Manpower planning documents;	
	Interviews	Manpower planning officials; Officials of Directorate of Vocational Training;

FIGURE 7.1 *Summary of field-work activities*

It is a coeducational school located in Banjul, the capital. It has a student body of 662 between the ages of 14 to 20 years in classes from Form 1 to Form 6. Its catchment area is mainly urban. Pupils enter the school after passing the highly competitive and selective Common Entrance Examinations from primary schools.

There are 41 staff spread across 14 subject departments. Their qualifications range from professionally trained graduate teachers, through untrained graduates to non-graduate certificated teachers.

The curriculum consists mainly of academic subjects in which students are prepared for the West African Examinations Council (WAEC) O level examination, and A level for those who get to Form 6.

The Secondary Technical School
The school is a coeducational school with a total enrollment of 800 between the ages of 14 to 19 years, from Form 1 to Form 4. There are eight departments covering 13 subjects. The 44 staff have a wide range of qualifications ranging from the untrained O level holder from a high school, through Higher Teaching Certificate holders, to teachers who have reached graduate, and even post-graduate levels.

Pupils enter the school after taking the nation-wide Common Entrance Examinations. Unlike in the case of the high schools, pupils do not select in advance the secondary technical school they would like to go to if they have the chance. Those who are unable to make the grade in the selection exam for the limited places available in the seven high schools automatically enter a technical school. In effect, entry into secondary technicals is more by default than choice. By the measure of the Common Entrance Examination the students in such schools have shown lower attainment than their counterparts in high schools. At the end of four years the students sit the Secondary Technical Leaving Certificate Examination administered by the WAEC. After this exam a few of those who passed well are offered places in high schools to start the O level course.

THE TWO SCHOOLS EXPLORED AND COMPARED

School Aims

In both schools principals and teachers identify with the officially defined functions of the schools. For the high school these are predominantly the provision of opportunities for further and higher education. For the secondary technical school they are concentrated on the acquisition of vocational/technical skills and on the role of the school as a feeder for some into high schools. Thus:

The school is a grammar school . . . that prepares students primarily for university. But circumstances have now caught up with that purpose. Generally, 20 per cent get some form of higher education, while the rest obtain certificates that might help to get employment, or of late middle-level training.   (High school principal)

To the principal of this school success is:

the extent to which more and more students reach further education. . . . The sixth form [of the school] is the only pool of students which will provide future doctors, engineers, etc.

In contrast the secondary high school principal argues that:

three things have basically been the aim: feed the high schools through those who repeat the common entrance in Form 1, or those who pass the secondary leaving exam well; secondly to prepare them for what could be described as a middle education certificate; with this we can get them employed in the lower sectors of government service; . . . thirdly there has been the aim of providing them with what can be described as a broad educational background so that if the student is able to utilise the opportunities he can be self-employed.   (Secondary technical principal)

His view on success also values examination achievement but significantly he gives far more weight to non-academic further education: 'I would like to point out that I am more proud of those students who get into a vocational training institution than those who make it to a high school'. Final-year students' aspirations in both institutions are consistent with these different definitions of purpose. Most high school students anticipate further and higher education and most technical school students expect to enter high school or technical forms of training. To this extent it can be said that each school's official purposes are recognised by students.

However, for each school, staff perceive problems with achieving the goals set for them. The main problem in the high school has been the poor transition rate to sixth form and possible further training. In the case of the secondary technical the 'pre-vocational' bias has never been fully realised, and the feeder function is seen to be in reality

TABLE 7.1   *Students' Intentions on Leaving*

	High School %	Tech. School %
Look for work	1.3	13.4
Go into training	3.9	12.2
Enter Form 6	60.5	8.5
Enter overseas training	34.2	13.4
Enter secondary high school	–	52.4

very marginal since it involves very small numbers and is outside the control of the school.

This can be seen from teachers' remarks on aims. In the high school these reflect predominantly the importance of certification.

The school is giving students the opportunity to compete in exams.   (Science subject teacher)

In preparing students to pass the WAEC exams, the school serves best those who enter Form 6 and proceed to university.

(Language subject teacher)

The school is mainly for the academically talented student.

(Art and craft teacher)

The majority are sacrificial lambs for the few who go to Form 6. No thought seems to be given to the majority.

(Technical subject teacher)

There is a weight of opinion amongst the academic subject teachers that supports the view of the principal that the school ends up with a lot of 'mediocre students who are not really high school material'.

Half of the teachers in the sample view the general educational aspects of the school as closely bound up with the certification process. This reflects their commitment to the inter-school competition with other high schools for external examination passes. The strength of this view is further indicated by the fact that less than 25 per cent of teachers in the sample appeared to be concerned about any adverse consequences of the examination orientation that this promotes within the school. Few indicated that the relative neglect of the 'less bright' students represented a problem or that any special provision should be made for them. Although it was this group that would perform least well on certification examinations and depress the overall performance of the school, there seemed on the whole to be little inclination to tackle the problem of student underachievement.

Perhaps predictably three out of the four teachers who were concerned about the neglect of students considered not to be 'bright' were teachers of non-academic subjects. This seemed to provide further circumstantial evidence that the school marginalises such subjects and discourages student interest in them if it is at the expense of academic subjects.

In the technical school the problems with curriculum orientation are reflected by the teachers' remarks that, for example:

Despite being a technical high school, the work is academically geared.... There is little chance for employment or self-employment for the leavers. Those who are fortunate enough go to high schools or get employed, and others roam about.

(Social studies teacher)

Most staff agree with a mathematics teacher who argued that: 'Students who continue to high school are very few. So we cater for those who do not go to high school'.

The lower level of external exam orientation apparent in the secondary technical appears to come from the realisation that successful student performance in the Secondary Technical Leaving Certificate Exam rarely leads to entry to high school. This has the effect of directing the attention of teachers to other aims that allow a broader conception of purposes. Partly as a result, the problem of the underachievement of students is viewed in a different way that is more sympathetic to needs other than those of examination performance.

These problems leave staff and the principals at least two options. The first is to attempt to reduce the gap between official goals and what is actually being achieved. The second is to use the lack of attainment of goals to define supplementary aims that are more realistic. The schools do seem differentiated by their responses to these problems and this reflects orientations towards regulation (the attainment of the goals as intended) on the one hand, and exploration of possibilities in redefining some of the purposes on the other.

In the high school several informants argue that the quality of the intake requires a reorientation towards more vocationally-orientated subjects and some movement in this direction has taken place, to the extent that 40 per cent of students do offer at least one of these subjects at O level. Nevertheless it is recognised that: 'At present subjects which are not of the academic type . . . can only provide the basics, and that is insufficient for employment' (technical subjects teacher). The dominant culture of the school values the academic subjects, and movements to diversify the curriculum have historically made little inroad in this school. The dominant aims remain examination success and access to higher education.

In contrast the secondary technical school has a principal with a personal dream to 'turn the students into job-makers and not job-seekers'. With the support of teachers he has been able to capitalise on the rural backgrounds of most students, which arguably make them more susceptible to practical learning of direct use in local occupations. The school employs a strategy of developing vocational awareness through involving students in school-based projects which are biased towards agriculture. For example, the school is embarking on a mixed farming project to introduce students to the idea of self-reliance with the aim of developing productive skills through a practical approach. Success in this endeavour is surrounded by reservations but there does seem to be a wider commitment to broader educational aims than in the high school.

> The idea is to relate a broad-based education to life after school. (Head of pastoral care)

> One of the most important tasks is to help students understand the value of some subjects. (Language teacher)

> We deviate a lot from the academic syllabus . . . to do more useful things like writing application letters. (Language teacher)

As the principal indicates:

> The school has to be given a new meaning. Students may be aware of their situation as those who 'failed'. But that failure should not be allowed to block any new meanings that could be given to their situation in this school.

There is therefore some evidence of greater openness to exploration that allows the redefinition of goals in the technical school to ones that reflect outcomes thought realistic for students.

Teachers' Roles

Data from teachers and students were used to categorise role expectations. These produced a similar overall pattern in both schools with some differences in emphasis.

In the high school three types of expectations of teachers in the teaching/learning situation were identified. These can be classified as:

(a)   Teachers as experts with knowledge to offer.
They expect me to be a good teacher who imparts knowledge to them.

They want to be sure that you know your subject very well.

Some are uncomfortable with this but accept the role given to them by the students:

I keep reminding them that my word is not gospel ... they take down every word I utter during lessons.

I point out references, explain difficulties ... students prefer to be taught ... not made to learn.

(b)   Teachers as instrumental guides to examination success.

They expect me to make them pass their exams.

I am supposed to always guide them and work according to the syllabus so that they will get good results.

This is a burden for some teachers who feel that it results in an instrumental dependence on the teacher that goes beyond reasonable expectations.

They expect so much, especially the examination classes ... almost everything is expected to be done by the teacher in the entire syllabus. I've even noticed that when we are short of time, they fail to cover topics on their own. Some even attend lessons without having brought the required text ... they expect the teacher to provide it.

(c)   Teachers as sources of affective support and motivation.

They expect you to give them your love and liking. This motivates them to treat your subject seriously.

The attention they give to the teachers is more than they give to their parents. They look up to you, they all listen and look at you in the classroom. You cannot but treat them and your work in a conscientious manner.

This view was not as common as the other two. All three views could be seen to overlap to some extent. The emphasis attributed to the role of the teacher in enhancing academic performance seems consistent with earlier evidence about the climate of this school.

In the secondary technical school, two main forms of expectation are noted by teachers:

(a)   Teachers as experts with knowledge to offer.

Students expect one to know everything ... even the definition of every word in the textbook.

When I turn my theory lessons into discussions, I have to do as much talking as during the dictation of notes.

(b)   Teachers as sources of affective support and motivation.

It looks like if you cannot have a fatherly or brotherly attitude towards them, they will not want to have anything to do with your subject. ... So you have to try and win them over.

I had a large number of entrants last year ... despite the maths phobia that students tend to develop, they expect maths to be difficult. I have decided not to be difficult. I accept as many irritating or apparently silly questions as I get in a lesson and severely discourage any mockery or laughing at each other's mistakes. The problem should not be me, or the fear to ask questions ... it is better for it to be the subject itself.

The view of teachers as instrumental guides to examination success did not emerge at all strongly in the secondary technical school. This seemed to reflect the lower priority given to it by the teachers who were not under the same kind of pressures as their colleagues in the high school. It seems also to reflect the different climate in the school where examination passes were not seen, at least internally, as the most important measure of effectiveness.

In the high school the strength of the external exam-orientation is evidenced by the predominance of the instrumentalist type of dependence on the teacher. The orientations identified showed the prominence given to the role of the teacher in determining syllabus treatment. And much as teachers appeared to dislike some aspects of this dependence, the stakes of external exam passes seemed too high to risk opposing them actively. The school's commitment to the inter-school external examination competition was so high that teachers were obliged to respond to it.

In the secondary technical school the orientations identified appeared more benign from the point of view of adverse examination 'backwash' on teachers' roles. For instance, the view of the teacher as a source of expert knowledge was linked to the inadequate antecedent primary school background of students, as well as the limited provision of textbook sources. It was not only referred to in relation to examination knowledge. More sympathy seemed evident with a supportive role in relation to motivation and confidence boosting to overcome the weaknesses of students.

Obstacles to Teaching

The teachers interviewed and given questionnaires identified a number of obstacles that they felt inhibited their ability to teach the curriculum effectively. In both schools equipment for teaching non-academic subjects, teaching aids for academic subjects, and lack of adequate subject-specific textbooks were frequently mentioned as problematic. But there were differences in emphasis and significance.

The high school staff recognised that compared to other schools they were well provided with textbooks but that nevertheless problems arose. In many of the academic subjects there are books written especially for the examination syllabus. Where these are in limited supply difficulties are created. Several teachers mentioned the effects of delays in textbook supply as opposed to availability in general.

When textbook provision is incomplete it can be crippling in subjects like ours. (General subjects teacher)

The general lack of textbooks affects the continuity of what is being taught. (General subjects teacher)

Because there are virtually no secondary school textbooks designed for Gambian students specifically, rather than for WAEC syllabuses in general, their lack of availability is a mixed blessing. The temptation in their presence is to use them rigidly as the best available support for examination success, discouraging creative approaches to subjects grounded in Gambian conditions. Yet their absence hampers both teachers and students, unsure of their ability to make curricular decisions and to cover the necessary material comprehensively.

The secondary technical school is in a different position since for most subjects apart from the academic ones:

> there is no coursebook. The teacher derives his coursework from the syllabus. (Metal work teacher)

Where there are materials, availability is a bigger problem in the school.

> We are restricted to one book ... and few students can afford it. Some even do work on pieces of paper instead of exercise books. (Language teacher)

> As a result, a few books of various types and standards are brought to school. (Agricultural science teacher)

In the secondary technical school textbooks are not considered as purpose-written texts for examination purposes. The school accepts that it is too expensive to require students to buy more than the bare minimum of books. The usefulness of the limited number of textbooks in the hands of the teachers is that they do help guide the conversion of the syllabuses into teaching activities. To this extent they are a fundamental resource for the teachers to draw on but their selection is *ad hoc* and uncoordinated.

In the high school five teachers mentioned the lack of teaching aids, like audiovisual facilities, and school trips to places of educational interest, as problematic:

> We lack a history room provided with relics to illustrate historical points, or which could be used for the showing of film strips. (General subject teacher)

> Inadequate funds prevent visits to places like an oil mill for the students to see how groundnuts are processed; or the veterinary department to see something about animal husbandry. (Science subject teacher)

However, the researcher formed the view that these were not a central problem inhibiting effective teaching, but rather a desirable optional extra.

Equipment for practical subjects was also lacking in the high school, reflecting the relatively low priority given to it in the timetable.

Tools, materials and machines are not mere teaching aids in our area; we need to have them in the first place.

(Technical subject teacher)

Home economics is not treated as a serious course; our best students drop it because it clashes with other subjects.

(Arts and craft subject teacher)

Equipment provision was a more serious problem in the secondary technical school as many subjects depend heavily on access to tools and machines:

Inadequate supplies of tools and machines . . . is the reason why there are no practicals in Forms 1, 2 and 3. Any interest . . . could well disappear by Form 4. . . . Besides, the practical element in the exam would be an experience that could be dangerous for students using unfamiliar tools.   (Head of technical department)

We have only one functioning sewing machine. The cooker and the refrigerator are out of use, because there is no electricity. For our practicals we make do with a charcoal stove . . . but it can take up useful lesson time to get it going.   (Head of home economics)

The schools were differentiated on the remaining obstacles to effective teaching which were identified. In the high school there was a body of opinion directed at the adverse effects of large class size on teaching and learning. This, it was felt, resulted in a reduction in individual student support and a diminution of the frequency with which work could be set and marked. Free periods for teachers were disappearing and lesson planning and marking suffered as a result of the recent growth in enrolment in the school without a commensurate increase in staffing:

Classes are too large . . . and in a subject like ours where we have a full class size and not a small set, it becomes impossible to keep to the former frequency with which we gave the students essays to write. To mark so many compositions or letters properly, you have to take more time.   (Language subject teacher)

In contrast, in the secondary technical school class size is not regarded as a key issue, although the staff-student ratio is higher (18:1 compared to 16:1). This may be because historically it has had a less favourable staff-student ratio than the high school and staff have become resigned to it. In the high school the ratio has recently been deteriorating. What is of concern as an obstacle is the background of the students entering the school. This did not figure prominently in discussions in the high school:

> Most (students) have been ill-prepared by primary schools. . . . They have poor reading habits, poor familiarity with the language, poor knowledge of grammár. Their English is often full of direct translations from their mother tongue.

Over 90 per cent come from outside the capital and its environs and are therefore from schools which are known to be frequently of low quality and under-resourced. One teacher living in the community reinforced the disposition of the secondary technical school towards a greater concern for underachievement by referring to the motivational handicaps associated with typical backgrounds:

> A lot see failure at common entrance as having made them failures. We can only try and change this . . . Some are keen but may be late developers. . . . For others, the fact that they stay with guardians leads to them being overworked, deprived of proper care, control and support. . . . Too many low marks make them relax . . . saying that they are not good in a subject.

Subject Choices

There are definite differences between the two schools on the matter of subject options and access to subjects. In the high school there is an official rubric for access to subjects imposed by the WAEC's subject grouping requirements. In the secondary technical the range of subjects that can be sat at the external exam is also restricted, but not the number of subjects that students can do. Within these restrictions there is room for each school to determine how many students, and which ones, can actually do which subjects.

The policy in the high school can be described as one of strong institutional control of access to subjects. The strength of the relationship with the WAEC subject groupings effectively controls and limits the choice of subjects. This is felt to be a disadvantage by many teachers:

> I am not satisfied with the limited subjects. We tend to cater for the 'high flyers'. The less fortunate fall by the wayside. We need more technical and vocational subjects, for both categories [of student]

to benefit. .... If you do not opt for a subject within a particular group you will not get a full school certificate.

(Teacher responsible for examinations)

The subject grouping restricts choice and places constraints on the timetabling of subjects. It also enhances the academic orientation of the school since:

pupils are more or less pushed into the technical side, an area which is more of a dumping ground ... whose subjects are chosen for fulfilling a combination of requirements.

(Technical subjects teacher)

A slightly different gloss is given to these issues by the science teacher who argued that:

in fact, they have too many options, considering all the subjects that they do up to Form 5. .... Subjects like art, metalwork and woodwork are not really necessary, considering the kind of school it is.

The major issue is about how to assign students the minimum number of examination subjects that have to be taken (seven) for certification, distributed across the 12 single subject departments. One result of this is that choice is really exercised by the teachers rather than the students. There is little counselling.

I would like to see more counselling, and not in the last three weeks of Form 3 ... when such decisions are being made. A lot of those students do not know what they are doing when they decide.   (General subjects teacher)

Although some teachers favour student choice as definitive, in reality the setting of minimum ability levels for entry into subjects and the mechanics of co-ordinating choice across subjects and the timetable give most influence to the teachers' views.

The teacher knows what the student is capable of ... and not necessarily as seen through examination results. .... Where the teacher has known a child for a year, his word should be given more weight than the child's belief that he/she can do the subject.   (General subject teacher/part-time counsellor)

This type of reasoning depends heavily on teachers' judgements. The high school has no standardisation of internal exams, and there is no continuous assessment of students, or other system of monitoring student progress, unlike in the secondary technical school. The pressure is on the school to manage student access to external examination subjects. In the process there is some evidence to suggest that the practical need to assign teachers appropriate set sizes, and to fit them in the school time-table, takes precedence over other considerations. Paradoxically this may exacerbate some of the other problems related to underachievement noted elsewhere. Given the wide range of ability of students, the combination of a student's lack of interest in a subject (that was someone else's choice) and the limited support given to less able students, there is a risk of worsening the performance of low-achievers.

The policy in the secondary technical is one of broad exposure to as many subjects as possible. There is encouragement of students to do the maximum number of subjects they feel capable of and there are fewer constraints than in the high school. The principal argues that:

> we do not provide any guidelines. We just tell them to choose. If the student seeks advice we will provide assistance . . . on whether or not he should do or drop the subject. . . . I believe students will be guided by interest or ability in the subject. We do not want the parents blaming the school when students flop the subjects that the school advised them to offer; it is a different matter when the child willingly chooses a subject.

Teachers who support broad exposure and student choice argue that there are advantages in the introductory value subjects can have for high school education; that it encourages balance with the general emphasis on technical subjects; and that it allows most students' needs to be reflected in their courses. However, a larger number of staff identify important negative side effects of the system of choice.

> It is impossible for all the students to do well in the subjects that they do. . . . Given the short period, the ones that are basically necessary should be identified and concentrated on.
> (English teacher)

> Students choose subjects . . . and the failure rate is increased. Teachers should recommend . . . as in high schools. It is no use allowing 200 to sit and get one pass. In needlework some girls come for the practical exam and skip the theory part.
> (Home economics teacher)

Students are unable to discover the worth of subjects. .... They say that some subjects are easier because they have objective tests. .... For that reason a lot of them opt for geography not history. .... I think the administration and subject head should recommend who should do which subjects.   (Teacher of history)

There is concern for the effects on lesson involvement and students' attitudes to subjects that are thought difficult. The data also indicates students are more attracted to subjects that are offered at high school than vocational/technical ones. This seems to be evidence of some ambiguity towards the secondary technical schools' official aims.

In sum, the subject option choice in this school is basically unplanned. Choices seem to be made on personal preference and a sense of how easy or difficult subjects are thought to be. This has to be seen as inconsistent with both the goal of balance and the special emphasis on technical and vocational education.

The Influence of Examinations

This is one major feature that differentiates the two schools. As far as the high school is concerned the most obvious reason for the strong influence of examinations on the curriculum in action is the school's commitment to offering O and A level courses. It is the exam itself that is the greatest problem for the teachers. The main complaints concern lack of consistency as a standard measure of attainment, its limited scope as a test of mastery of syllabus facts, and its power to reduce curriculum outcomes to answering exam questions.

The exam is limited in what it tests. .... Skills tested vary from year to year. They should devise methods to test more effectively. .... There should be uniformity from year to year.   (Science teacher)

Most of it is facts ... It is difficult for a student to produce original material. It then falls to a teacher to be looking around for more facts.   (General subjects teacher)

The students expect me to teach and stress what the examination requires.   (Language subjects teacher)

Many teachers admit to concentrating on syllabus coverage, and most indicate that they do give prominence to exam performance skills in their teaching. Their problem is that although in general terms they are examination-orientated and suffering 'diploma disease' backwash on their teaching, the nature of the examination is inconsistent and they have little control over it or access to the thinking behind its form, since this is a WAEC concern.

Throughout the data on the high school there is corroborating evidence testifying to the high level of examination orientation. Students are 'very conscious of the syllabus . . . other things do not matter'; many essays are set 'in order to illustrate the different ways in which a question could come'; teachers make it known that 'this is what WAEC is looking for' and 'the exam constitutes a target . . . this has to be understood'. This is consistent with the overall orientation of this school and its aims but there is uncertainty in teachers' minds about how best to respond to these pressures. This can be illustrated by the general subjects teacher who opined: 'it is necessary to give them guidelines on the topics that need to be covered on the syllabus . . . but it is impossible to identify them with any accuracy'.

Of course the range of topics is clearly identified in the syllabus document, but the ones that may be included in an examination for a particular year are not. The dilemma does induce stress in teachers caught between the conflicting expectations of covering the syllabus while also paying special attention to those parts that lead to specific questions in a particular year.

In the secondary technical school the influence of examinations is perceived in somewhat different ways. There is little mention of unpredictable aspects of the examination creating uncertainty in what to teach. Many teachers indicate that the exam does not restrict their teaching because success in the exam does not necessarily lead to high school entry. This creates opportunities to extend the curriculum beyond the confines of the formal syllabus.

> The second part of the paper does provide for problems on the commercial and technical and modern aspects of maths . . . but this has not made the syllabus comprehensive enough. . . . I would have preferred more of the commercial and technical components . . . because if you compare the numbers of those who get to high schools they are outnumbered by far by those who drop out.   (Maths teacher)

> The students want a certificate that comes from passing the examination . . . this does not come easily for the vast majority. I try to strike a balance. . . . I try to add the missing links, emphasising more on areas that affect us . . . Even if the exam does not specifically deal with rainfall and farming, this has relevance for the majority of students from farming communities.   (Geography teacher)

The main criticisms are about how the exam is unsuitable for the kind of students who attend the school. Several point out that the examinations follow those of the high school exam too closely. Others argue that they fail to take account of the quality of student in the school. Many referred to the constraints of background, teaching material and equipment not being recognised in the way that questions were set.

Both theory and practical are adequately tested . . . If anything, the lack of suitable facilities is the problem. (Home economics teacher)

To cover the required topics whilst there is a textbook shortage is quite a job. Supplementing, improvising or searching for the occasional substitute text is given most attention; there is hardly time for other things. (Teacher of history)

The exam is set to measure academic achievement of students for whom the understanding of the very examination question is often a problem in itself. . . . The question is only understood after translation into the vernacular. There is little certainty as to whether what the exam is testing for is in there.
(Head of social studies)

Thus in both schools examinations are seen to be important influences on teaching and learning. In the high school these appear as constraining factors that restrict action and in large part ensure teaching is bound to the syllabus. In the secondary technical school this is less so and the concerns are more with relevance and the adequacy of assumptions of antecedent conditions implied by the nature of the examinations.

CONCLUDING REMARKS

This chapter has explored the development of educational policy in The Gambia that has resulted in the establishment of a two-track secondary school system. It was designed to illuminate features of both types of school in action, to gain some grounded understanding of differences between them. Five areas were identified for presentation here: schools' aims; teachers' and students' expectations of teachers' roles; teachers' perceptions of obstacles to effective teaching; students' preferences in selecting subjects; the influence of external examinations. The data analysed above offers insights into all of these and the reality of policy implementation in the two case study sites.

Several tentative conclusions can be reached. First from the narrative that investigates the development of the policy that created the schools it is clear that ambiguity over purpose has been an enduring feature of both parts of the dual system established. This seems to have affected each in different ways. The high school has retained its central identification with a 'grammar school' tradition, despite experiencing significant changes in the quantity and quality of its intake and despite substantial changes in the career opportunities for its graduates. Attempts to vocationalise some parts of its curriculum have withered in practice and there seems to have been little serious attempt to resource them. The secondary technical school, on the other hand, has the problem of a set of purposes that it cannot fulfil through, again, lack of resourcing, unrealisable outcomes (the transfer into high school is minute), and an ambivalent attitude to the relationship between academic and vocational and technical subjects. From the case studies there is evidence on the ground that policy continues to be made on the basis of a view of what happens within the schools that diverges from reality. The image of what ought to be is more powerful than the reality of what is (Lewin 1985).

Second, in both schools there is general recognition of formal aims consistent with public policy but the response to them is different. The high school enthusiastically embraces its brief to prepare an élite and maximise examination success, to the extent that it seems to neglect the needs of average and less than average students. The secondary technical school is not so driven by certification and attempts to offer a broader and more balanced practically-orientated curriculum. In so doing it demonstrates a more flexible approach to meeting the needs of its students, at least at the level of intent, than does the high school.

Third, in the high school the strength of the external exam-orientation is reflected in instrumental dependence on the teacher. The school's commitment to the inter-school external examination competition appears so high that teachers are obliged to respond to it, though some recognise the problems that this creates in the school in meeting the needs of all the students. In the secondary technical school, on the other hand, the teacher role orientations identified appeared more benign. More sympathy seemed evident with a supportive role in relation to motivation and confidence-boosting related to the weaknesses of students.

Fourth, the obstacles identified to effective teaching showed some common features – lack of textbooks, teaching aids and equipment. Equipment did seem a more significant problem in the secondary technical school since the practical subjects had a high demand for it. An important difference was the emphasis given to class size-related problems in the high school (though their staff-student ratio was better) and the problems arising from student backgrounds in the secondary technical.

Fifth, approaches to subject option choice varied. WAEC-prescribed groupings and teacher choice predominated in the high school. The secondary technical school gave weight to students' preferences in an apparently *ad hoc* way. Neither provided significant counselling opportunities to inform choice.

Sixth, examination orientation was a feature of both schools but appeared much more virulent in the high school. The syllabus-bound nature of teaching was evident in the latter, though uncertainty surrounded many aspects of what WAEC might demand in terms of performance on particular topics. In contrast there were examples of practice in the secondary technical school that, at least sometimes, went beyond the syllabus to meet the perceived needs of students defined in relation to likely occupational futures.

Reflections on the Research

This research did manage to capture some of the realities experienced by teachers in the two schools. It fell short of the kind of insight that might be accessible to an 'ethnographic' style of research but choices had to be made. There simply was not the opportunity nor time to adopt this style, so case study with non-participant observation was chosen as the most viable approach to explore research questions that emerged.

The researcher feared that his own biography as a student and teacher in the system under study would create some problems of preconceived explanations and significant issues. All he could do was to guard against these by adhering to open interpretation of the data and seeking corroboration of the expected as well as the unexpected.

Some of the difficulties experienced in tracing baseline data and policy documentation were not originally anticipated. In The Gambia documents, even official ones, are often produced in small quantities and not always stored in accessible forms. It was necessary to search hard, often through contacts and acquaintances, as well as libraries, to trace things through and this absorbed a lot of time.

The researcher thought initially that he might meet some appre
hension or even hostility in the case study sites as an inquirer who
might uncover unpalatable information. These fears proved ground
less and a lot of helpful co-operation was received. It did take some
careful explanation to students to get them to understand that he was
not teaching them but wished to explore their opinions and experience
since this was an unfamiliar event when undertaken by a 'teacher'. In
introducing himself he tried to give a general impression of his
concerns without giving away particular value positions that might
influence informants' responses. This seemed to work well.

Some problems were encountered with the observational aspects of
the study. Gambian teachers are not used to observation by research
ers and it was thought they would change their normal practice as a
result. The researcher could not do enough observation over a long
period to be representative, so he chose to depend mainly on inter
view data and other sources (such as students' work) to get a picture
over time of teaching approaches. Knowledge of a teacher's teaching
repertoire was also considered valuable in this respect.

Questionnaire administration had unanticipated problems. Dis
tributing them was easy, getting the returns took a long time and
more than a week had to be devoted to just one group of student
questionnaires to get a reasonable response rate. (105 were given
questionnaires and 76 responded.) Interviewing difficulties centred
on appropriate places in which to hold them. In one of the case
studies an office space was allocated which seemed to give a formal
air to the proceedings that was not conducive to open discussion. The
researcher tried to minimise its use when he realised this.

The study emphasised teacher data and this was one of it
limitations – but also perhaps one of its strengths, given that choice
had to be made about orientation. Furthermore, the emphasis is an
apt recognition of the high visibility and centrality of the teacher in
Gambian classroom situations. The study of the life history of the
policy decisions that resulted in the dual system was limited by the
accessibility of those involved. Many were unable or unwilling to
grant interviews.

The Future

This study opens an agenda for subsequent work and is the first of it
kind on schools in The Gambia. In summary it points to needs for
policy-makers to take account of curriculum reality in the school

system that they are planning for. Some of the problems identified could be ameliorated by closer attention to the official goals of schools, clearer specification of these, and realistic appraisals of what it is possible to achieve. Central to this is an appreciation of the central role played by examining systems in determining patterns of teaching and learning. Perhaps the effects of WAEC certification need re-examination; the quality of internal information on student progress certainly does. The study also draws attention to the inconsistent usage and uneven availability of text material which affects practical subjects in particular. The rationale for option choice, and the mechanisms through which it is achieved, need refinement if they are to result in achievement of the outcomes to which the different types of schools are formally committed. Finally the study has exposed weaknesses in the conceptualisation of the dual system that strike at the heart of its viability. It is this question perhaps more than any other that requires persistent, open and informed debate.

The idea of middle schools is being fully implemented with effect from September, 1992. The main benefit seen in restructuring secondary education is to offer a uniform kind of education during the first 9 years of formal education. This may take some time to achieve. There are more secondary technical than high schools and each group of schools has different traditions as is clear from these case studies.

Part IV
Systems Reforms

The final two studies concern attempts to implement large-scale changes in educational systems. One involves a small island republic and the other a Nigerian state.

During the early 1980s the secondary education system in Nigeria was reorganised. Florence Nwakoby's study concerns one part of this: the attempt to introduce a more vocationally-oriented curriculum into the Junior Secondary Schools in Anambra State. Insofar as she was professionally part of the State education system, hers is the view of a participant observer, though as an official rather than a teacher. This was extended by interviews at several levels, documentary analysis and school case studies.

Nwakoby investigated how far the education system was able to implement this innovation successfully. She pinpoints major gaps and inadequacies in the system in the setting of goals, in the implementation management, in the organisational structures and in the classroom implementation. The study analyses how the planned changes were not clearly conceptualised, and how there was a very serious lack of communication between many different parts of the system. The classroom observation showed that the ideas set out in the National Education Policy, such as integrated approaches to subject matter, student involvement and problem-oriented teaching methods, were not being put into practice by teachers. Neither training nor resources had been directed towards helping the teachers to change.

After the 1977 revolution in the Seychelles, the education system underwent a radical reform process in three stages. Ian Haffenden focuses on the second stage, the introduction of the National Youth Service (NYS). This was a two-year progressive educational programme open to all 15 to 17 year-olds, designed to act as a catalyst for social, economic and political change. The students were to live in residential 'youth villages' where education would be combined with production and where they would develop skills and attitudes suitable for a socialist society.

Haffenden describes how the government, overcoming initial opposition, set up the first village and recruited a heterogeneous body

215

of expatriate staff to teach there, of which he was one. He was therefore also a participant observer and from this standpoint he analyses how the school management and different groupings of teachers came into conflict with one another due to the different expectations and perceptions of what organisational and educational structures were needed. The 'co-ordinators' (management) were concerned primarily with getting the organisation under way, while the teachers, who were at first given control over the curriculum, were interested in developing radically new forms of teaching and learning. By the end of the first year, however, control was becoming centralised in the co-ordinators' hands and gradually the curriculum moved back towards more traditional patterns. Haffenden concludes that both external and internal pressures were responsible for the problems faced by this innovation.

The studies make an interesting comparison on several points. In the Seychelles as in Nigeria there were inadequacies in the management and organisational structures necessary for implementation, and a lack of consensus about goals. But in the Seychelles case the teachers took on the role of initiating change in the classroom: although both innovations were directed from the top, in the NYS there was also an element of bottom-up, teacher-led change. In the ensuing clash, the teachers were overruled; it is an open question whether they were more in line with the policy makers at the very top than the middle management whose views eventually prevailed.

Another question is about endogenous versus externally-stimulated changes. The Seychelles is a small island country, newly independent and open to external pressures. The innovation studied was part of an ambitious attempt to restructure a whole society; the impetus for this seems to have been a combination of internal dynamics and external ideas and assistance, exemplified in this case by the enthusiastic foreign staff. Haffenden suggests a combination of internal and external pressures caused the failures in implementation.

The Nigerian study concerns a more mature and self-confident education system and the innovation was more narrowly educational in its intentions; it does not appear to have owed much to external pressures or to expatriate personnel. The weaknesses were those internal to the system. It is perhaps also relevant that the NYS was not at that time part of the educational bureaucracy, but a self-contained project under the President's office, thus less vulnerable to being hampered by the system, but more open to external threat.

Time is necessary for change to become established. Both these studies were conducted at the very beginnings of the planned changes, and both reveal the great difficulties in implementing the original ideas. Yet in both cases, the innovations went on. Nwakoby found a wide consensus about the need for change, and a strong commitment to it; she highlights the persistence with which it was carried through in spite of all the problems. In the Seychelles, there was by contrast little consensus about the need for or the direction of the innovation, but it too has persisted – while the radical curricular innovations were not firmly established, the institution of the NYS itself, eight years later continues to exist and to develop. The end of both these stories has yet to be told.

8 Vocationalising Secondary Education: A Study of the Junior Secondary Schooling Innovation in Nigeria

Florence Nwakoby with Keith Lewin

INTRODUCTION

The decision to undertake this research was a response to the debates which followed the introduction of a new secondary education system in Nigeria. The innovation was designed as a complex package offering an integrated approach to changing educational values, orientations and learning outcomes. The research was planned to investigate this innovation during its first life cycle between 1982 and 1985 to see how much foundation there was for the doubts being expressed.

One element, the vocationalised curriculum, caused immediate concern at the time because of the discouraging evidence of the impact of previous attempts to achieve this in Nigeria and other countries. The research reported here was part of an extensive study, carried out in Anambra State, which included other aspects of the innovations at secondary level – in the examination system, in the new structure of Junior Secondary Schooling (JSS) and in the new emphasis on guidance and counselling. The research reported here sought to explore the state of readiness that existed to support the implementation of the vocational elements of the Junior Secondary Schools curriculum introduced into Nigeria from 1982. The study shows how the innovation evolved through different phases and identifies the strengths and weaknesses of the approach adopted.

The chapter is organised in five parts. First the general characteristics of the pre-vocational elements of the JSS are outlined. Second, the research methods are described. Third, research evidence is

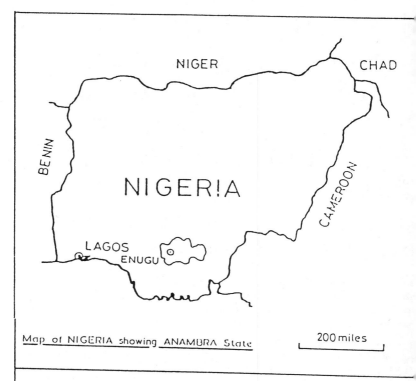

Map of NIGERIA showing ANAMBRA State

200 miles

Map of Africa with NIGERIA

presented on three selected aspects of the innovation – conceptualisation, dissemination of information, and on the curriculum in action. Fourth, some reflections are made on the limitations of the research methods. Finally some summary conclusions are reached.

THE VOCATIONALISED CURRICULUM INNOVATION

The new curriculum for the JSS as explained by the *National Policy on Education* (NPE) (Federal Republic of Nigeria 1981) is designed to offer a pre-vocational as well as an academic education which will enable students to develop both cognitive and manipulative skills with which they can acquire further knowledge for their future use. Students are expected to learn 13 subjects altogether, made up of 12 core subjects including two Nigerian languages and two pre-vocational subjects, as well as one non-vocational elective.

Core Subjects	Pre-vocational Subjects (select 2)
Mathematics	Woodwork
English	Metalwork
Nigerian languages (2)	Electronics
Science	Mechanics
Social studies	Local crafts
Art and music	Home economics
Practical agriculture	Business studies
Religious & moral education	*Non-vocational electives*
Physical education	(select 1 only)
Pre-vocational subjects (2)	Arabic studies
	French

SOURCE   Federal Republic of Nigeria, (1981) *National Policy on Education*

FIGURE 8.1   *List of subjects in the JSS curriculum*

The JSS curriculum thus has the following characteristics:

(a) a pre-vocational base for vocational training;
(b) an academic base for training in cognitive academic skills;
(c) a content designed to reflect an integration of school and societal values and needs;

(d) a syllabus geared to achievements covering a range of levels of cognitive, affective and psychomotor domains;
(e) teaching/learning strategies to stimulate interest, enquiry and experimentation.

The *Blueprint for Implementation* (Federal Republic of Nigeria 1979) is complementary to the NPE and gives specifications for the new curriculum. The *Blueprint* advises on the mode of implementation. Two approaches are suggested for designing the pre-vocational curriculum: a subject approach and an integrated approach. In the first situation the student studies three pre-vocational subjects for two years and then in the third year specialises in only one of the subjects. In the second approach the student is introduced to a wide range of subjects which he studies for the three years. Emphasis here is on generalisation. Decisions about which approach to adopt are to be made locally depending on such conditions as the employment situation, availability of teachers and facilities. There is a requirement that, whichever method is used, States must introduce the pre-vocational subjects not later than the second year of the JSS.

In consideration of differences in educational needs and in the availability of resources among States and among schools, the *Blueprint* allows considerable autonomy in the adaptation of curriculum content and time allocation to subjects. However, it recommends that:

> At the JSS level 'introductory technology' should be taught as part of general education for every pupil. The subject should be designed as an integrated subject including elements of woodwork, plastics, metalwork, ceramics, elementary building technology, elementary mechanical and electrical technology related to common domestic appliances, bicycles etc., technical drawing and simple agriculture. It is recommended that 8 periods per week should be allocated to introductory technology.

There is a provision that:

> until the curriculum for the integrated subject introductory technology is devised, and where facilities and teachers are limited, every school should have at least woodwork and technical drawing, with metalwork being added as soon as possible. All schools should also spend two or three periods per week on agriculture, except in the heart of an urban area where land may not be available.

Instead they should do gardening and learn to grow vegetables, peppers, etc. which take little space.

Thus the innovation seeks to diversify secondary school curricula by introducing vocational subjects and making them part of the compulsory core to be studied in the first three years of secondary school.

RESEARCH QUESTIONS AND METHODS

The research questions relevant to this chapter that were identified from the preliminary enquiry and analysis undertaken were as follows:

(a) How far does the system appear to have accurately identified its problems and specified reasonable solutions to them?

(b) To what extent can the system be observed to have adequately exploited channels for negotiation to establish a common understanding about the innovation?

(c) How far does there exist the management capacity for efficient marshalling, deployment and co-ordination of resources and information to support the innovation?

(d) What evidence is there that the system possesses the expertise to carry out and sustain implementation?

A range of research methods were used to explore the questions identified above. These included interviews, questionnaires, case studies, documentary evidence from official sources and a literature survey.

Interviews

Altogether 55 actors from different levels were interviewed during different periods of the field work in order to elicit relevant information about the innovation. These interviews included staff of the Federal Ministry of Education (FMOE), State Ministry of Education (MOE), principals and school teachers, employers, and some parents. The strategy was to keep the questions at a general open-ended level from which the discussion could then be further explored during the interviews. A semi-structured interview schedule was used. It was possible to tape-record several of these interviews, especially those with colleagues who knew me well. However the majority of the interviewees outside the MOE were hesitant about being tape-recorded, an attitude that was not unconnected with the highly repressive tendencies of the military regime between 1984 and 1985. Any talk that was in any way critical of Government was regarded as punishable treason, as two journalists found to their cost just as I started my fieldwork:

I therefore made notes which I filled out soon after each interview. I was careful not to schedule more than one interview a day where recording was not possible to allow sufficient time for note-making at home. In addition to the first phase of interviews, I also had the opportunity during the case studies in schools to engage in further interviews with principals and school teachers whom I met at schools. These form part of the case study reports.

Case Studies

An illuminative evaluation procedure was adopted for use (Parlett and Hamilton 1976). The purpose of the case studies was to carry out an in-depth investigation to see how the 'instructional system', that is, the planned innovation, was being operated in the different learning milieux represented by the selected schools. The case studies permitted me to undertake an analysis of the innovation in action. This enabled contrasts to be made with perceptions at higher levels in the system. The studies were carried out in three phases spanning October to December 1984, May 1985 and January 1986.

The first phase was a preliminary fact-finding exercise. I wanted to ascertain the status of the innovation in the schools and therefore spent three weeks talking to principals and teachers and observing activities in three schools selected for the purpose within Enugu urban centre. The schools were chosen because of their ease of access. It was also to these schools that I returned to pre-test the questionnaires I used. There was no evidence of the implementation of the innovation in the schools during this period and so it was necessary to plan for a full-scale study later in the session.

The second phase case studies were carried out in the month of May 1985. It was hoped that by this time the schools would have settled down and would have begun to think seriously about the JSS and how to implement the new policy before the examinations in June.

Altogether seven schools were used for the case studies which included six State schools and one Federal school. (All schools in

Anambra State are government managed). Five criteria were used to select schools for study:

(a) one school was selected from each of the five education zones in the State;
(b) each school must have been issued with equipment for introductory technology between 1983 and 1984;
(c) rural and urban subsystems were each represented by two schools in the study; a third semi-urban subsystem was represented by one school;
(d) the selection also had representation for all-female, all-male and coeducational schools;
(e) one school was included to represent the Federal school system.

Activities for the case studies were planned to include interviews with key members of staff and with students, observation of classroom activities, collection and examination of documentary evidence from official school records and assessment of the general atmosphere in the school. These seven schools were also among a wider target group of 14 schools to which questionnaires had been administered just before the case studies took place. It was hoped that the interviews would get the views of different key actors in order to gain perceptions from different points of view.

Classroom observation was undertaken to see the innovation in action. This additionally gave access to samples of student work. The level of facilities available could also be established.

The approach at this level of enquiry became eclectic. An illuminative approach was used for investigating school environments and antecedents. Taba's (1962) objective evaluation model was applied to the examination of the curriculum and its operation in the classrooms. The analysis of curriculum materials was based on the Sussex model (Eraut 1975) while the strategy for classroom observation was adapted from Walker and Adelman (1975) and Delamont (1976).

The level of implementation of the innovation in all the schools studied in May 1985 was still inadequate to support detailed analysis. I therefore had to return the following session to repeat the investigation, with the hope that there would then be an innovation to study!

The third case study research period took place throughout the month of January 1986. This time the number of schools was reduced to three – two boys' schools and one coeducational; one school from the Enugu urban centre and the other two from rural areas. The same strategy of interviews, documentary analysis and classroom observation was used.

Questionnaires

Pre-tested questionnaires were used to provide complementary data to that collected from the interviews and case studies. Over 500 were returned from a sample of final year JSS students in 14 different schools (response rate 94 per cent), more than 150 from teachers in those schools (response rate 85 per cent), and from 150 parents randomly selected (response rate 60 per cent). They are not discussed further here since this chapter predominantly uses data from other sources. (For a fuller discussion see Nwakoby 1987.)

Documents

Documentary materials from the Ministry of Education and other educational establishments in Anambra State were accumulated and analysed. Intensive library work was undertaken to review relevant materials. Newspaper reports provided a very useful secondary source of information, representing public opinion about the innovation.

THE CONCEPTUALISATION OF THE JSS VOCATIONALISED CURRICULUM

> It is amazing that the thing has been running for two years and it is only in this second year that I am beginning to understand it. Now the emphasis is to orientate the child to be able to use his hands to help himself, be able to understand the machines that surround him in his world. We had wrongly thought initially that the emphasis was on acquisition of employable skills.
> (Chief Inspector of Schools (Secondary), Interview: October 1984)

This quotation dates from early in the third year of the JSS. The Chief Inspector of Schools (CIS) vividly presents the doubts and difficulties that were being experienced in getting the concepts of JSS clear at the highest echelon of the implementation subsystem two years after the programme was supposed to have started. The evidence presented here shows how far the ideas and assumptions of the national policy on education (NPE) appear to have been clearly understood and correctly interpreted at different levels. The analysis is undertaken at the Federal, State and school level.

Conceptualisation at the Federal System Level

The NPE made the following provision in its section on JSS:

> The Junior Secondary School will be both pre-vocational and academic; it will . . . teach all the basic subjects that will enable pupils to acquire further knowledge and develop skills . . . (Federal Republic of Nigeria 1981:17)

This specification seems clear enough in establishing the nature and purpose of the new curriculum. However the Joint Consultative Council (JCC) Reference Committee on Secondary Education had long held a different view and stated the aims of the new curriculum in a report in 1978 as follows:

> The aim is to make him/her achieve some level of competence in the chosen vocation that will make him immediately employable at the end of the years of JSS education.

This position seems in direct contradiction to the 1981 NPE position. It may be that the definition of objectives was still being evolved in 1978. The view in the *Blueprint for Implementation* suggests this when it insists that:

> students at JSS level cannot be expected to acquire skills with which they can immediately find a job. Instead they would at this level build up a wide base of vocational understanding and knowledge from which they can later on select a more specialised direction. (Federal Republic of Nigeria 1979:77)

The seeds of some confusion seem to have been sown early on in the development of the policy.

In May 1983 a national workshop on Introductory Technology was organised by the Implementation Committee for Technical Teachers in Lagos. The Chairman of the Implementation Committee, the Honourable Minister of Education, and the Director of Planning in the Federal Ministry of Education each addressed the workshop and each restated the aims and objectives of the new curriculum. Their interpretations confirmed the specifications as outlined in the NPE and the *Blueprint*. Nothing could be clearer than the statements of these officials in the highest decision-making level at the FMOE that the curriculum would be pre-vocational in character.

Yet the Presidential Assistant was reported in December 1982, three months after the JSS started, to have told a meeting of secondary school principals from all states of Nigeria, in Yola that 'the new system would reduce unemployment problems among secondary school leavers'. Again, in February 1985 the then Federal Minister of Education was reported to have told newsmen in Lagos that: 'the essence of the new system was to prepare students who might not be able to go beyond the JSS level to be able to take gainful employment or proceed to technical colleges' (*Punch*, 14 February 1985).

From evidence so far presented it would seem that those who had interacted closely with planning and policy formulation at the FMOE Headquarters had reached a consensus about the pre-vocational, non-employment orientation of the new curriculum, while the political appointees, who were not at all involved in the policy formulation, had tended to focus on the employable skills.

What emerges from this analysis is the confusion in specifications and interpretations at the Federal level, a tendency not uncharacteristic of similar attempts at vocationalisation elsewhere, as the literature has shown. (See, for example: Bacchus 1980; Blaug 1973; Dodd 1969; Foster 1965; Lillis and Hogan 1983.)

Conceptualisation at State Subsystem Level

Evidence of the earliest attempts to conceptualise the vocationalised curriculum at State level is contained in the *Report of the Committee of Implementation of the NPE in Anambra State with Respect to Technical Education in the JSS System*. The Committee adopted the recommendation of the *Blueprint* on 'Technology in Secondary Schools' (Federal Republic of Nigeria 1979) that a syllabus for an integrated subject, 'introductory technology', should be devised and taught as part of the JSS curriculum. The orientation in the Committee's recommendation is pre-vocational. The report acknowledged the influence of colleagues who had been very closely involved at national level with the drawing up of the new curriculum. It is not a surprise therefore that the specifications of this Committee are as clear as those of officials of the FMOE.

During the fieldwork in October and November 1984 I sought through interviews to find out what different actors at various levels of the education system in Anambra State saw as the purpose of the JSS curriculum. The most senior Chief Inspector of Education (CIE) in charge of Secondary Division, who also co-ordinated the work of all other divisions for the MOE, told me that the idea of the JSS system is 'not for training in a particular vocation but to get ideas about skills needed'. The Chief Registrar (CR) in charge of the Exam Development Centre (EDC) supported this view.

On the other hand the Permanent Secretary in Anambra confidently claimed that:

> the three years will equip them to make a living after leaving school. The graduates of JSS can't be called drop-outs because they have been prepared for being useful even after three years.

A basic conceptual problem seemed to be emerging. Despite the clarity in the definitions given at the Federal and State MOE levels there was evidence from the interviews undertaken for this study that staff not closely involved with the planning of the new vocationalisation policy developed differing views of its key features.

Two years after 'take off' the State Education Commission was still not certain what was expected of the schools. Five months before the end of the first cycle of the JSS system the Commissioner for Education found it necessary to explain to principals of secondary schools what the new curriculum was supposed to be achieving, stressing its pre-vocational nature.

The most dramatic demonstration of the difficulty in conceptualisation comes from a biology school teacher I had interviewed in October 1984 at a girls' high school. She explained that the:

> purpose of the new system is to give those who can't carry on academically the chance to go out and find another means; perhaps to get a job and not waste time and money trying Class 5.

Then she turned to ask me:

> Will they be given a choice? That is, is the child to choose whether to remain or pass out, or is it the teacher who selects those to stay or leave? Some children will resist this. What is the prospect of getting jobs for them? What of equipment? Are they providing the equipment necessary for preparing them for jobs on leaving school? But will it work here when those well-qualified have not got jobs?

Through the interview, this teacher suddenly became aware of a whole range of implications arising from her conception of the JSS system. She had raised the kinds of questions and consequences which needed to be carefully considered before specifications could be deemed clear and well reasoned. Indeed the CIE (Sec) rightly assessed this conceptual problem in an interview in October 1984:

> The curriculum of introductory technology clearly sets out the required outcomes and tools needed. But the idea of local crafts as part of the whole package has not been well stated in the document, eg, the use of local craftsmen and knowing whether they exist ie, local crafts are dying out: basket making is being replaced by plastics.... Returns from basket making are not sufficiently attractive to be an incentive for people to pursue them for remuneration.... Learning has to take into consideration the relevance of what is being taught to actual needs ... There wasn't any real study of local needs. Only national conferences that decided on national needs for technical and vocational education. ... The curriculum was drawn up before people started thinking of the problems they would be facing.... It is at this stage of the implementation that problems are being thought of.
>
> (CIE (Sec) MOE, Enugu, October 1984)

It would seem that there had been a failure to develop interconnections between what was proposed as a curriculum and needs expressed through the aspirations of parents and pupils. Thus while the Chief Inspector could clearly see a relationship between the curriculum and what he thought offered viable job options and so an incentive for study, the school teacher could clearly perceive an antagonistic relationship between the new school system and the aspirations and options available to students. 'They will resist it' she had pointed out.

These two actors at different system levels of responsibility had been able to perceive implications of which the planners did not seem to have been fully aware in their curriculum specifications. The data here bear a direct relationship to the problems of curriculum design and how to match it against the aspirations of consumers; they also reflect the realities of the socio-economic world.

School-based Data on Conceptualisation

Two of the pre-vocational subjects were examined at school level in this research; business studies and introductory technology. An illustration from the introductory technology course will suffice to indicate some of the confusions of conceptualisation that arose at the school level.

The objectives of the introductory technology course can be summarised as follows:

(a) to provide pre-vocational orientation for further training in technology;
(b) to provide basic technological literacy for everyday living;
(c) to stimulate creativity.

During my school-based research I tried to explore student perceptions of the curricula they were following, to see how far these aims were being realised. Two contrasting perspectives emerged. In Udoka High School in Enugu students seemed to be grasping the inter-relationship between introductory technology, other subjects and the world of work. For instance, although all of those inter-viewed did not doubt that they would go into senior secondary school, most did argue on a hypothetical basis that they would become better craftsmen and be able to set up viable businesses on account of their experience in introductory technology. One student confidently assured me that he did not consider time spent on introductory technology as wasted. In fact he had found it helpful in applying knowledge gained from introductory technology to other subject areas in a practical way. Mathematics was cited as an example. Because they needed to design and measure everything they produced during their workshop sessions, he claimed that he was able to understand maths much better and considered introductory technology as an extension of the maths lesson.

In contrast students in Akwata High School, also in Enugu, did not see this relationship. When visiting the school I found the students in front of the workshop queuing up to pay their JSS exam fees. I asked several how they found doing practical work and they promptly told me that they had never done any practicals. 'But you have both equipment and workshop and must be using them', I insisted. They revealed that their first visit to the workshop was that morning and it was to register for the examination! The workshop is opposite the kitchen in front of which stood a water tank. The tank had a crack from which water flowed to waste. I asked why they could not have done something to repair the tank. They were very amused by my suggestion and told me that a welder or plumber could do it. When I pointed out that they learned these things in introductory technology and should be able to apply what they learned they insisted that it was a plumber's job and had nothing to do with them. Then they mischievously pointed at one boy whose father, they told me, was a plumber and could repair the tank. They were now teasing the boy who was very embarrassed and denied hotly that his father was a plumber.

Next, I asked how many of them owned the homemade cart children drive for fetching water called a 'borress'. Again there was a roar of laughter as they pointed at the same boy again saying that I should ask him to bring his to show me. They said he made it himself. Once more the boy denied it. It was clear to me that these boys had not been encouraged to acquire a positive attitude towards vocational skills promoted by introductory technology. They just had no understanding of what it meant, unlike boys in Udoka School. Among the boys in Akwata School there seemed to be little change in perception or attitude to manual work. The truth is that many of the boys in Akwata could in fact construct useful things they use around the home but could not see any relationship between what they thought of as the labourer's craft, 'ogwuaja' (digger of sand, that is a labourer) as they said to me, and school learning. But when I proposed the possibility of making some of these useful things during the introductory technology period and suggested something like a trolley for their grandmothers to help them pull their loads in the villages, they became interested. They made some discerning comments such as:

that they would require small wheels to fit the trolleys and these were not easy to get;

you need to search the mechanic's dumps for them;

one could ask the mechanics as a favour to reserve any they might get;

but some mechanics demand payment;

the wheels must run on tyres to avoid being caught in the sand as the village roads are not tarred and so one could not use wheels made out of cans as are used for the water cart.

With a little direction the Akwata boys began to demonstrate as much capability at effective problem solving as their colleagues at Udoka. The difference between the two schools is that while Udoka School had had two teachers, both graduates in Industrial Technology, and had access to workshop practice, Akwata School had a teacher who was a science graduate who never organised any practical work. Most teachers in the State schools have similar backgrounds to the teachers in Akwata School. For them the syllabus has not provided sufficient guidance in order to enable them to interpret the concepts of introductory technology effectively and be able to convey them to their students.

Emergent Conceptual Issues

The main issue that emerged from this analysis was the lack of coherence in conceptualising the new JSS curriculum. All data sources threw up evidence of different interpretations of the purpose and objectives of the JSS curriculum. Even as late as 1985 actors at all system levels were still grappling with the task of concept definition and specifications. A major conflict was posed by the contradictions implicit in the assumptions of the policy statements:

(a) that the JSS should be terminal for the majority of students and therefore –
(b) the curriculum should cater adequately for this group to prepare them for life outside school but at the same time –
(c) the curriculum should provide a general education with basic pre-vocational orientation.

The issue of clarity and logic in solution definition, specification and choice became problematic as a gap was created between the need to provide full vocational as well as pre-vocational training under general education. The evidence demonstrates the difficulties in bridging this gap in logically conceptualising real needs against what are feasible, thus replicating similar problems found in other studies (for example, Lillis and Hogan 1980, Lewin 1981).

CURRICULUM IMPLEMENTATION DATA: DISSEMINATION AND COMMUNICATION ACTIVITIES

This section explores data on dissemination and communication at the Federal and State levels.

Communication at Federal Level

'Do we have anything from the Federal Ministry of Education (FMOE) on the innovation?'
'No, nothing special.'
'No literature.'

'We stumble on facts by reading what people say in general.'
'I have not heard of JSS till now, only 6–3–3–4 system.'
'The Inspectorate Office here is not put in the picture.'
(Inspectors of the FMOE, Zonal Inspectorate Office, Enugu,
November 1984)

These quotes are excerpts from my group interview with the Inspectors of the Zonal Inspectorate Office of the FMOE in Enugu in November 1984, showing their reactions to my request for any information or materials they might have on the innovation. The interviewees had included the Chief Federal Inspector in charge of the office and three Assistant Chief Federal Inspectors.

I tried to probe these surprising answers by insisting that their responsibilities as inspectors must surely include managing the implementation of the innovation in their area of operation. Their specific assignment, they assured me, involved only 'monitoring the quality of education, ie, to see that every school maintains minimum standards'. I went on further to establish in what ways, if any, they had been involved in the innovation. They claimed that they were in no way involved, not even in conferences, seminars or anything concerning the innovation. When I asked how delegates to conferences were selected they said it was all handled by Administration at the Headquarters in Lagos. 'How much interaction is there between the Inspectorate Office and the two Federal colleges in Enugu and Onitsha?' I asked, and was further surprised to hear that there was none whatsoever, an assertion later confirmed by the Vice-Principal of the Federal Government College in Enugu.

This was strong evidence that there was hardly any communication between the various departments of the FMOE organisation. It appeared that the organisational structure of the FMOE had helped to aggravate the situation. An organisational chart showed a typical bureaucratic structure divided up into several vertical departments that seemed to function independently, only bound by their common allegiances to one chief executive at the peak. Communication flowed along the vertical columns from top downwards. There were no horizontal information flows and therefore no interdepartmental communication. There was thus a communication gap between the Inspectorate Division of the FMOE and the Division for Schools and Educational Services.

The mode of operation of the Implementation Committee further helped to create a gap in communication. It was a body set up

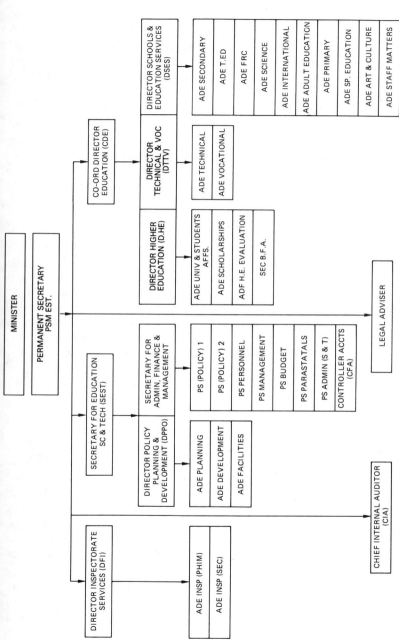

FIGURE 8.2 *Nigerian Federal Ministry of Education: organisational chart*

especially to manage the implementation of the NPE. But it would seem from the calendar of programme implementation, that its concern was only for teachers and schools and resources (Federal Republic of Nigeria 1979). Communication was left out entirely from the plan, which made no provision for general enlightenment about the innovation.

The communication gap at the Federal system level extended to its dealings with the states, thus demonstrating not only an intra-system inadequacy in information flow but also an inter-system gap. An incident amounting to a 'diplomatic' *faux pas* will illustrate better the extent of the communication hiatus between States and the FMOE. In 1983, the Implementation Committee had organised a workshop for teachers of introductory technology using the model workshop at the FGC, Enugu. The Minister of State in the FMOE and the Secretary of the Implementation Committee had been involved in the workshop. It was only from press reports of the workshop that the CIE (Coordinating), and the Permanent Secretary and Commissioner for Education in the Anambra State MOE, Enugu, got to know about the workshop. A protest letter was despatched from MOE Enugu to Lagos against what was regarded as a grave insult.

At the Federal level, then, available evidence of awareness creation showed a high degree of tendency to intra/inter-system fragmentation through a lack of an articulated policy to facilitate information flow to ensure effective participation at all levels.

Communication at State Level

The CIE (Sec), summarising communications within the MOE, perceived the crux of the problem to be system breakdown due to fragmentation and compartmentalisation: what he called a lack of 'systematic plan', that is, no system, no integrated action to facilitate information flow. While he deplored the effect of decentralisation on communication and internal cohesion within the MOE, on the other hand the four Zonal Inspectors (ZIEs) interviewed all regretted the difficulty they encountered in getting headquarters in Enugu to give heed to their opinions when making decisions about various implementation activities.

There was a feeling among the ZIEs that power was being concentrated in the office of the co-ordinating CIE in Enugu in a manner that impinged on what they perceived as their logical functional boundaries. The most common complaint of the ZIEs was that instructions were issued from Enugu demanding that they carry out programmes that were not feasible because those at Enugu had not bothered to study information available from the zones in order to reach more realistic decisions about implementing the innovation. For example, if reports from the zones had been taken into account regarding the situations in the schools, headquarters would not have insisted on imposing the JSS examination in June 1985. Efforts to send up information from the bases in the zones were thwarted and side-stepped, thus causing a blockage in the information flow.

The CIE himself provided evidence to support this claim from the ZIEs that their functions were being usurped by the centre. I found him sitting encircled by the mound of files around his table with his head just peeping out above the files – and he is among the tallest men in the Ministry. He had even had to provide extra tables to create more space for his files.

Noticing the amazed look on my face as I contemplated the daunting pile of files this particular morning, he tried to explain in exasperation that nobody else ever wanted to work any more in the Ministry: everything got pushed to him. The files had been dumped while he had been away to an NCE meeting. As he spoke one of the drivers came in with an application from an inspector seeking the CIE's approval for transport. This was surprising because the organisational structure in the Ministry did provide for a transport unit under the administration division.

It would seem that the role and responsibilities of a co-ordinating Chief Inspector in the Ministry had not been sufficiently differentiated to enable inspectors to understand more clearly what was expected of them. Even the CIE himself did not seem quite so certain about what his responsibilities were from his complaint against the inspectors and from the way he had angrily sent the driver away.

One consequence of this inadequacy in infrastructural configuration is that bottlenecks develop in the communication flow. Inspectors have to wait for unduly long periods before decisions are communicated to them; meanwhile vital information cannot be circulated to the grassroots as the files may be at the bottom of the pile, or the CIE may have to be away for another meeting. At a time when the CIE was ill, an inspector wondered how the MOE could cope without him 'for he is the only officer in the Ministry with up-to-date information about what is happening in the Ministry. He knows everything about every section of the Ministry' – a remark significant for this analysis of communication flows.

Emergent Issues from the Communication Data

Four major problems are thrown up by the data on communication strategies and these are:

Late start and poor maintenance
It was revealed that activities to generate awareness for the new curriculum actually did not start until implementation was well on its way. The earliest effort from the Federal level to inform teachers, by means of a national orientation workshop, was made in exactly the month, September 1982, that the innovation was supposed to come into effect. Nothing else was done till a year later, when a one-day State-run workshop was held for senior and middle management, and this was for just one subject area: introductory technology. In 1985 a similar workshop for teachers was held. Such efforts had been sporadic – they had not been sustained, and as a result it was difficult to expect those involved to remember the information that they had been given. The long distances and cost discouraged States from participating fully in federally-organised activities. The States for their part made very few efforts to provide any inservice training.

Poor integration
This factor has two aspects: a low inter-system information flow among actors in different subsystems; and a low inter-system information flow between subject disciplines.

The research strengthens the view that whatever communication was initiated from official quarters flowed within bureaucratic functional boundaries. The organisational structure was of the 'Greek temple' variety, encouraging information flows from the top down. Thus at Federal level, the Federal Inspectorate Division was isolated from the activities of the Implementation Committee and of other Divisions. The Federal Government College in Enugu remained an island by itself refusing to interact with the Federal Inspectorate as well as with State schools. At State level Inspectors also experienced difficulty within the MOE organisation of directing information from the base upwards. Involvement of the schools and the teacher training institutions was minimal as shown from very low levels of participation at conferences or workshops.

The second problem of inter-system integration was that most efforts initiated by the MOE gave pride of place to introductory technology, almost in total exclusion of other subject disciplines. No attempt was made to place introductory technology in relation to other subjects. Officials, and subsequently teachers, failed to demonstrate the relevance of an integrated approach to learning. The result was that school learning was organised without the benefit of experiences that could have been drawn from other subject areas in order to enrich the learning process.

Inadequate exploitation of the media
Key people interviewed pointed out this deficiency. The planners and implementers should have used the media for effective communication but had failed to do so. From parents particularly I heard that little effort was made to communicate officially with the public. Information that did get out was at the initiative of the various news media particularly the radio and television. Even parents in the rural areas had heard the news from radio. This shows the immense potential of the media which must be tapped and incorporated in official strategy to generate awareness.

Parent teacher associations, town unions and the community
In spite of the impression created by the MOE that these were dispensable and could be taken for granted, evidence in this study demonstrated the contrary. These bodies were very much involved in implementation activities yet they were amongst the least informed about the innovation. Similarly, employers were not approached with information, although they were bound to be affected by the changes in curriculum.

CASE STUDIES OF THE CURRICULUM IN ACTION

Phase 1

In late 1984, two years after take-off, there was no evidence of the innovation in schools in Enugu, and very little awareness about it. The old secondary syllabus was still being taught since there was nothing new to replace it. The general position was vividly captured in the reaction of school principals at their meeting with MOE officials in November 1984. They had listened with disbelief as the Commissioner for Education informed them that they had to prepare their Class 3 students for the examination in the following year.

Phase 2

By April 1985 there were noticeable signs of implementation. Teachers for pre-vocational subjects were deployed in schools between January and April. Most of these had either BSc, HND or OND qualifications in engineering, architecture, survey or allied subjects. Almost all, however, lacked pedagogical training. All five educational zones had had a one-day induction course for the new recruits. The case study schools with equipment were still not using it owing to a range of reasons that included lack of skilled teachers, funds and workshops. In five out of the six State schools studied during this phase, the equipment was still in its cartons either in the general store or in the principal's office. In several instances teachers who were supposed to be teaching the subjects were not aware of the existence of the equipment. The Federal school was obviously different, having two professionally trained teachers in Industrial Technology and being the proud owner of one of the three model introductory technology Workshops provided by the contractors in 1983. But they, like the Anambra State schools, had only obtained the syllabuses between December 1984 and February 1985. Textbooks were still not available and the classrooms were completely devoid of any audiovisual aids except for the chalk and blackboard.

Given the inadequacy of teaching aids, including books, it is no wonder that the teaching method resorted to proved to be rote learning. The method was geared towards increasing student efficiency in recall. There was no involvement whatever in any of the classes observed to encourage any effort in analysis and synthesis; there was no evidence of discussion or discovery or experimental approaches to the learning situation. In no class did I hear any cross-references to other subject areas to bring together related concepts.

The highlight of this period was a technical drawing lesson I observed at Adaugo School, where for the first time, I saw students actually react with interest and enthusiasm to the lesson. The teacher later explained that it was their first lesson ever on technical drawing and they had been thrilled because they were able to get their measurements and designs right. The students later assured me that they were confident of passing their examinations which were barely 12 days away from the date of this encounter on 20 May 1985.

Phase 3

In January 1986 I spent one full week in each of three schools,

(Akwata High School, Hillside School and Central School), for the third phase of the case study work. The main purpose of this period was to find out what was happening to the innovation in the classrooms. I shall therefore summarise the general situations in schools at the time, before I examine evidence from the classroom observation.

Some slight improvements were observed in some aspects such as the workshop provision. Central School already had completed its workshop conversion and had had the equipment installed. Hillside School was on the verge of completion but equipment was brought into class for lessons. Akwata School had a finished workshop but it was not in use as yet. The local zonal committee was busily engaged in various innovation activities, including the collaborative drawing up of schemes of work in various subjects. Some publishers had brought out textbooks in the new subjects such as introductory technology, business studies and social studies.

Teacher Readiness

Perhaps the progress with implementation can be typified by the concerns expressed by members of staff at Hillside School. I attended an interesting discussion about the development of teaching aids, which indicated possible improvement in this area. During a staff meeting the principal reported to his staff that teachers were now going to be assessed for promotion on their performance as observed by SEC supervisors. They would be judged on their overall application to work, including the use of teaching aids. This led to a full discussion on teaching aids, notes of lessons and schemes of work, matters that seemed to bother many of the teachers who were new and untrained.

The teachers were not familiar with audiovisual aids or how to use them, and showed little capability for improvisation. Another problem was the lack of funds to provide the necessary materials for producing aids, and the principal seemed unwilling to commit himself to the necessary expenditure.

The teachers also raised questions about how much they should include in the notes of lessons and how much of the syllabus they should cover in the scheme of work because some of the subjects were too wide to be effectively covered. To this the principal answered:

You are not expected to finish the syllabus. You draw the scheme on what you feel you can complete under normal circumstances –

enough to keep teacher and students very busy during the school term.

In this brief meeting it was clear that the teachers realised their weaknesses and were willing to find ways of improving. This can be seen as commitment, but cynics may suggest that it is because they had been threatened with assessment from the SEC on which their promotion was said to depend. Overall, this staff meeting discussion did not give the impression that the teachers possessed the level of competence which the innovation anticipated. I shall now turn to see how the teachers' skills were displayed in the classroom.

Evidence on the curriculum in action at the classroom level was acquired from two main data sources: written curriculum materials, including schemes of work, lesson notes and textbooks, and interviewing about and observation of the classroom transactions.

Curriculum Materials

Schemes of work and notes for lessons represented the teachers' working documents for implementing the innovation. They provided indications of the extent to which teachers had been able to assume direct responsibility for converting the 'given' curriculum and localising it in the form of schemes and notes of lessons for application to their specific context. These materials thus indicated the degree of initiative teachers had taken, and how they conceived the innovation.

I was able to study closely schemes of work and lesson notes prepared by teachers at the three schools in two subject areas: business studies and introductory technology. All the schemes without exception displayed a dogged lockstep adherence to what had been outlined in the textbooks and syllabuses. In none of the materials examined in the three schools was there any significant attempt to try to localise the lessons in order to relate them to the experiences drawn from the immediate environment. Teachers' notes did not seem to provide evidence of their ability to apply themselves creatively to adapting the innovation.

The sample schemes and notes used did not go beyond recall of what was in the book. Using Bloom's (1956) classification, analysis showed that the teachers were not aiming above the comprehension level of learning, whereby the students summarised and used their own words to recall what they had read. The teachers rarely if at all planned lessons that involved application, analysis and synthesis. In addition they failed generally in their schemes and notes to provide for practical activities that would enable students to develop the relevant affective and psychomotor skills.

Where notes from Central School included teaching aids, the only ones mentioned were the blackboard, chalk and diagram; the three-dimensional aids that had been supplied in the form of introductory technology equipment were left out completely. In general, their preparation showed no attempt to take the lessons beyond the classroom by exposing students to learning experiences that lie in the environment outside.

Direct personal experiences at Akwata School during my January 1986 visit supported these observations. Road construction work was going on right outside the school gate using all kinds of machines. Students had shown great interest and even missed lessons to watch the bulldozers and diggers, whereupon the principal arrested some of them for truancy. When I later asked both the introductory technology teacher and some other students what opportunities they had had for making contact with the road builders for their lessons the answer was 'none'. My reaction was 'What a colossal waste of opportunity'.

In the same school, such opportunities were also wasted in other subject areas such as business studies. A student's shop was doing brisk business and a mobile bank service drove in during break. The shop was run by an outsider, not by the students themselves, and neither the operations of this shop nor of the bank had been considered for inclusion in the teaching strategy for business studies, where topics included retail trading and banking.

Classroom Transactions

In observing transactions in the classroom the following issues provided the main focus:

(a) how well the teachers were able to design and organise classroom experiences that reflected the integrated nature of the new curriculum;

(b) to what extent teachers effectively managed lessons to communicate with and involve students;

(c) to what extent teachers adopted problem-oriented approaches to the organisation of learning which would stimulate active enquiry, initiative and experimentation in the learners.

Evidence of integration
I shall start by examining evidence of an integrated approach to
learning design. It was intended in the new curriculum that
integrative relationships be developed at three levels: intra-subject
inter-subject; and school – society. What evidence is available, for
instance, that lessons in business studies were shown to be clearly a
part of previous topics/units of the subject and could be further
developed if considered alongside other subject areas and linked to
what happens outside the school?

The evidence from my observations shows that every lesson in each
school started with a revision of a previous lesson or test. However
such revisions stood as separate activities complete in themselves
aimed at ensuring students could recall facts; they were not used to
establish relationships between past and future lessons.

In none of the lessons was there any reference to topics in other
subject areas. The topic Transportation, which I saw taught in a
business studies lesson in Akwata School, is actually also included in
social studies, but throughout there was no mention of this fact either
by the teacher or the students. Similarly, social studies has a topic on
technology as part of economic development, but this was not
recognised by either introductory technology or business studies
This disjointed approach would explain why students, according to a
teacher at Central School, found it difficult to understand why
questions which they perceive as belonging to a particular subject are
asked in a different subject altogether. They have been ill-equipped
to make such knowledge transfers. The teachers themselves seem
largely unable to demonstrate the value of this.

Evidence has been already cited above to show how teachers failed to
link lessons to activities going on in the world around the classroom
As a result of this gap in perceiving linkages and devising procedures
for integration of concepts and topics in the learning process, the
achievement of the aims of secondary education as specified by NPE
(Federal Republic of Nigeria 1981) become problematic.

Management of communication flow in the classroom
The evidence demonstrates the nature and manner of communication
management in the classroom so as to show how far teachers and
students were involved in classroom dialogue.

In the lessons I observed, teachers tended to dominate the class activi
ties entirely. Students made only token gestures of following the lesson
None of the activities were initiated by the students. Figure 8.2

Social studies	0–10 minutes	10–20 minutes	20–30 minutes	30–40 minutes
Teacher's behaviour	Introduces lesson topic: Origin of Man Lists themes: myths, legends, religion, evolution	Tells story of Yoruba myths Tells of Chinese myth of origin of man	The scientific story of origin of man – evolution: Charles Darwin Igbo myth, Christian religious myth	Other religions and Igbo religious myths Calls for questions from students but without waiting asks instead 'Who is the Champion of Evolution' 'That's right.' As he leaves class asks prefect to come and arrange for the notes to be copied
Student behaviour	Listening No writing Small hums of agreement with what teacher is saying	Still listening Laughter at the sound of the name of the Chinese God Pau Ku	Still listening	Listening Two boys raise hands to ask question but the teacher asks instead. Students chorus 'Charles Darwin' to teacher's question. They say 'thank you' as teacher leaves

FIGURE 8.3 Lesson profile, Hillside School

shows a typical lesson profile, a social studies lesson seen at Hillside School. In this lesson, the students did not even make their own notes – that had to be arranged by the teacher, who had come late to class and so could not give the notes there.

During a business studies class at Akwata School the teacher actually discouraged students from writing anything on their own because she said she would give them notes later. At the appropriate time she said to them: 'Now sit up straight and take down the notes'.

There was very little evidence of initiative being exercised by the students, and even on the rare occasions when this happened, there was no encouragement from the teachers. In one example, at the end of the lesson the teacher called for questions from the students. Two boys actually raised their hands to ask but the teacher instead put in his own question and thus the students lost their chance.

No incidents of discussion ever featured in any of the lessons observed in the schools in three phases of the study, nor was there any interaction among students during the lessons. The only form of interaction occurred between (a) the teacher and the class as a whole when he was delivering the lesson, and (b) between the teacher and an individual student when he asked a question. Communication flowed mainly in one direction, top-down from teacher to class most of the time, and, very infrequently, from bottom-up from individual students back to the teacher in response to direct questions from the top. A horizontal communication flow was hardly ever observed during the lesson.

And yet this was contrary to what was observed in the absence of the teachers. Several times in different schools I had sat through periods with the students when the teachers had not turned up for the lessons. During such periods I had seen students consulting one another on assignments, borrowing notebooks, textbooks and various items of stationery. At Akwata School consultations centred on social studies and English assignments. A boy whose father worked for a travel agency had brought a map of the world transport system and this was enthusiastically consulted by many of the students. They had been given an assignment in social studies to draw some international air routes. The gap in inter-subject relationships was particularly emphasised for me because the next lesson was business studies and the topic that day was 'Transportation'. No mention was made of the social studies assignment and it struck me that the students had not bothered to identify this linkage.

This and other similar incidents showed me that in the teachers' absence students tended to band together and help each other out:

here was a good deal of peer support and free flow of information. It was difficult to establish any instance during classroom activities conducted in the teacher's presence that exploited this informal relationship among students to advance the learning process. The only time something different was observed was in an introductory technology lesson at Akwata School. Students obviously considered the lesson a waste of time, so they engaged in other activities like noise-making and doing assignments in other subjects. t was only when a new topic was introduced towards the end of the period that the class became quiet and attentive but this did not last as the teacher had exceeded his period and the students were not prepared to let him get away with it. It was noticeable that on at least four different occasions students actually took the initiative to ask a question, offer an example or in fact to terminate the lesson by calling out pointedly for submission of an assignment. An explanation for this might be found in the teacher's style. He seemed to have built up an easy kind of relationship with the students in which they could openly show their opposition to the progress of the lesson.

The only conclusion from the evidence before us is that most teachers had yet to acquire the capabilities required by the curriculum innovation to organise classroom interaction in such a way that there was full and meaningful participation by most students. There were no opportunities provided in the lessons I observed for learners to develop their powers of expression, thinking for themselves, and confrontation with other people's views, as contained in the innovation's specifications.

Approaches to learning

The next section explores the data which showed how far teachers presented learning experiences to stimulate originality in tackling problems, seeking alternative solutions and in improvising resources. Evidence has been difficult to find because most teachers concentrated on giving out the 'facts' of the subjects as they were found in the syllabus, scheme of work, and the textbooks. There were no examples of creativity on the teachers' parts in designing and organising the lessons. None of the teachers observed in these schools seemed to aim higher for their students than the level of simple knowledge mastery; rarely did they advance into the level of comprehension.

The teachers' questioning techniques showed this clearly. Excerpts from business studies lessons from Akwata and Central Schools will be used to illustrate the level of competence existing in the classroom in this regard. They show the following characteristics:

(a) the concentration on the part of the teachers on getting out the facts of the lessons;
(b) lack of any attempt to develop or follow up the facts when they have been given, even if students, from their reaction or often non response, would seem to demand a follow-up;
(c) the frequently stilted language in use which would seem to be the consequence of trying to 'give back' the facts as they have been taught, and as seemed to be demanded by the teachers' questioning mode;
(d) questioning mainly at the level of recall; there is no instance of probing to raise the level of the learning process to application, analysis, synthesis and evaluation of the knowledge learned.

Extract 1: the importance of transport
   Teacher: Transportation is important to the world of business. Do you agree with me?
   Class: Yes.
   Student 1:   For example, a businessman can't carry all his good off head.
   Teacher: (*correcting*) On his head.
   (*Class laughs at the mistake*)
   Teacher: (*writes on blackboard*)
      'Importance of Transport in Business'
      1. Helps to distribute products to customers – goods and services.
      2. Helps in location of industry eg, Nkalagu.
      3. Encourages specialisation and division of labour.
      4. Encourages large scale production.
      5. Raises, improves standard of living, by making available to consumers different products from different places.
      6. Helps and affects choice of location of office to make it accessible.

   Now will someone give me back these last three points mentioned.
   Student 2:   (*answers from the front*)
   Teacher asks a boy at the back to repeat. He has not heard. So Teacher makes Student 2 repeat his answer and gets the boy at the back to say it. Two other boys give the remaining two points.
   Teacher then asks class to sit up and take notes.
          (From class observation notes at Akwata School, 9.1.86)

In this example, after making a good start the teacher failed to seize the opportunity to prod the students into actually providing insights into the importance of transportation in business. Rather she was more eager to give them her own 'correct' version of the list which she wrote down on the board and promptly demanded that they 'give her back'. Satisfied after getting the 'correct' answers which the students had read from the blackboard, she then went on to give more detailed notes to be copied. The points were not discussed. The students seemed to know what to do: memorise the list and give it back. It is significant that this was the same group of boys who had been more responsive in the introductory technology lesson mentioned above. This bears out my argument that students tended to take their cues from the teachers once they were able to assess the teachers' style and demands.

Extract 2: home trade: the retailer
Teacher: A retailer buys from wholesaler and makes small profit. He breaks the goods into small quantities and makes them available to the consumer. Who is the retailer?
Student 3:   A retailer is one who buys in small quantity.
Teacher: What are the functions of the retailer?
(*No response*)
Teacher: (*writes on blackboard*)
The retailer provides:
1. The link between the wholesaler and the final consumer.
2. Makes goods available to consumers.
3. Studies the needs of the consumer and informs wholesaler.
4. Gives credit to consumers.
5. Saves people trouble and expense of looking beyond the locality.
How do you save time and money by buying from close range?
(*No response*)
Teacher: People don't have to travel long distances to buy. Remember that the retailer is operating at home. Who can tell me the special features of the retailer's operation?
(*No response*)
Teacher: (*enumerates and writes on blackboard*)
1. No language problems.
2. There is common currency.
3. Retailer operates under the same laws as his customers.
Before you take down the notes let me give you some more questions.

Who can tell me the nature of our markets? What form do our markets take?

Student 4: Shops.

Student 5: Open market.

Teacher: Who is a retailer?

Student 6: A retailer is a tradesman who buys in small quantities from wholesaler and sells to consumer.

Teacher: (*correcting*) 'Trader'.

Student 7: (*also attempting to correct*) 'Businessman'.

Teacher: Who can tell me one function of a retailer?

Student 7: To know the wants of the consumer.

Teacher: That's good. Another? Nathaniel?

Student 6: He renders local service.

Teacher: Good. Another one?

(*No response*)

Teacher: Now let us write them down so that you can remember them.

Student 8: How do you explain a market?

Teacher: That's a very good question. A market is where people come together for the purpose of buying and selling. I hope this is clear. When we include 'situation' it means any time when people arrange to buy and sell, eg, by phone.

Student 9: What about those people who carry their goods about to sell?

Teacher: They are called 'hawkers'. Any other questions? None. So it means you have understood the lesson. Now you can take down the notes.

(From researcher's notes during observation of Class 3B business studies lesson, 16.1.86 at Central School).

In this extract it is clear that the teacher's questions were all aimed at recalling the facts that had been given. Several times the questions did not receive any answers but the teacher proceeded regardless. Thus for example instead of a discussion of the functions of a retailer with the class, the teacher took the easy way out by simply ignoring the silence to his question and just writing out a list of functions for students to copy. When students did answer the questions they came as near as possible to the language used by the teacher, as is shown in the latter part of the extract.

Even when students raised questions the teacher failed to develop the problem by getting the students involved, as in identifying other 'situations' where buying and selling could take place. The example of the telephone is hardly applicable in a rural setting and would not be well understood. Also because of lack of development of the subject matter this teacher left out 'hawkers', an important group of retailers which many of these boys might join after school. Even when a boy pointed out the omission, the teacher did no more than give it cursory treatment, dismissing hawkers in one brief sentence. One other aspect of the classroom transaction that needs to be highlighted is the kind of language in use. The excerpts show something of the kind of notes given, the manner in which the teachers presented the 'facts' of the lesson, and how students were required to 'give back' the answers. The language in operation for most of the time was stilted 'jargon' culled from the teachers' lesson notes, put on the blackboard and then transferred into the students' notebooks after being recited by both teacher and students. There were few opportunities for students actually to attempt to put the information received into their own words: they were not challenged to try to interpret what they learnt so as to make it their own. How far the learner has then assimilated what he has learned becomes problematic.

LIMITATIONS OF METHODS

The very nature of the study presented certain constraints on the research methods. Some of the more important limitations which may have influenced the course, and possibly the outcomes, of the study will now be briefly discussed.

The Scope and Complexity of the Study

The scope of this research, of which only a small part is presented here, led to problems of management of diverse pieces of information derived from a wide range of sources. It was a considerable organisational task to keep track of information relevant to a particular problem and ensure that gaps had not been left. The logistic arrangements for interviewing and questionnaires required careful planning. The scope of the study was physically taxing for the researcher because of the sheer range and volume of activities that were generated.

Time Constraints

Constraints on time were felt particularly during the case study periods because of external pressures on the schools. These included a sudden massive retrenchment of teachers and the flurry of last-minute activities precipitated by the sudden realisation by schools that the JSS innovation would be publicly examined. Readjustments in scheduling had to be frequently made.

Finance

The cost of this study is yet to be reckoned but most of it including all the expenditure for the fieldwork which involved two separate visits to Nigeria and local transportation while there, has been borne personally by the researcher. This was a situation that was found exceedingly stressful.

Questionnaire Status

During the pre-testing and re-testing of the questionnaires, it was discovered that some types of questions were never well responded to. No specific reasons could be identified and it was not simply attributable to inappropriate phrasing. It may have been the result of unwillingness or suspicion. In the end, the design of the question-naires had to be much simplified. This is a phenomenon that calls for future investigation into the limit of questionnaire use in research studies in the Nigerian context.

Researcher Role Conflict

My role as a member of the State MOE subsystem in general proved most advantageous in gaining access and information, particularly within the MOE organisation. But there were occasions, especially during the school visits, when my status as a member of the MOE tended to be detrimental to the research. This perception of my role among the school heads and teachers threatened to distort informa-tion as they tried to treat me as an inspector, on 'inspection' duty, and would try to 'stage-manage' situations for my benefit. I therefore needed to play down my image as an 'inspector'. I assumed the less well-known identity of an officer from the CDC, highlighting its research and problem-solving role and also emphasising its status as an ally prepared to share the problems of the school.

SUMMARY OF FINDINGS ON THE JSS CURRICULUM INNOVATION ELEMENT

A general impression of overwhelming inadequacies has been created by the available data but before these are discussed there is a need to emphasise those areas of success or strength that have been identified. Otherwise one can find oneself so paralysed by the failures that one is tempted to abandon a potentially important innovation.

One such area of strength was the unanimity among various groups of actors in perceiving the innovation as 'a good thing', that a change was required: in other words there was a general agreement at all levels of the system to the effect that the old school curriculum had outlived its usefulness and needed to be replaced. This common perception of need for a change may help to explain the second strength of the innovation and this was the level of commitment observed in the adoption stage of implementation among actors at both Federal and State system levels. I found evidence that actors had planned and engaged in activities that committed them to implementation. So, in spite of immense difficulties, the first cycle of the innovation had proceeded to its conclusion.

Apart from this compelling need and commitment to change it has been difficult to locate any more strengths from the data. One can only conclude that the one most important positive tendency identifiable in the system was the persistence with which implementation was carried through. This was despite a full awareness of severe inadequacies in several crucial areas which suggests an awareness of considerable organisational pain, the cause of which may not necessarily be linked to the problems for which the JSS vocationalised curriculum innovation has been chosen as a solution. This therefore requires that more effort be made to give a more accurate diagnosis of the origin of the pain.

The rest of this section will concentrate on the gaps that have been identified. It should be borne in mind that the full significance of each issue raised may properly lie in the extent to which it is related to other issues that have emerged. The following are the major gaps that have been identified.

Inadequate Clarification of Concepts Manifested as:

(a) insufficient clarity in the identification and specification of problems for which the curriculum innovation has been chosen as a solution;
(b) insufficient clarity and emphasis in the specification of the basic concepts and assumptions which underlie the rationale for the innovation;
(c) insufficient specification of goals and objectives to guide appropriate curriculum design;
(d) inability of the curriculum as designed to reflect the concepts, goals and objectives as intended.

Inadequate Implementation Management Shown as:

(a) lack of provision for a communication policy;
(b) insufficient planning capability;
(c) inefficient resource management;
(d) inefficient curriculum implementation.

Inadequate Organisational Structures Shown as:

(a) ineffective deployment and co-ordination of existing organisational structures within the education systems at Federal and State system levels for implementing the innovation;
(b) insufficient capability in integrating available structures to achieve stronger cohesion within the school and also in establishing linkages between the school and society.

Inadequate Implementation at the Classroom Level Shown as:

(a) lack of change in teaching styles;
(b) lack of understanding of new aims and objectives;
(c) unwillingness to adapt materials;
(d) failure to use the local environment;
(e) inability to integrate curricula.

These findings corroborate the conclusions shown in the literature of curriculum innovations in other locations such as the studies by Havelock and Huberman (1977), Adams and Chen (1981), Lewin (1981) and Lillis and Hogan (1983).

The evidence in this chapter indicates the lack of an adequate conceptual and implementational capability for supporting a successful change process. The pieces of evidence have persistently manifested the absence of the basic elements of the systems concepts of interdependence, interaction and integration among system parts which are the essential characteristics of a high level of system completion and goal achievement. It has further been shown that a poor management capability was demonstrated in co-ordinating and facilitating effective linkages between system parts; a deficiency that tended to lead to system fragmentation and low coherence in the problem-solving process.

The viability of an innovation therefore in systems terms is the product of a process of communication which facilitates a continuous flow of dialogue at all phases of the innovation among all subsystem parts. This allows a 'negotiation of shared meanings' between planners and practitioners which occurs during debates on intentions, and also during the practice of implementation. The findings demonstrate the dynamic interdependence and integration of the procedures of the innovations problem-solving process and their limitations.

The implications of this for theories of the implementation of innovations have been developed in detail elsewhere (Nwakoby, 1987). The findings of this chapter provide the basis for reconsidering the adequacy of existing models. Any effort to secure a more satisfactory evolution of the curriculum innovation must take cognisance of the conceptual and management gaps which must be bridged in order to generate the level of infrastructural capabilities necessary to support effective and successful innovation.

9 The National Youth Service in the Seychelles

Ian G. Haffenden

INTRODUCTION

The research on which this chapter is based sought to evaluate the implementation of the Seychelles National Youth Service (NYS) during its first two years of operation – the duration of the first student cohort. The overall aims of the study were:

(a) to identify what, at the grassroots level, affects teachers' experiences of the change process and to monitor their responses to them;

(b) to assess the extent to which the National Youth Service of the Seychelles as a planned change was realised in practice.

Following an account of the research approach adopted this chapter will focus on just two areas of the study. Firstly, the national socio-historical context will be considered and the socio-political environment in which the NYS was planned and implemented: the NYS was to be an institution central to the curriculum reforms introduced by the Seychelles Government in the early 1980s. Secondly, the chapter will outline selected findings of the study in relation to the implementation of the NYS management structure and curriculum organisation and development.

The Research Approach

The research approach adopted in the study on which this chapter is based is that known as 'illuminative evaluation'. This approach draws on the methods described by Parlett and Hamilton (Parlett and Hamilton 1972) and focused on the change process as seen from the participants' perspectives. In particular, the study of the Seychelles National Youth Service was to identify the teachers' experiences of the implementation process and how these experiences came to affect their expectations and commitment to the new ideas and practices. As Berger states: 'Every human being knows his own world better

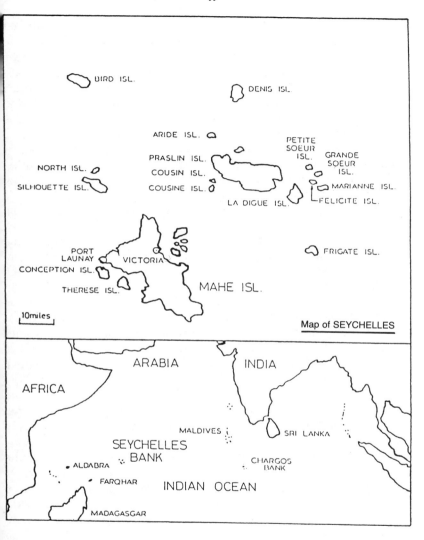

Map of SEYCHELLES

than any outsider (including the experts who make policy)' (Berger 1974:13).

Parlett and Hamilton describe four stages in a typical illuminative evaluation study. The first stage is concerned with the researcher negotiating entry into the field of study. In this study the fieldwork was undertaken during 1981 and 1982 when the researcher was a participant observer, spending 15 months in the field as a practitioner and participant in the change process. Moreover, permission to undertake the study was only sought after the researcher had taken up his post and established himself as a member of the teaching staff. He was thus recruited in a similar manner to other staff. Hence the data was collected and analysed by someone who was an 'insider' to the change process and accepted as such. This allowed the interpretation of key events 'in a manner that extends beyond the available documentary evidence' (Yin 1982:47). The field notes consequently reflected insights and feelings that were qualitatively and quantitatively different from those available to a researcher who was not intimately involved in the change process.

The second stage of the illuminative study is known as the exploratory stage. This stage was undertaken in the present study as a goal-free (Scriven 1972) exploration of issues and concerns that the participants held regarding the implementation of the NYS innovation. The information was initially conveyed to the researcher during his induction and socialisation process at the start of the fieldwork. During this stage a range of data was collected and recorded in the field notes. In addition to the collection of documentation, direct observation, interviews and the analysis of records and files, other data were also gathered to throw light on emerging areas of concern and to prepare the way for the third stage of the illuminative evaluation.

In particular, an understanding of the structure underpinning the social relationships between the students was identified as one area for some further exploration. It was important to understand this in order to comprehend the teacher–student classroom interactions. This led to recording and analysing, for example, the seating positions of students in a number of classrooms against their academic ability, previous school, NYS dormitory, age and region of the country from which they came. From the findings of this work, and that derived from a number of student sociomatrices constructed, it was possible to identify the key areas for more detailed analysis in stage three. To support this area of exploration two primary schools (one urban and one rural) were also visited for one day each and the teaching observed. This gave insight into the type of teacher–student relationships previously experienced by the students before entering the NYS.

The third stage of the illuminative evaluation study is known as the focused enquiry. Following the six months of open-ended exploration this stage of the research centred on the significant issues emerging from stage two. Here the researcher, whilst continuing the on-going participant observation, was to focus more specifically on:

(a) extensive classroom observations with a specially prepared observation schedule. This was to evaluate the extent to which the curriculum guidelines written by the teachers were subsequently implemented in the classrooms and the stated assessment procedures adopted;

(b) extended periods of observation and involvement with the students in their dormitories and during their leisure time. This enabled a clear understanding of the factors affecting their interpersonal relationships to be uncovered.

During the nine months of focused enquiry data was gathered from a range of sources – students, teachers, animateurs (youth organisers, or pastoral staff, in charge of dormitories, domestic affairs and extra-curricular activities), and co-ordinators – using a variety of means from note books and diaries (the researcher's and those written by students for the researcher), to formal, semi-structured and informal interviews, to extensive classroom observation using a specially designed schedule and a number of dormitory sociomatrices.

The final stage of illuminative evaluation is to analyse and report on the findings. In this study the major analysis was undertaken following the completion of the fieldwork. A grounded theory approach was adopted (Glaser and Strauss 1967) with the focus of the report and the research questions it addressed generated out of the analysis, although draft questions had been developed between the second and third stages of the fieldwork. This chapter will, however, be confined to reporting on the institutional organisation of the NYS and its effect on the curriculum development process. Firstly the study will be placed in its wider socio-historical context.

HISTORICAL AND CONTEMPORARY BACKGROUND

The Seychelles: The Socio-Historical Context

The social and economic development of the Seychelles islands was influenced in its relations with the outside world by three factors – location, size and resources (Kaplinsky 1980). Situated 990 miles from the nearest mainland coast of Kenya and between four and eleven degrees below the equator, the 115 small granitic and coraline islands have come to support a contemporary population of less than 65 000 (Foreign and Commonwealth Office 1986). The islands' isolation was to be an important factor in their slow development. During both the French (1756–1814) and British (1814–1976) colonial rule (and particularly during the latter) the Seychelles were considered economically insignificant and neglected. Interest was only taken in the islands when world affairs at large made their location significant. This occurred initially with the colonisation of East Africa and the Far East, which brought the first settlers from Mauritius to inhabit the islands in the 1770s, and again at the time of the Napoleonic wars, when the islands' colonial rulers were to change following the French defeat. Under British rule the Seychelles were to remain strategically significant until the opening of the Suez canal in the late nineteenth century. With its subsequent closure in 1967 and with the post-World War Two advent of 'airborne nuclear weapons' (Le Brun and Murray 1980) the islands have recently become once more of potential strategic significance. At all other times, however, the islands and their small population were virtually ignored by outsiders. In fact until the late 1960s the only regular link with the outside world was provided by a supply boat on the Mombasa–Bombay run, calling in at the islands once every six to seven weeks (Mancham 1983).

In 1971 the situation was to change with the completion of the Seychelles' first international airport. For the first time the Seychelles became accessible to visitors from all around the world. The massive investment that followed, promoting the Seychelles as a tourist paradise, further enabled some Seychellois (and foreign investors) to become prosperous at a time when many other countries were suffering the effects of world recession. The new-found prosperity was nevertheless to have far-reaching effects on the local economy, employment market and traditional culture. There was, for example, increased dependency on imported foods and luxury goods, while a twilight zone of prostitution and touts developed alongside the hotel industry. Moreover, following independence (in 1976) little was to change, with the new ruling party happy to maintain the status quo. Things were only to change for the Seychellois workforce when Albert René's socialist party took control by *coup d'état* in 1977.

Following a period of stabilisation, the new regime set about establishing a new system of government and supporting (social) administration. However, the new infrastructure alone was not sufficient to bring about changes in the basic attitudes and beliefs – the superstructure – of the society at large. After 200 years of colonialism and colonial-capitalism attitudes, values and beliefs were firmly implanted in the minds of the people and the structures of society. As René observed whilst practising law in the Seychelles (between 1957 and 1961), during colonial rule justice and equality were functions of power and wealth and both were restricted to the upper classes:

> [There were] three years during which . . . I mixed with every section of the population, from the labouring class to the so-called upper class. In those years I learned my lesson. First of all I learned that if you want to get on in Seychelles you had to belong to the upper class. Otherwise you were doomed to one of two things: either to remain in the middle class, which was what many people did, particularly civil servants, policemen, nurses, teachers, Cable and Wireless employees – these were kept on tenterhooks, so to speak, because for them it was a continued aspiration to climb up and become a member of the upper class . . . as we all know this never happened. The other alternative was to live as a member of the working class. I discovered that if you wanted to get on, you had to belong to the upper class. And you had to be careful with whom you mixed . . . I got into trouble for mixing with all three classes. I did so, however, because I had to find out what was going on in this country.   (Seychelles People's Progressive Front 1978:1)

The strength of the inbuilt attitudinal and normative class values amongst the influential, identified above, meant that the introduction of socialism would not be easy. It required changes in the Seychellois system of values at the most fundamental level. In particular, to eliminate the prevailing class system the economy would need to be reconstructed. This would take time during which contradictions would inevitably exist and be experienced by society at large. As such, long-term planning required the re-education and re-motivation of the people into a new system of values appropriate to the new regime.

However, the René Government's reform strategy did not specifically address attitudinal change. In fact in three very important ways the new regime mirrored that of the old and in doing so sustained the prevailing value system. Firstly, the nature of the political unity established during this period essentially replaced one small power élite with another – the 'grand blanc' and rich merchants of the old regime were replaced by the party hierarchy and its Central Executive Committee. Secondly, the continued maintenance of capitalism was to result from the government-sponsored parastatals, who were to operate on similar lines to private enterprise. Finally, the nation's continued economic dependency on tourism an 'oligopoly capitalism of a slightly different kind' (Lacey and Haffenden 1985:190) led to a social and economic context where:

> All the social inequalities and negative attitudes have not been eliminated. In the state of capitalism which prevails, during a period of transition, society reflects the beliefs and ways of the capitalist classes.   (*Nation*, 1 May 1982)

Accepting this, the new socialist government looked towards the education of the young to change attitudes and values for the future – the next generation:

> The education of the young is therefore the focus in the building up of socialism in the Seychelles. The new generation who leave Seychelles schools must be equipped with the ideology, professionalism, and moral and civic values prepared to leave their mark on the Revolution of 5th of June 1977 – the building of the socialist society.   (*Nation*, 1 May 1982)

Education was thus seen as playing a central role in the establishment and transmission of the new set of goals and values to the population. The existing education system was therefore to undergo major reform in the years following the socialist revolution. Central to these reforms was the creation of the National Youth Service (NYS).

Educational Reform

The NYS was set up to cater for all Seychellois 15 to 17 year-olds. It was further to stimulate changes in the primary education sector and to dictate a new standard and new expectations for the system of further education to follow it. In particular, it was to act as a test-bed for the development of ideas that would support the preparation of young adults for a developing socialist society. As claimed by Lacey, the NYS:

> was the result of one of the most fundamental reappraisals of the role of education in a modern state and ranks with the early experiments in Russian education, and Cuban education.
> (Lacey and Haffenden 1985:171)

Thus, while the NYS in concept was to share many of the characteristics of contemporary innovations of the time (Smawfield 1984) – attempting to link production and education and theory to practice – its scope was far wider. The NYS was to be instrumental in developing 'a new type of person' (Seychelles Government 1980) for a new and very different Seychelles society from that previously known. The skills, knowledge and values that the NYS was to transmit were not those prevalent in the society at large. The skills, knowledge and values were those needed to change that society and to build a new one.

Nevertheless, while the NYS was to form the focus for curriculum reform, the creation of a new, free, unified and national system of education for all Seychellois children was given first priority – a system that was both just and equally accessible to all. The introduction of the educational reforms took place in three phases. The objective was to replace the existing system, where:

(a) the primary provision had been non-compulsory and unavailable in many districts;
(b) the secondary sector was largely fee-paying and serving only the top 10 per cent of the population; those who could afford it (Le Brun and Murray 1980).

The Three Phases of Reform

Phase one
The first phase of the reforms was introduced between 1978 and 1983, and saw:

(a) The introduction of creche facilities to all districts, enabling mothers to work.
(b) The introduction of a common, free, compulsory system of primary education for all children between the ages of six and 15 years.
(c) A programme of construction which enabled a 'zoning' policy to be introduced such that primary education was localised in each district.
(d) To support this, an increase in the number of primary teachers by one-third in just three years.
(e) The introduction of Creole as the Seychelles national language (with English second and French third). This decision was followed by the introduction of adult Creole literacy classes and the

subsequent introduction of Creole, stepwise, into the first four years of primary education.

(f) The phasing out of the two secondary grammar schools over a period of four years (1980–83). This enabled the second phase of the educational reforms to be introduced.

Phase two

The second phase (initiated in 1981) saw the introduction of the National Youth Service (NYS). The NYS was set up by a newly created Department of Youth and Community Development. This Department was contained within the President's Office and was therefore able to be responsive to change and was not restricted by the existing bureaucracy of the Ministry of Education and Information, for example. The NYS was to become a two-year residential youth programme free and open to all 15 to 17 year-olds who had completed nine years of primary education. The NYS was both to educate and discipline the young – who were 'in need of direction' – as well as reduce the number of 15 to 17 year-olds seeking work (during the mid-1970s 45 per cent of the Seychelles population were below the age of 15). At the time it was reported: 'Unemployment is concentrated mainly in the 15–19 and to a lesser extent 20–24 age groups' (Seychelles Government 1978:7).

Further, the NYS was to act as a means through which a corps of young people would emerge qualified and motivated to support the new regime and work towards its goals. In short the NYS was: 'a two-year progressive educational programme especially designed for the Youth of the Seychelles as they step into adulthood' (Seychelles Government 1980:3). The NYS was thus central to the government's plans for enabling and maintaining its socialist transformation and as such was to act as a catalyst for socio-economic and socio-political change. Its programme was to be 'pre-figurative' of the 'new socialist society' and was to develop 'new forms of social relations' relevant to changing the economic organisation. In particular, it was to aim at stimulating a revival in agricultural production, to introduce co-operative practice, and the principles of 'self-reliance' (see Lacey and Haffenden 1985). Moreover, in the purpose-built residential youth villages (there were to be four in total by 1984) the youth of the Seychelles were to develop into 'a new type of person', a person who would be able to create 'new ways of doing things, which will serve as models for the country as a whole' (Seychelles Government 1980:4).

Phase three

The final phase of the educational reforms (started in 1983) was the creation of a Seychelles Polytechnic. This institution was to be open (through selection) to all NYS leavers and provide a range of academic and vocational courses. The Seychelles Polytechnic was set up and maintained within the Ministry of Education and Information. Thus the new system of education was unified. It offered nine years of free compulsory schooling to the age of 15 years followed by two years free and residential pre-vocational education at the NYS. Following the NYS those students able to benefit could continue vocationally orientated education at the Seychelles Polytechnic.

The NYS Development Context: from Conflict to Constraint

Of the three phases described above, it was the creation of the NYS with the abolition of the secondary grammar schools that generated the strongest opposition and resistance. In particular, those sections of the population whose power and influence had been displaced by the new regime were keen on reducing its impact and rate of planned change. These sections of the community, comprising the 'grand blanc' and 'bourgeoisie', were thus naturally opposed to changes in the secondary education system; a system to which their children had a privileged access. More specifically, their direct opposition to the government's plans to implement the NYS, in 1979, led to demonstrations and riots when an anti-government newspaper (legal at that time) published an article that claimed that the NYS would be compulsory, involve substantial periods of manual labour and be situated on the island of Coetivy – a small island some 130 miles from Mahé. As it was this information was not entirely false, as the National Development Plan of that year had stated:

> that as many as 1000 young people may be undertaking National Service at any one time. Because the emphasis of National Service is on production a considerable amount of equipment will be needed, and permanent camps will be established, one on Mahé and one on an outer island. It is envisaged that this scheme will be self-financing after one or two years, through construction works. (Seychelles Government 1979:132)

However, the intense conflict stimulated by the article was further fuelled by rumours, increased suspicion and anxious parents. Finally the concerns reached a climax with the students rampaging through the streets in opposition to the scheme.

The Government's response to the deteriorating situation was to attempt to prevent its escalation through reporting in the government newspaper – the *Nation* – that Coetivy had been bought by the government so as to allow 'parents and children or teachers and children to go camping on' (*Nation* 12 October 1979). However, this was not sufficient to stop the student rioting the following day and the government was forced into a further compromise which resulted in a declaration that:

> those who do not want to take part in it [the NYS] will be permitted to continue their secondary education without hindrance.
>
> (Seychelles Government 1980:2)

This promise stopped the rioting, but the effect of the student opposition was to delay the initiation of the NYS for a year. During this year the Government's policy on the innovation was fully reappraised with the reformulation drawing not only on the ideas and the experiences of other nations linked to the Party doctrine, but also on external professional advice from UNESCO.

The new policy for the NYS was based on research undertaken by UNESCO and grounded in the belief that only through the full participation of the students in every aspect of the organisation and running of the youth village could appropriate new forms of social relations be achieved. Additionally it was hoped that through careful co-ordination the national youth village would act as an exemplary model for the society at large (Le Brun and Murray 1980). In particular, the NYS would attempt to reunite work, daily life and education and develop a curriculum that sought to relate education to production and theory to practice.

Once formulated these ideas were piloted during the middle part of 1981. The pilot formed the first part of a nation-wide student recruitment campaign, which, carefully planned and implemented, turned the tide of opinion in favour of the Service. However, it resulted in some 60 per cent more student volunteers coming foward to join the NYS than had been expected. This additional student register was to create problems. The most pressing of these problems was the need to recruit extra teachers late in the day, along with the need to build more housing.

In the case of the former, the problem could only be overcome by the acceptance of teachers from a range of sources including many who had been initially recruited by the Ministry of Education and Information for the existing Seychelles secondary school sector. The effect of this was that the NYS was to open with a teacher register drawn from a range of different countries and personal backgrounds, each with widely differing levels of initial exposure, preparation and understanding of the NYS.

To summarise, the above sets out the historical and the contemporary background to the development of the Seychelles National Youth Service. The purpose has been to provide a clear understanding of the problems and constraints facing the René government's attempt to introduce the NYS as part of its development plan. The Service was set up to promote social justice and equality, and to reduce unemployment, whilst supplying the newly liberated nation with a trained manpower sympathetic to its national development goals. In short: (a) the Seychelles National Youth Service was – in the end – a carefully prepared and piloted innovation which sought to support planned national development of a radical and far-reaching nature; and (b) due to an unexpected swell in the student register, extra staff were required and recruited late in the day. This recruitment was, however, unsystematic and undertaken in a largely *ad hoc* manner leading to the heterogeneous body of staff differentially prepared for the task ahead.

THE IMPLEMENTATION OF THE NYS

Reuniting Work, Daily Life and Education

To fulfil the aim of reuniting work, daily life and education in the NYS a management structure would be required which brought together all categories of participant, both staff and students, in a structure that would enable each category to become actively involved in the implementation process. As stated in the government brochure: 'There will be a democratic structure of staff and students responsible for the day-to-day running of the youth village' (Seychelles Government 1980:12).

Clearly to facilitate this the relationship between different categories of staff and students would need to be co-operative and supportive. A set of relationships akin to Likert's 'principle of supportive relationships' was necessary where, for example:

The leadership and other processes of the organisation must be such as to ensure a maximum probability that in all interactions and all relationships with the organisation each member will, in the light of his background, values and experiences, view the experience as supportive and one which builds and maintains his sense of personal worth and importance.   (Likert 1961:103)

Yet, as identified by Smith and Keith:

The process of inventing new roles, the determination of their mutual relations and of structuring the field of rewards and sanctions so as to get maximum performance, have high costs in time, worry, conflict and temporary inefficiency.
(Smith and Keith 1971:148)

Not surprisingly the task of developing 'supportive relationships' in the NYS was to prove difficult. In particular, the heterogeneous, multi-national staff meant that learning of new roles would 'rely heavily on social relations among strangers' (Smith and Keith 1971:150), and in many cases strangers of a different culture and who spoke a different language. Moreover, without supportive relationships amongst the staff the development of a common set of expectations would prove difficult.

The importance of the staff's initial expectations lies in the fact that the NYS was to be developed empirically, allowing the staff to adapt it (and freely experiment) within a framework provided by the government brochure (Seychelles Government 1980). Thus the success of the NYS in its early days, would depend on both the staff's initial motivation and on their expectations. As stated in the guidelines:

The outline we present attempts to embody these values and the government's perspective on the NYS as the seedbed of new social relations. It should be read and discussed in this spirit, not as a blueprint to which all must conform. For in initiatives of this kind the advances cannot be made in the head. They are made by the practice of those involved, working towards common ends, listening to each other, remaining tolerant, expecting short-term difficulties as a necessary cost of long-term success. While then we cannot foresee all the eventualities, what we can do is to prepare ourselves critically.   (Le Brun and Murray 1980:26)

In short, the successful introduction of the NYS would depend on the political negotiations between the project designers, the policy-makers and the different categories of staff employed. The success of the Service would depend on the extent to which the chosen participants could create and maintain appropriate structures and processes through which the set policy goals could be achieved.

As identified above, the different categories of staff at the NYS brought differing levels of skills, language, socio-cultural backgrounds, understandings and expectations with them and the first three months of the innovation's implementation was found to be a difficult period by all. It was a time during which the NYS was found to be 'inconsistent' by co-ordinators and teachers and other staff alike. The problem was made worse as a consequence of each group of staff having received a separate programme of induction to the NYS. Each group was thus to perceive the aims and direction of the innovation differently – they all held contrasting agendas for action. The co-ordinators and teachers, in particular, as the key groups involved with the design and delivery of the new curriculum were to place very different emphases on the status of the NYS policy guidelines, for instance, and become differentially orientated toward the process of implementation.

The co-ordinators, for example, were to give the NYS policy goals and theoretical guidelines a low profile, as a result of the multitude of immediate problems they faced. This is not uncommon for those in charge of managing change, as Sarason points out:

> up until the opening of the school the principal is not concerned with such issues as what life in a classroom should be, how teachers will be related to decisions and planning about educational values and goals, the role of parents and neighborhood community resources, the handling of problem children, the purpose of evaluation, and other issues that bear directly on the educational experience of all those who have or should have a vested interest in a school.   (Sarason 1971:116)

To the co-ordinators the essential priority was to establish a managerial structure that would invest in them control over the innovation's development and wider publicity. They were – as Party members – all clearly aware of the political significance placed on the success of the Service. Thus to achieve their ends the co-ordinators were to centralise all major decision-making to their Coordinators' Committee and this was to form the NYS executive body.

In contrast the teachers were to give high priority to the NYS policy goals and theoretical guidelines as a result of their induction programme led by the UNESCO adviser (and co-author of the policy guidelines). They had been led to believe that the NYS was to be theory-led and based on the ideas set out in the policy guideline document (see Le Brun and Murray 1980). However, problems arose once they attempted to put this theory into practice. Due to the absence of an organisational framework (democratic and participatory) within which problems and issues could be addressed very little progress could be made. The teachers were left no option but to resolve their difficulties by use of the only structure available to them – their own teachers' weekly staff meetings.

As a means of supporting the development process the teachers' weekly staff meetings were to prove inadequate – very little was achieved. The problem was that the resolution of issues was painfully slow due to the number of teachers involved in this forum (40 teachers in all) and the need for all statements to be translated three ways (English, French, Creole). The result was high levels of frustration, resulting in conflict and divisons among the teachers. Firstly, they became divided into three language groups: the groups in which the debates took place. Secondly each of these groups further fragmented into two sub-groups – 'idealists' and 'conformists'. The divide here was a result of the different levels of expected involvement in the innovation's development process as perceived by certain individuals and national groups. The idealists expected, for instance, to play a leading role in the organisation and running of the youth village – at all levels – and that the innovation would approximate closely to the theoretical guidelines. This group originally contained Canadians, British, Mauritian and some Seychellois teachers. On the other hand the conformists were more willing to accept the co-ordinators' definition of the situation and to be responsive to requests and direction from above. This group initially contained Guineans, Sri Lankans and some Seychellois teachers. The fragmentation of the teachers into these sub-groups was to split their power base and was to prevent them from forming a united front on issues that concerned them.

Thus, in conclusion, the principal participants in the creation and implementation of the NYS's 'new education' were to develop quite different and conflicting orientations toward the 'natural order of things' (Silverman 1970:33) to follow. The relationship between the teachers themselves, and between the co-ordinators and the teachers (the essential relationships involved in defining the curriculum programme) were thus strained during the early period of the implementation process. For, although both groups were aware of inconsistencies in the situations they faced – incomplete buildings, high teacher–student ratios, and limited resources – as a result of the absence of a common programme of staff induction, both teachers and co-ordinators were to perceive the way forward differently. Individual commitment to the ideology was not alone sufficient, practical support and guidance were required as well as a management structure to facilitate this.

As a result of the differing expectations, the co-ordinators (administrators) and the teachers were not to work together in harmony. Instead, the management structure set up by the co-ordinators excluded the teachers (or any other category of non-co-ordination staff for that matter) from taking any part in the essential decision-making processes. Even when a Village Committee was set up representing all categories of staff and the students, it became dominated by the Chief Co-ordinator. As is so often the case in newly developing organisations, the:

> requirements of leadership and the demand for representation are often in conflict and not easy to reconcile in decision-making – their true relationship is too frequently cloaked in the language of rhetoric or public ritual.   (Sarason 1971:60)

Moreover, the day-to-day running of the youth village – work, daily life and education – were to become fragmented into six parts (production, education, health, security, personnel, and animation) each under the separate administration of a different assistant co-ordinator. Each assistant co-ordinator was then responsible to the Co-ordinators' Committee. However, while this management structure supported the needs (expectations and intents) of the co-ordinators it did not include a joint staff forum to support the development of an integrated curriculum across the work, daily life, and education domains (see Haffenden, forthcoming). The teachers were thus left with no means of supporting the implementation of the policy aims as they understood them.

As the first year of the innovation progressed the differences between the teachers' and co-ordinators' orientations and expectations, identified earlier, came into conflict. In particular, during the second period of the year – from April through until June – as the co-ordinators began to introduce their definition of the 'natural order of things' for the NYS, so the teachers began to experience the emergence of the management hierarchy in the form of a management structure that distanced the teachers from the co-ordinators and the decision-making process. As the teachers' involvement and participation in the decision-making process became limited so the organisation that emerged did not provide them with a structure through which their needs could be supported. This led, in turn, to frustrations and the widening awareness of some teachers' unrealised expectations. The growing concerns of the teachers were addressed in the mid-year summer recess workshops.

The first two weeks of the NYS's summer recess were given over to a workshop. The workshop was set up to allow staff an opportunity to address and resolve some of the on-going problems they were facing. In addition, it was also seen as providing a further period of staff development; it had always been understood that the initial period of staff development – the teachers' induction programme – had been insufficient and inadequate to satisfy all the teachers' needs. The workshop was, however, to become the medium through which the conflicting orientations and expectations of the staff were expressed. The teachers, in particular, were to ask for a clarification of their role in the NYS organisation and its development process.

The Chief Co-ordinator in her response made it clear that she held the dominant role in the management structure. 'Power is in the hands of the Co-ordinator', she explained and it became clear to the teachers that they were powerless to influence her. The power and control over the innovation had become centralised. The effect of this formal realisation by the teachers of their subordinate role was a substantial drop in their commitment and morale. They had come to expect (following their recruitment and induction programme) that a more 'open', democratic, and participatory framework of organisation and management would have existed. As a result of the mismatch many of the more committed 'idealist' teachers resigned. They were unable to accommodate the gap that had emerged between their expectations (expected role models) and that which could be realised in practice (the realised role model).

To the co-ordinators, however, it should be noted that the expatriate resignations only confirmed their earlier suspicions over the extent to which these teachers were really committed to the NYS, especially those who had not been recruited by NYS staff. Further, since it was these teachers who resigned first, at a time when thing appeared to be getting tough, it did little to strengthen the position or value of those teachers remaining.

In short, the organisational arrangements and management structures evolved in the NYS did not support the developmental needs or expectations of the staff at the grassroots in their attempts at reuniting work, daily life and education. More specifically there was no 'cognitive participation' in the sense that:

> Those who are the objects of policy should have the opportunity to participate not only in specific decisions but in the definitions of the situation on which these decisions are based.   (Berger 1974:13)

As this did not occur the personal expectations held by teaching staff were to differ considerably from the co-ordinators' expectations of them. These differences in perspective subsequently led to conflict between the two groups and the resignation of those teachers finding the situation intolerable.

Thus to conclude, the findings of this study support those of Havelock and Huberman in that planners and managers of change need to address:

(a) infrastructural considerations to ensure that all the participants understand the rationale behind the organisational structures and the levels of accountability and responsibility enshrined in them. Furthermore, the infrastructure must facilitate the effective flow of information between the different groups of staff at and within different levels of the organisation;
(b) staff consensus, so that the new ideas and procedures are established in negotiation with those responsible for carrying them out. It should be recognised that consensus at one level of an organisation does not necessarily lead to consensus elsewhere;
(c) leadership authority must be clearly established if planned change is to be maximised. Moreover, the authority invested in meetings, committees and working parties must also be clearly stated. The status and value of such groups must be made explicit. There is no better way to demotivate staff than to involve them in working parties whose recommendations are ignored.

(Havelock and Huberman 1977)

Further this study would suggest that if the expectations of those involved at the grassroots is carefully managed by those responsible for implementing change many of these concerns can be overcome.

CURRICULUM ORGANISATION AND DEVELOPMENT

The Linking of Production to Education and Theory to Practice

In contrast to the innovation's management structure the arrangements pertaining to the curriculum organisation and development were – following the early period of inconsistency – more supportive of the teachers' needs. In particular, while the involvement of teachers in wider issues relating to the innovation's implementation were to deteriorate, their control over experimentation with the curriculum organisation and development was to improve through the introduction of a Block system of education.

The Block system of education as introduced vested in the teachers complete autonomy – in the first instance – in its development. The Block system represented a move away from traditional curriculum organisation and development based on academic disciplines. It saw the introduction of seven vocational blocks – each of four weeks' duration – and a core curriculum of English, Mathematics and French. The blocks were: agriculture, animal husbandry, construction and technology, health, fishing and agriculture, information, and culture and political life. Within these blocks the teachers organised, timetabled and developed the curriculum (see figure 9.1).

The teachers' early efforts did not, however, lead to the successful linking of production to education as hoped. Because of communication difficulties experienced between the teaching staff and production workers (due to differences in language, culture, status, and wage differentials), only in those blocks able to overcome such problems was any real progress made. Furthermore, in such cases success was only achieved through personal effort (animal husbandry for example, where the Mauritian teachers were able to converse with Seychellois production workers in Seychellois Creole) and where the teachers were able to address both the production and related education opportunities themselves (the Radio Station set up in the Technology Block for example).

The difficulties faced by the teachers in relating production to education was subsequently reflected in the curriculum development process. In particular, since production was (in the main) only superficially related to education, the teachers were unable to relate effectively the students' experiences of practice to theory in the classroom. Moreover, the duration of the first year blocks (four weeks) further prevented the establishment and continuity of project-

ased approaches to the curriculum, depth of subject study, and the
levelopment of good teacher–student relationships.

To address these concerns a review of the progress made by each
lock during the first three months of the Block system was
undertaken. This review took the form of each block producing a
3lock Report, reporting on the successes and failures experienced.
These reports then formed a basis on which the staff could identify
any changes to the system necessary to maximise its success. The
3lock Reports were then addressed by the teachers during the mid-
year recess workshop.

However, although the issues and concerns raised in the Block
Reports were addressed and debated in full, following the mid-year
recess the teachers were not involved in the reformulation of the
3lock system based on their recommendations. This was due to:

(a) teachers' resignations – due largely to their dissatisfaction with
the NYS management structure (as described in the last section);
(b) a loss of confidence by the co-ordinators in the ability of the
teachers to effect the desired changes;
(c) the co-ordinators' need to secure: (i) a common curriculum
framework by the start of the second year so that it could be
utilised by both the second year of the first NYS village and the first
year of the second village (due then to start), and (ii) a set of
curriculum guidelines – for the Seychelles Polytechnic – that
defined the scheme of work the students had followed.

The reformulation of the Block system was thus undertaken by the
UNESCO adviser in consultation with the co-ordinators. Hence,
although the teachers participated in the identification of a range of
changes necessary to support the curriculum implementation process,
they were not involved in the interpretation of those changes into
policy statements. Furthermore, with a change over in UNESCO
adviser at the start of the second year of the innovation, the
implementation of the finalised changes to the Block system were to
be facilitated by someone who had not been involved at all in the
ormative development process.

Consequently, whilst many of the teachers' suggestions were
included in the reorganised Block system the changes were set within
context of wider changes not of the teachers' making. In particular,
the new system whilst increasing the length of the blocks – from four
weeks to eight weeks – removed the timetabling flexibility essential to
project-based teaching (one of the main reasons for extending the

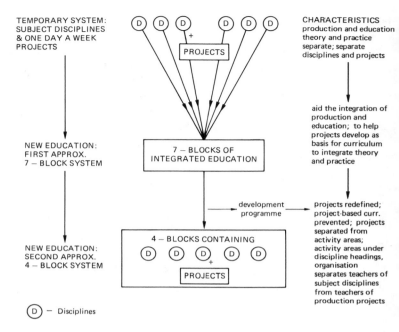

FIGURE 9.1   *Evolution of the educational organisation*

duration of the blocks in the first place). In setting a largely rigi
timetable for all subject areas the development of links betwee
education and production was essentially prevented from takin
place at all. Furthermore, the new subject areas were now defined b
the co-ordinators and allocated to the teachers and not developed s
as to reflect (as far as possible) the practical experience of th
students. Finally, in addition to the centrally-defined organisation o
the curriculum its development process also became standardised a
the start of the second year. Each subject teacher was now require
to write a curriculum activity guideline for each of the subject area
allotted to them – based on an exemplary guideline provided
However the development of the curriculum activity guidelines, b
the teachers, took place at the start of the second year at very shor
notice and with very little additional support or guidance. Moreove
as many teachers recognised that resources required to implemen

their guidelines would not be available, it became an exercise for some in providing what they believed the co-ordinators wanted to see – an Ordinary Level General Certificate of Education course in eight weeks.

Thus, in summary, the formalisation of the curriculum organisation and development that took place at the start of the second year of the innovation reduced the teachers' ability to unite production and education and to relate theory to practice in the classroom. The reorganised system did not specifically support the identified needs of the teachers, and the reintroduction of subject disciplines only increased the academic orientation of the blocks, making them less relevant to the daily life of the village, although satisfying more closely the O level standard entrance expectations of the Polytechnic. Thus, the teachers' control of the curriculum organisation, choice of appropriate subject area and development structure was lost. The only real power they retained by the start of the second year was in the classroom delivery of the curriculum.

REFLECTIONS AND CONCLUSIONS

Review of the Fieldwork Stance Adopted

This study sought to (a) identify what, at the grassroots, affects teachers' experiences of the process of change and to monitor their responses to these influences, and (b) assess the extent to which the planned educational changes represented by the NYS were realised in practice. To achieve these aims the researcher adopted an approach which emphasised the teachers' perspective. Firstly, this provided an insight into educational change that was poorly represented in the literature. As Fullan notes in relation to research on educational planning, 'there is not nearly as much research available on implementation processes within schools' (Fullan 1985b:412).

Secondly, understanding the teachers' perspective is crucial to the production of clearer specifications of the conditions under which change takes place (Marsh and Huberman 1984) and there is no better way of understanding this perspective than becoming a teacher involved in the change process. For these reasons, coupled with the fieldwork opportunity provided by the Seychelles National Youth

Service, the researcher entered the field as a teacher and undertook the study as a participant observer.

The major strength of this approach was that the researcher was accepted as a full participant in the innovation. As such, he was subjected to the same socialisation processes as all other members of the NYS teaching staff. Consequently he experienced first-hand all that was involved in being a teacher in the NYS and was able to share in a common understanding of the concerns and issues perceived at this level of the NYS organisation. In short, the research stance adopted enabled the change process to be experienced and examined from within the teaching staff group, with the findings reflecting the felt strength of the issues encountered.

However, there were also some limitations in the stance adopted in that 'how one describes and experiences the school culture is largely determined by one's relationship to it' (Sarason 1971:234). In the case of the research reported here the relationship of the researcher to the NYS was one of expatriate and teacher. As an expatriate the researcher was by definition a foreigner and was to experience all the problems of an unfamiliar language and culture, problems that were compounded by the multi-national composition of the teaching staff group. The effect of this was that for the researcher much of what was said and exchanged between co-ordinators, students, production workers, animateurs and some of the other teachers was unavoidably missed.

Further, as a teacher, the researcher had limited access to certain events and information. Whereas a non-participant observer might have been able to observe a range of key events, discussions and meetings involving staff groups at different levels of the organisation, the reseacher's role as a teacher prevented this. Moreover, as the teaching staff's participation in the NYS decision-making processes became restricted and distanced from the co-ordinators', so the information readily available to them as a staff group, and to the researcher as part of this group, became narrower. Whilst this did not prevent the key issues from being examined from the teachers' perspective, it did preclude his developing an empirically-based understanding of the whole organisation and decision-making context in which the teachers' actions and problems were set, and prevented these being viewed from other perspectives.

In summary, by taking a teachers' perspective the researcher was able to gain access to a more intimate understanding of the problems and issues encountered by this group during the implementation of educational change, but opportunities of gaining similar insights from other staff groups were restricted.

Some Conclusions

Following the Seychelles socialist revolution of 1977, changes were introduced into the nation's political and educational systems as a means of reforming the society as a whole. However, as Lillis has pointed out (Lillis 1981), a nation's educational independence is dependent on its cultural independence, which is dependent on its economic independence, which is dependent on its political independence. In the case of the Seychelles, political independence did not result in economic independence due to the nation's economic dependence on the capitalist-dominated tourist sector. As a result the Seychelles economy remained essentially capitalist within a socialist political structure. As such the identified needs for changes in cultural values and the social relations of production were unobtainable. Moreover continued resistance to change in the economy and political spheres of the society at large – including the South African-backed mercenary invasion in November 1981 and the civil war in July 1982 – all meant that the planned national development was behind schedule, which made more difficult the integration of the NYS graduates into working life and society.

In addition to the difficulties identified above, the NYS was itself to come under pressure as a result of its position in the education system, sandwiched between the primary and further education sectors. The need for the NYS to become integrated into the educational system as a whole and accountable in its ability to prepare students for further education, resulted in its ideals becoming weakened in favour of more traditional educational organisation and content. Hence, the fate of the innovation was heavily influenced by external expectations placed upon it by both the needs and values maintained in the economy at large and the requirements of the wider education system – which had remained largely unchanged in terms of its course organisation, content and standards. The problem for the NYS was that the education system, as with the society at large, had not been sufficiently prepared for the extent of the changes it was originally set up to bring about. So whilst the rhetoric of change was maintained in the NYS, it was not practised in the everyday reality experienced by the (largely expatriate) staff and by the students; consequently the radical ideals were effectively reduced during the implementation process.

Thus, to summarise, the study suggests that:

(a) the process of educational reform in a small country needs to be supported by a body of trained local staff, whose language, culture and aspirations are germane to the task. Dependence on expatriate staff is less likely to be successful due to communication and cultural difficulties;

(b) changes to one part of an educational system are not sustainable unless the rest of the system is concurrently changed and/or modified to accommodate them;

(c) changes in the education system at the school/labour market interface are not likely to be successful if the new social relations for production (emphasised by the education system) are not supported and reinforced by employers.

Finally it should be noted that the educational reforms in the Seychelles are ambitious, radical and on-going. Through successes and failures the momentum of change has been continued by the willingness of the government to learn through the analysis of its experiences. In reporting this study it is hoped that others may also learn from the Seychelles experience.

10 Postscript
Keith M. Lewin

A long, varied and thought-provoking journey through radically different attempts at innovation in different contexts has now reached completion. The introduction of this book argues that its main value lies in the experience of travelling through the case studies, rather than arriving at a set of neat conclusions. It should be clear by now that there are no 'quick fixes' to many of the problems that arise in the process of innovation. But that is not the same as saying that these are no more than idiosyncratic accounts bound completely to their context. To admit that is to deny the possibilities of planned change, and accept impotence in the face of growing needs.

In conclusion this postscript turns to two theoretical debates. The first encapsulates different approaches to innovation to be found in the literature. It tentatively links these to aspects of the case study material. The second approaches a major debate within the education and development literature which concerns, at its simplest level, the tension between conflict and order perspectives on social change. These are offered to tease the reader further into speculation on and reflective analysis of the case studies.

SOME APPROACHES TO INNOVATION

The innovation literature is now very extensive and is based on a considerable accumulation of empirical studies and theorising about different aspects of change.

There are many reviews of the educational change literature which need no repetition here (Slater 1985, Fullan and Pomfret 1977, Fullan 1982, Papagiannis, Klees and Bickel 1982, Bolam 1978, Dalin 1978, Hurst 1978, Huberman 1973, Hoyle 1970).

Much of the early work developed from studies in areas outside formal education systems and was based on the experiences that were beginning to accumulate in development projects which sought to promote planned change. Thus for example Rogers and Shoemaker (1971) explored social system innovations cross-culturally using many examples drawn from different fields in the development literature.

American perspectives on innovation and the linking of research and development with practitioners were heavily influenced by the development of the Land Grant Universities and agricultural extension practices. Another strand in the innovation literature was inspired by psychological studies with a Utopian (Skinner 1948), group participatory (Lewin 1947) or psychoanalytic basis (see Chin and Benne 1969). Organisational psychology and sociology have provided other inspirations, for example the 1930s Hawthorne studies (Roethlisberger and Dickson 1939), the Mayo Human Relations School (1945), Likert's work on organisations (Likert 1966) and that of Katz and Kahn (1978).

The most accessible educational change literature relates to experience with education systems in industrialised countries. Thus much seminal work (for example, Gross *et al* 1971, Smith and Keith 1971, Havelock 1973, Huberman and Miles 1984, Becher and MaClure 1978) reflects the organisational ecology and social system characteristics of educational institutions in the North. Case study accounts (for example, OECD 1973) are often drawn from industrialised countries. As Havelock and Huberman (1977) note in their foray into the problems of innovation in developing countries:

> These problems [of educational innovation] have given rise to a considerable theoretical literature in which research workers have tried to explain change phenomena in order to help practitioners better to organise for change. However, most of this work relates to industrialised countries, and tends to reach a degree of abstraction or complexity that reduces its applicability . . . the case study literature and the empirical research that we expected to find in rich abundance were not really there.

Given the arguments about what might count as valid research pertaining to educational innovation in developing countries and the problems of its accessibility, one might add that Havelock and Huberman could not identify it in forms usable by them. Happily this situation is changing and case study material which probes inside the 'black box' of innovation and looks beyond inputs and outputs is beginning to emerge.

Many models have been developed for different phases of the innovation process. At the most general level there are those which identify overarching theories encompassing initiation, development, implementation, and evaluation of outcomes. The models which have most currency in the literature and are most widely quoted are those related to the work of Havelock (1969), and Chin and Benne (1969). The former initially identified three dominant patterns in approach – research, development, diffusion; social interaction; and problem-solving. The latter classified innovation strategies into rational-empirical; normative-re-educative; and power-coercive. This has led to several subsequent formulations and attempts at synthesis (Havelock and Huberman 1977).

Without wishing to cloud the waters of competing models further, the synthesis offered below attempts to assimilate key elements of these, and other strategies, into a single simple typology that can be juxtaposed with the case study material.

Six approaches can be identified that have distinct characteristics (Lewin 1988a):

(a) systems;
(b) bureaucratic;
(c) scientific;
(d) problem-solving;
(e) diffusionist;
(f) charismatic.

Systems approaches

Systems approaches view educational institutions as subsystems which are part of a wider system that has formally specified goals. Innovation from this point of view is initiated as a result of a commitment to achieve these goals. The goals are generated by systems (political or otherwise) outside the education system and the innovator's role is to design and implement programmes that will achieve these goals. Educational systems and institutions have to be re-tuned to deliver appropriate educational outcomes for changing circumstances. Innovation is therefore a goal-directed process towards defined ends that requires the detailed working out of learning programmes and their evaluation against the pre-set goals. Poor goal achievement needs to be identified and remedial action taken to increase the efficiency with which the system performs.

Key features of these approaches are that educational innovation takes place within open social systems; these systems have identified goals which are shared by system members; goal achievement is the result of a systematic process which builds on the performance of subsystems to culminate in the desired outcomes; specialisation

occurs in subsystems related to function; stable systems are homeo-
static and exist within a dynamic equilibrium.

The systems perspective is related to Chin and Benne's rational-
empirical approach and less closely to Havelock's research, development and diffusion pattern. It has affinity with Katz and Kahn's
(1966) views on open systems. They contrast closed systems
(mechanistic, vital, independent of events outside the system
boundary) with open systems which are defined by input, throughput,
output, differentiation, and equifinality (reaching the same final state
from different starting conditions and through different pathways).
These systems import inputs from the environment outside the
system and interact constructively with it. They are dynamic and
recycle information and experience to improve performance. The
latter are typical of education systems.

From a systems viewpoint initiation of innovation arises from
changed external conditions or mismatches between input, throughput and output. The development of an innovation is a rational-
empirical process, taken step by step, and guided by logic, trial and
feedback. Implementation of innovations occurs through those
systemic structures that are designed for the purpose and which
essentially prescribe good practice to the clients of the system.
Evaluation of this kind of innovation is implicit in its initiation. Is the
response adequate to meet system needs to maintain homeostasis and
dynamic equilibrium in the face of changed external conditions? Are
the mismatches resolved? Criticism that individuals rather than
systems have goals leads to, amongst other things, the development
of theories of 'goal displacement' where institutional goals are
replaced by those related to the needs of individuals, particularly in
organisations under stress. Silverman (1970) and others have attacked
the reification that systems theory gives to organisational constructs
and have developed the idea of an 'action frame of reference' which
partly resolves some of the problems they perceive.

Systems approaches to innovation seem to fit some aspects of the
China case study. The Chinese education system since liberation has
always been very centralised. The system has a highly organised,
specialised and inter-related set of agencies responsible for implementing change initiated in the political and ideological system. The
process through which the People's Education Press developed and
disseminated new geography texts illustrates this. Recent attempts at
decentralisation and increased local autonomy in curriculum development have yet to really take hold. Both Nigerian case studies also

have elements of a system approach in their planning and in structures adopted for implementation. But in these cases the balance of evidence suggests that the systems simply do not function in ways that would result in the intended outcomes. Kano State seems to fare a little better than Anambra State on this but to say so is to ignore the fact that the former case study was looking at an innovation much more limited in scope than was the latter. In both cases confusion of authority, poor information flows, and inadequate supporting infrastructure contributed to the limitations of the implementation that took place. System completion was an elusive goal that was never achieved. In Malaysia a cascade model for inservice was adopted which suffered from some of the well-known difficulties of this approach. The planning appears to have been formulated within assumptions related to systems theory once the needs had been identified centrally.

In all these cases, however, strong elements of bureaucratic approaches coexisted with systems assumptions, and arguably proved more influential.

Bureaucratic Approaches

Bureaucratic approaches to innovation are directed by goals identified at the system level. Unlike a systems approach they tend to have static rather than dynamic characteristics. In particular, directive circulars, rules and regulations, agreed procedures, and legal obligations provide the benchmarks against which innovation is judged and the needs for it are identified. As these change, innovations may be appraised against criteria which are more administrative than educational. Innovation then takes place to satisfy approved procedures where the regulatory purpose is given a conspicuous prominence. Though bureaucracy is often used in a pejorative sense, as an organisational form it is, like other forms, effective for some purposes but not for others.

Key features of bureaucratic approaches include the definition of goals by hierarchical organisational structures; the delineation of individuals' roles in innovation by their positions in the organisation; the conditioning of the interactions between organisation members by role cultures; information tends to flow down the system more easily than up it or across it from substructure to substructure; power is drawn from position, expertise and control over resources; rules determine actions rather than judgement.

Innovation from this point of view is initiated almost invariably from the organisational apex, drawing for its legitimacy on the position power of incumbents. Development takes place as a result of delegated authority and functions according to rational, technocratic procedures without close consultation with client groups. Implementation is viewed as a largely procedural problem of disseminating information and instructions. The evaluation of outcomes is usually based on internally approved criteria sanctioned by the hierarchy.

Bureaucratic approaches are often associated with power-coercive strategies for implementation (Chin and Benne 1969). They capitalise on both the advantages and disadvantages of bureaucratic organisations (Blau 1955, Weber 1947, Handy 1985).

In the China case study most elements of this approach are present. Implementation was essentially power-coercive. Information flows were 'convectional' up the bureaucratic structures but were not definitive. Those that were came from the top down, and were backed by positional power and hierarchy in both political and professional spheres.

The Nigerian case studies both show a preponderance of bureaucratic solution-seeking after the battles had been fought to establish the special Science Schools programme and the vocationalised Junior Secondary Schools (JSS) innovation. However, the evidence on the efficiency with which the bureaucracy functioned shows it had great difficulty in conforming to bureaucratic procedures. Personal power often dominated power based on expertise, decision-making at most levels was as much political as bureaucratic in character, and formal procedures were often ignored or only partially adhered to. Malaysian KBSR inservice provision seems to have conformed to a bureaucratic style in the sense that central initiation was followed up by delegated responsibility through the educational bureaucracy to organise state level programmes using officers already employed in suitable positions. Their roles and responsibilities were defined positionally and their performance, as represented in the case study, illustrates the kind of concern for accountability (covering the material, circulating the information on what is to be done, lecturing from a prescriptive standpoint) that characterises bureaucracies. Speculatively it could be suggested that this may have led to the kind of goal displacement that sees the clients of innovation as its initiators and controllers, rather than the teachers or students who are the end users. Though the Gambian case study shows that the development of policy has been *ad hoc* in important respects, its elements seem to reflect bureaucratic styles of attempts to innovate more than others. So also in Leach's study do some of the Sudanese recipient organisations experiencing technical co-operation display strong elements of bureaucratic approaches.

Scientific Approaches

Scientific approaches to innovation claim that research and evaluation on the needs of learners, the learning process, and curriculum effectiveness are at the centre of the initiation of change. This approximates to the research, development and diffusion sequence sometimes applied to innovation in science and technology. The curriculum developer in this model must undertake basic and applied research on teaching and learning to arrive at the more effective design of learning materials and curricula. More sophisticated models have feedback built in to them so that formative experiments feature prominently and development is planned as a meticulous process of trial, evaluation and revision.

Key features of this approach are that there is a rational, basically linear, sequence to the innovation process; research and development should take place before implementation; the division of labour in research and development tasks is both necessary and desirable; consumers are essentially passive and rational; high initial costs in money and time are justifiable by long-term benefits of quality, efficiency and viability. Innovation is therefore driven by curiosity, theories of how learning takes place, and the appraisal of the effectiveness of existing practice according to criteria embedded in learning theory and the achievement of educational goals.

This approach is most adequately represented in Havelock's research, development, diffusion approach and also relates to Chin and Benne's rational-empirical approach.

There is very little evidence in any of the case studies of research acting as an initiating feature and shaping the form that the various innovations took. Where it does seem to have played a role it has been less important than other factors and it appears in several characteristic forms. Research involving the analysis of foreign geography texts did influence the debate on the new Chinese geography curriculum but it was of an international comparative nature and not concerned with primary data derived from clients of the innovation. Preliminary research of a needs analysis type was not evident in the innovations studied, with the exception of the Sudanese projects which had experienced feasibility studies prior to disbursement. But these attracted a mixed reaction concerning their validity which was called into question by subsequent events. In Stuart's study the teacher researchers did undertake research on their own practice, but, as argued later, other aspects of their work exclude it from classification within a research, development and design strategy.

Problem-solving Approaches

Problem-solving approaches offer a fourth alternative. In these 'organisational pain' and individual dissatisfaction are important. A problem may be experienced within educational institutions, and the innovators' first task is to find out what problems have arisen and what their causes are. Alternatively, problems may be recognised by individuals in their own practice. The problem-solver diagnoses the difficulty, searches for a solution which may or may not involve innovation, and then offers it to the organisation, or applies it to their own practice for trial and refinement.

The innovator in this approach may be more of a process helper than a solution giver, a change agent offering suggestions and deepening the problem analysis to the point where those suffering the problem realise what action has to be taken. Problem-solvers may themselves be participants and the clients of change guided and assisted by others.

Key perspectives here are that clients' needs are paramount, careful problem diagnosis is a necessary first step, internal resources should be mobilised first and fully; and that self-initiated and self-applied innovations have the greatest chances of success in the long run.

This is closest to the normative-reeducative approach of Chin and Benne and Havelock's problem-solving and relates to models proposed by several others (Argyris and Schön 1974, Stenhouse 1975).

Stuart's action research study in Lesotho characterises some elements of this approach. Her change agent strategy as a consultant was client-centred and her research group identified and tried out changed practices to respond to the problem areas that they themselves had identified. By employing cyclical problem diagnosis, problem-solving and re-evaluation strategies, progress was made by members of the group. They became more 'reflective practitioners' able to analyse their own problems and to try out action to overcome them.

Leach's case studies illustrate the importance of the problem-solving approach to understanding innovations that take the perspectives of actors as central. The projects she studies have basically bureaucratic and systems assumptions built into their organisation. Her work indicates that failure to see development and innovation problems from the perspectives of different groups and in terms of the human relationships involved can precipitate conflict and ambiguity, loss of motivation and commitment, and confusion of professional roles.

Haffenden's study suggests that at the outset the National Youth Service (NYS) in the Seychelles had a strong element of problem-solving strategies embedded in the original concept. To some extent this later came to be supplanted partly by diffusionist practices (see below), and partly by bureaucratic structures that appeared, at least from some perspectives, to reduce the role of teachers in problem-solving.

Diffusionist Approaches

Diffusionist approaches place the stress on the processes through which innovations are disseminated and adopted. This is seen characteristically as the result of social interaction between actors existing within networks of communication that provide access to information. This model assumes that behaviour is heavily influenced by the social networks to which actors are linked; that position in these networks is a good predictor of acceptance of innovation; that personal contacts are central to the spread of innovation; and that diffusion of new practices will follow an S-curve of growth with early adopters and laggards.

Havelock characterises this as the social interaction model and it relates to Chin and Benne's normative-reeducative approach.

The conferences that shaped the Chinese geography innovation do seem to have served as forums where networks began to form and new ideas were debated and diffused as participants mixed with their professional peers. But this process seems to have been restricted to the initial phases of the innovation and not subsequently utilised as a central strategy.

In Nigeria both case studies indicate the relatively weak basis for the diffusion of ideas through professional networks and journals. Where it occurs it seems more often by accident than by design and random rather than systematic in any way. Sarr's study in the Gambia indicates that in the absence of more systematic procedures ideas have diffused and decisions have been made autonomously at the school level outside those areas that are regulated bureaucratically. The Lesotho teachers formed a micro-network and there is some evidence that this spread beyond the immediate group to influence others.

Charismatic Approaches

Charismatic approaches are difficult to classify since their nature makes them unique to individuals and circumstances. Strong beliefs, convincingly articulated by those in influential positions, are often the initiating activity. When they succeed in carrying other people with them they can generate development activity which reflects their educational philosophy. Their motivation comes from conviction rather than research; their goals may not be those of the organisations in which they work which they may often seek to change.

These approaches are linked to the inspirational insights of individuals and seek conversion to a new set of beliefs largely unsupported by systematic analysis. Conviction, force of personality, public relations skills, refined mastery of the arts of persuasion, and single-minded drive towards goals are all characteristic of the proponents of change of this kind. As an idiosyncratic phenomenon charisma is difficult to incorporate into models of change. Mahatma Ghandi, Paulo Freire, and Patrick van Rensburg are just three examples of individuals whose educational ideas have influenced many attempts to innovate in developing countries, and some proportion of that influence has come from the charisma they have been able to project.

Charismatic individuals are significant in several of the case studies. In China the key roles played by Deng and Hua in the political debate are evident. So also is the influence of actors like Chen Erzou and Li Yudan. Though holding positional power these individuals drew influence from the considerable charisma that surrounded them. In one of the Nigerian case studies events were strongly influenced by the appointment of a new commissioner for education whose inputs to the innovation process were critical. Haffenden's account shows that there were charismatic figures involved in the development of the NYS and that their contributions partly depended on this attribute. Without understanding aspects of the personalities involved in the stories of the innovations, the accounts would be much less penetrating and critical dimensions would have been missed. In different ways the experiences of innovation analysed by the contributors touch on the application of all these models. It has to be said that there is little evidence from the studies that the models were consciously applied by many of the actors involved in the evolution of the innovations. On the other hand they do seem to offer useful structures to analysis of the innovation. And, as might be expected, different actors seem to behave according to the assumptions of different models and the same actors shift between them at different points in time. So the convenient separation offered above is not as simple as it seems.

PERSPECTIVES ON EDUCATION AND DEVELOPMENT

An earlier paper written with Angela Little explored some of the central issues which inform neo-classical and modernisation views of education and development on the one hand and neo-Marxist and dependency perspectives on the other (Lewin and Little 1984). This discussion tries to link these ideas with the case studies. These deal with education systems subject to very different ideologies, culturally-grounded beliefs and power relations, and all our contributors have their own ideological and epistemological perspectives. This postscript is therefore offered from my perspective alone.

The innovation and social change literature recognises two distinct orientations to innovation that are associated with philosophical and sociological traditions of long standing (Paulston 1976, Karabel and Halsey 1977, Burrell and Morgan 1979) and are mirrored in distinctions drawn in the development literature (Toye 1987). These in essence counterpoise functionalist and conflict theories. The former see change as essentially incremental, equilibrating, and consensual; the latter discontinuous, unstable, and characterised by conflict rather than consensus.

In the following discussion functionalist approaches are associated with the theories of modernisation, while conflict perspectives are linked to Marxist, neo-Marxist and dependency theorists. In so doing this glosses over important differences, but in the interests of making this debate accessible to a non-specialist audience this seems inevitable.

A Level of Agreement

Proponents of both perspectives are in considerable agreement about the nature of relationships between education and social and economic development in a more general sense. Thus the 'correspondence principle' advanced by Bowles and Gintis (1976) from a neo-Marxist position, which asserts that educational structures replicate those found in the production system, echoes the view of one of the founding fathers of functionalist sociology 70 years earlier (Durkheim 1969) that: 'educational transformations are always the result and the symptom of the social transformation in terms of which they are explained'.

To some extent the human capital theory beloved of post-war neo-classical economists writing on education, and part of the inspiration of some of the innovations discussed in the case studies, was an aberration of the dominant functionalist tradition. The latter essentially defined educational spending as consumption rather than investment and viewed education as having a basically conservative role in preparing students to enter and adjust to the adult world rather than transform it (Seers 1983). The ideological prestidigitation involved in creating a class of capitalists without physical capital (every individual is a capitalist since they can invest in their own human capital) was a neat, if disingenuous, trick. The radical view amongst neo-Marxists similarly extended their reasoning to incorporate the possibility of education systems acting as vectors of change rather than simply reflecting wider structures.

> Despite its (the education system's) primary function of selection and socialisation, it does produce individuals who are not only agents of change within the dependent (education) system but also some who want to break the dependent system. Through increased schooling the dominant groups in society may unintentionally create forces opposed to dependency and the dominance of groups who live off the dependent system.   (Carnoy 1974)

From both viewpoints educational change comes about from mismatches between educational and socio-economic structures. For the functionalists such mismatches are 'dysfunctional' and deviant change is designed to harmonise them. For neo-Marxists they are the inevitable consequence of conflict between interest groups and the task is to resolve the contradictions that arise.

In the Chinese case the planned innovation in geography was

largely the result of mismatches seen to exist between China's development needs and the existing curricular provision. Somewhat paradoxically for a Marxist state this was publicly argued in terms of the needs of the Four Modernisations and the need to catch up with industrialised countries in science and technology. Echoes of human capital theoretical assumptions are clear. This becomes understandable in terms of the politics of post-cultural revolution China where the Dengist pragmatic line came to occupy centre stage. The initiation of the NYS in the Seychelles conforms to what might be expected in a post-revolutionary context. Innovation was precipitated by political events that led to the establishment of a socialist government. This latter began to change radically the power relations between groups in conflict with each other and sought to match aspirations for a fairer society with the organisation and purposes of the education system.

The Malaysian case study is illustrative of a rational-empirical view of relationships where the introduction of a new programme created the need for inservice support for it. This appears to fit a functionalist interpretation. So also does The Gambia case study where manpower rationales have figured prominently in the development of policy. School organisation and curricular form have been seen as a potent force to meet the needs of national development for trained school graduates with academic and practical skills.

In Kano State the mismatches between education and society that initiated the special Science School Project had additional dimensions. National manpower needs for science and technology trained personnel were prominent but they were seen as particularly acute in the context of the internal political debate. The North historically depended on trained manpower from the southern States and this dependence was brought home during the Biafran war when many Southerners left their posts, leaving Kano with few scientifically-trained staff. The need to promote indigenes of Kano State was therefore seen to be paramount to balance the educational disadvantages that had their origins in early missionary policy and Lugard's dual mandate. In addition the innovation hoped to change attitudes to ones more favourable to scientific and technological careers and to balance the needs for this with the conservative Islamic reaction to modern schooling.

The rationale for introducing vocational elements into Nigerian schools had a prominent element of responding to labour market needs. However, there were strong differences of interpretation as to the extent to which it was to promote skills of direct use in employment or skills which would lay a pre-vocational foundation on which to build. JSS as a whole could be seen as a response to growing demand following in the wake of Universal Primary Education which greatly increased the numbers reaching secondary school entrance level. At the same time politicians defended it as capable of ameliorating the problems of rising school leaver unemployment.

Stuart's study sees relationships much more in terms of the individual's relationship to professional practice than in terms of needs identified at a system level. She promotes reappraisal within existing conditions and argues that change should come from the motives and aspirations of actors within the system who are the practitioners. From a related perspective Leach's Sudanese case studies stress the viewpoint that change in social systems comes about through changes in the behaviour of the actors involved. The need for the projects in the Sudan arises from the drain of competent staff and the lack of resources, though a dependency-type interpretation of events casts the high level of foreign aid in a more sinister light.

Exploring the approaches further leads us to identify six key dimensions on which the approaches differ. These are:

(a) consensus or conflict;
(b) groups or individuals;
(c) certification of competency or legitimation of inequality;
(d) historical determinism or ahistorical equilibration;
(e) beneficent modernisers or conspiratorial hegemonists;
(f) the evaluation of intentions and outcomes.

In reading the case studies these categories can be used to explore the ideological and theoretical sub-texts that underlie the analysis offered. It should be noted that the case studies were not designed with this as an organising framework. All the more interesting, therefore, to establish whether these theoretical perspectives are useful.

Consensus or Conflict

Modernisation theorists assume high degrees of normative consensus within societies. Conflict is a pathological deviation from consensus (Paulston 1976) and thus changes that do not arise from social needs as articulated through that consensus are 'dysfunctional'. Clark (1962) illustrates this view well:

Greater schooling for greater numbers has brought with it and evidently implies a greater practicality in what the schools teach and what they do for students. The existence of children of diverse ability calls forth the comprehensive school.

Neo-Marxists see consensus as a pathological deviation from conflict. Where it does occur it is to be regarded with suspicion since it may be the product of co-option (adoption of the values of a dominant group) or of false consciousness (failing to see what is in the real interests of the group). Educational change from this perspective is a continuing 'struggle' of competing interests, and policy and innovation reflect the dispositions of groups that have power.

The China case study illustrates elements of this. The ideological debate over the geography curriculum revolved around whether the education system should be regarded as part of the superstructure or part of the base. Consensus was assumed once a party line had been established. Events in the Seychelles conform to a view of change based initially on conflict and realignment of power relations. Haffenden shows how this occurred at the start of the project and how the forms of establishing consensus changed in its formative years.

The KBSR case study of inservice in Malaysia indicates a high expectation of consensus about the new programme and its aims. The fact that these were not readily demonstrated subsequently in teachers' opinions was taken by many as an indication that more work had to be done in disseminating ideas about the courses. The implementation strategy was not developed in a climate of competing points of view about the KBSR programme. In The Gambia consensus seems to be assumed and the dominant value system is accepted in both the schools studied. Policy has not emerged from conflict between groups so much as from perceived needs to maintain equilibrium and reduce mismatches of school output and labour market demand. Though consensus was assumed in the need for the introduction of JSS in Nigeria, Nwakoby's analysis suggests that there was little subsequent consensus about key aspects of the innovation. In Adamu's work a 'forced consensus' was achieved in the wake of the military coup. This ensured that implementation would proceed despite the initial opposition of the Ministry of Education, but later analysis illustrates its fragility in relation to the curricular elements of the innovation.

In contrast, Stuart's action research study places the teacher and pupil clients at centre stage in the innovation process, arguing that consensus should be negotiated by them prior to action to improve implementation of the development studies curriculum. Consensus is not assumed. Leach's study similarly highlights the idea that perception gaps in project actualisation are a key determinant of performance. Formal consensus may be combined with unresolved conflicts in views.

Groups and Individuals

For the modernisation theorist normative consensus is essentially an expression of convergence of individual interests. Consensus, conflict, competition, and reward are all viewed as individual level phenomena. For the neo-Marxist, on the other hand, group or class interests are the definitive characteristic of social and economic interaction. Consensus, conflict, competition and reward are first and foremost group level phenomena.

The China case study illustrates a strong element of competition and conflict between factional groups in the development of the new geography curriculum. The professional debate, like the political one which preceded it, was characterised by groups promoting different views of appropriate curricula and struggling to get their own accepted through debate and the mobilisation of power. The NYS in Haffenden's study was seen as an initiative to ensure more equitable access to educational provision for the population as a whole. The development of the project is characterised by the formation of different groups over time which represent different interpretations of how best to achieve this. In Leach's work in Sudan groups which compete to interpret project tasks and benefits are identified. A three-fold division is apparent in the projects which counterpoises project staff, local management and expatriates, and their interests.

In the Kano case study individuals played a key role in the development of the project. But its origins were embedded in the politics of competition between groups – the North and the South, modern education and Islamic values, the needs of the élite schooled in urban areas and those of the mass of children in rural schools. Nwakoby's study attributes individuals with having pivotal influence on the development and implementation of the JSS innovation. Groups of actors do not seem to have asserted themselves and their interests strongly in the development of the programme. In Lesotho individuals' professional practice and its improvement is central.

Through the medium of a collaborative group common problem areas are identified.

Certification of Competency or Legitimation of Inequality?

Modernisation advocates stress selection and allocation of individuals through meritocratic competitions. Achievement certifies ability and effort, provides access to opportunities, and justifies differential rewards on a relatively impartial basis. Clark (1962) argues that:

Sorting must take place at some point in the educational structure. If . . . it does not take place at the door, it must occur inside the doors . . . the college offers the opportunity to try, but the student's own ability and his cumulative record of performance finally insist that he be sorted.

In contrast neo-Marxists accept that selection of this kind may be inevitable with division of labour in production, but they interpret its social significance differently. Far from allocating opportunities fairly to students, selection systems merely:

legitimise existing economic inequalities by persuading workers that their own economic success, be it great or small, is deserved on the basis of fair scholastic competition . . . since the ostensible objectives and meritocratic entrance standards favour the economically advantaged.   (Bowles, Gintis and Simmons 1976)

In Carnoy's (1974) terms:

Neo-classical development theory views schooling as a 'liberating' process in which the child is transformed from a 'traditional' one to a 'modern' one. This transition is supposed to enable the child to be creative as well as functional. . . . But in dependency theory, the transformation that takes place in school cannot be liberating since a person is changed from a dependent role in one system to a different role in the same system. . . . Rather than being a means through which individuals fulfil their potential the schools are reduced to being largely selectors and socialisers.

The role of subjects in selection and allocation figures as part of the story of most of the innovations examined. The resurrection of meritocratic examinations leading to university entrance was a key step in the pragmatists' attempts to reduce the importance of ideology in favour of competence in post-Maoist China. Though contradictory in the sense that many would guess that this would inevitably lead to the regeneration of patterns of access that favoured and legitimated the promotion of children of intellectuals and urban dwellers (the Marxist critique of selection as a legitimator in an unfair competition) this view temporarily at least held the day as a backlash to the excesses of the Cultural Revolution. Recent work here by Leung and others (for example, Lewin and Xu 1989) does suggest that examinations have once again begun to dominate teaching and learning and that selection and access are unevenly distributed by class background. In the absence of much social science research on achievement and social background in China it is difficult to take this analysis further.

In Kano selection and allocation on the basis of competency were represented as the way forward. The opposition that saw in this a Machiavellian conspiracy of elitist practice lost their battle in the wake of the military coup which took influence away from the professionals and gave it to the military governor. It incidentally brought closer the relationship of educational and economic policy-making. The JSS innovation in vocationalisation was accompanied by the introduction of new school-based assessment methods in Nigeria which are explored in detail elsewhere (Nwakoby 1987). This background was significant for the way in which the vocationalised subjects developed, if only because there was even greater confusion and delayed implementation surrounding the new assessment arrangements. As a result the dominant concern for selection which characterised the schools could not be easily used to reinforce the implementation of the new curricula.

Selection and allocation were important considerations in the formation of the NYS. As it was to be 'prefigurative' of new patterns of social relations based on socialist ideals, it sought to balance selection through academic performance with that in other arenas of human development, and especially those connected with useful living and working skills. Selection and allocation figure prominently in the exploration of school climates in The Gambia. The high school curriculum is controlled by the demands of external examinations and the school climate is heavily influenced by pressures to produce examination results. In the secondary technical school direct influence seems less but the 'second chance' opportunity provided for access to high schools academicises parts of the curriculum. The selection and allocation of local staff for opportunities within the Sudanese projects is clearly a source of potential conflict. Those who benefit appear to defend the legitimacy of the process; those who do not, see it as reflecting power alignments and patronage.

Historical Determinism or Ahistorical Equilibration?

Modernisation theorists attribute less significance to historical experience than do neo-Marxists. The models of development that shaped economic thinking in the 1960s (for example, Rostow's stages theories) were historical in a comparative sense but did not seek to explain current development problems as a result of historical processes. The emphasis was on what were thought to be domestic problems such as capital scarcity, feudal institutions and land reform. Neo-Marxists and later dependency theorists elevated historical relations to centre stage. Thus Sunkel (1979) could argue that:

> Even if one must still begin from the particular country that one is interested in, its specific historical development process must be put in the context of the evolution of capitalism generally globally and of its local internal manifestations. These have typically been the determining factors that have triggered off profound processes of structural transformation.

The significance of the history of Chinese political development is evident from Leung's case study. Recent events can also only be interpreted in the light of this. Kano State's science education problem was clearly conceived of in a historical context by most of those involved. The 'under-education' of the North of Nigeria was seen as a result of successive colonial policies, described politely as benign neglect, which created a much lower level of enrolments than in the South. In contrast the history of attempts to vocationalise Nigerian education do not seem to have had much significance – institutional memories were too short and crisis management punctuated by successive compromise seems to have dominated the pattern of development. In Malaysia institutional learning from previous inservice programmes also seems to have been limited. Traditional expectations of teacher's and pupil's behaviour play a role in creating the baseline for the Lesotho action research initiative. So also does the positivist view of knowledge attributed to pupils and teachers identified by the group as problematic. But in this case historical influences are shown to be open to change.

Historical context is important in the Sudanese case studies for its relationship to socio-cultural differences between the groups

identified. Both Sudanese and expatriates bring with them to project
a cultural baggage of social interaction conventions which are a resul
of historical processes as well as roles within the projects. In Th
Gambia the high school is strongly influenced by its development as
grammar school. The secondary technical school seems less bound b
history as it has a relatively short one. History both recent an
colonial was of great significance in shaping the form that the NY
took in the Seychelles. The embedded privileges of the 'grands blancs
created a focus of dissatisfaction and a motivation for restructuring

Beneficent Modernisers or Conspiratorial Hegemonists?

Both traditions regard the formation, behaviour and attitudes o
national élites as important determinants of social change. The label
attached to élites differ. Modernisation theorists perceive no neces
sary contradiction between the interests of national élites and thos
of the people that they claim to serve. Modernisation is generall
conceived of as in the interests of all groups in society even if th
'trickle down' (Chenery 1974) effects of élite-led growth have bee
more like drops into sand than rivulets of redistribution. The view
that what is good for the élite is necessarily good for the masse
necessarily presupposes some consensus about individual and societa
level goals. Since modernisation is implicitly attached to imitativ
patterns of development it is not surprising that this perspective see
little to criticise in the replicative introduction of educational innova
tions that reflect recent developments in metropolitan countries.

Neo-Marxists use the language of class stratification and conflict t
refer to comprador classes and bourgeois élites acting within
framework of national and transnational exploitation. Some go as fa
as to relegate local élites to the status of a 'lumpenbourgeoisie
incapable of independent accumulation and blind to their rea
interests (Frank 1974) who are incorporated into a system of globa
exploitation. The development of a transnational community i
argued to be made up of:

> people that belong to different nations but who have similar values
> beliefs, ideas (and a lingua franca – English) as well as remarkabl
> similar patterns of behaviour as regards career patterns, family
> structures, housing, dress, consumption patterns and cultura
> orientations in general. (Sunkel and Fuenzalida 1979

But dissenters find this insulting and culturally demeaning as an Indian reviewer observed:

> There could be no greater slur inflicted on our capabilities: we are nincompoops, we are unable to ensure a local supply of exploiters, the process of exploitation has to be initiated elsewhere ... this itself is neo-colonialism of a sort.
>
> (Indian Economic and Political Weekly, 23 April 1977)

The case studies reveal differing perceptions amongst key groups of roles and the interests of groups. In most there is a familiar division between those who claim to have subordinated individual and group interests to the collective good, and those who interpret action to reflect these. Thus it seems clear that China's élites, though part of a Marxist–Leninist state, seem to see themselves as beneficent modernisers who act in the interests of the masses. They would claim they are driven by dialectical materialism and the ideology of scientific socialism. Whether this view is shared by the masses is in question as the old guard impose a revolutionary style that seems to clash with the aspirations of the post-Cultural Revolution generation.

In both the Nigerian case studies the key role played by military intervention in government makes unfashionable reading. The military government and its appointees seem to fit into the role of beneficent modernisers as judged by their own accounts. Action-orientated and power-coercive by orientation, this is perhaps not surprising. Expatriates in the Sudanese case study represent an élite and are resented for it. Collectively their defence is also that of the benevolent moderniser. Sudanese project management staff are often reluctant to delegate and feel entitled to discharge duties on behalf of others. But project staff often interpret actions in terms of the self-interest of those with power.

The Gambian case study makes the point that the high school is the traditional location of the children of the local élite. For this reason, and the connection with access to overseas universities, the school climate has continued to reflect its elitist origins. The secondary technical school creation was regarded by this group as a kind of cooling-out device. Since it did not threaten the grammar school concept it was neither opposed nor resourced properly. To the current Seychelles government, its predecessors were hegemonists intent on maintaining control over production and the distribution of the wealth generated by it. Their self-image appears to be that of well-motivated servants of the people, the party of the vanguard of a new society.

The Evaluation of Intentions and Outcomes

These differences are probably the crudest to articulate but also the most fundamental in importance. They have two elements.

First is the evaluation of the intentions of the agents of change. Modernisation theorists see the motivation of the initiators of change as benign. *Noblesse oblige* is the guiding light of élites striving to extend the benefits they enjoy to the rest of the community at a rate governed by what is prudent and can be resourced. Individuals are attributed with different psychological needs which can be hierarchically organised (Maslow 1943). Changes come about in response to these. More particular change has a strong individual basis since it is driven partly by those with high psychological needs to achieve, the entrepreneurs with high N-ach (need for achievement) in McClelland's terms (McClelland 1961).

Dependency theorists cast the verb 'to underdevelop' in transitive form implying conscious mal-intent by groups intent on enhancing their hegemony (Dore 1977). Class stratification necessarily creates a divergence of interests that can only be resolved through power struggles where those with most power enforce their interests on the remainder of the population. Motivation to change is thus seen as driven by the logic of self-interest of groups rather than commitments to public service and the greater good. These arguments are applied to both intended and unintended change, it being presumed that there are consonant underlying motives that explain changes that were not intended.

Second is the evaluation of the results of change. This is a complex set of issues but some differences are apparent. Modernisation theorists encourage convergence of 'modern' dispositions and systems of production, and value international standards and integration into global market places. They value growth more than distribution, and pluralism more than ideological purity. Neo-Marxists take the view that changes that result in continued transfer of wealth and resources to the relatively rich, continue the dependence of the masses on an élite and undermine national identity are antithetical to development. Distribution is thought more important than growth, and pluralism may be a luxury for a later stage of development.

These different evaluations cannot be simply catalogued since they need interpretation within different developmental contexts. They are of great importance to innovations since it is on them that appraisal of relative success or failure depends. It matters a great leal, for example, whether increase in enrolments in secondary chools is seen as a successful and valued outcome that increases the low of secondary educated workers who can contribute to industrialsation, or is seen as a failure if it conceals the fact that such nrolments are from already privileged families and result in a net ransfer of resources away from a primary school system where access s more equitably distributed.

It is appropriate to end a book on educational innovation which eeks to explore rather than prescribe with a list of questions. These an be used to interrogate the evidence in the case studies and rovoke further research. It is therefore left to the reader to begin to nake judgements from the case studies about the intentions and esults of the innovations described.

Is China's leadership adopting an ambiguous stance towards innovation which tries to reconcile openness, critical debate and increased local autonomy with older values that sanctify the centralised authority of the party, seniority and hierarchy?

Are the costs of innovation in Nigeria born at the expense, or in the interests, of those at the margins of the system?

Did inservice training in Malaysia result in the best preparation of teachers for KBSR that was possible, or did it offer too little too late?

Does Stuart's emphasis on teachers' ability to critically reflect on practice offer a valuable strategy for change or is it a potentially risky avenue of development that may lead some teachers away from the expectations parents and governments have of them?

Are the expatriates and the nationals in the Sudan victims of the social relations of donors and recipients or are they willing accomplices?

Is restructuring in The Gambia frustrated by lack of resources or ambivalence in policy formation?

Will the realignments that catalysed the NYS in the Seychelles survive its maturity, or will its radicalism be dissipated by consolidation, routinisation, and the redevelopment of powerful interest groups?

Bibliography

*Indicates written in Chinese.

Adams, R.S. and D. Chen (1981) *The Process of Educational Innovation: An International Perspective* (Kogan and Page/UNESCO Press).

Adamu, A.U. (1988) *Science, Schooling and Manpower Production in Nigeria: A Study of Kano State Science Secondary Schools, 1977–1987,* unpublished D.Phil thesis, University of Sussex.

Aikenshead, G.S. (1984) 'Science Teaching at Prairie High School', in J. Olson and T. Russell (eds), *Science Education in Canadian High Schools, Vol. 3: Case Studies of Science Teaching* (Ontario: The Science Council of Canada).

APEID (1976) *Towards Strategies of Curriculum Development: Report on an Asian Workshop* (Bangkok: UNESCO).

Archer, M.S. (1984) *Social Origins of Educational Systems* (Sage Publication).

Argyris, C. and D.A. Schön (1974) *Theory in Practice* (London: Jossey-Bass).

Asiah, A.S. (1981) 'KBSR – Beberapa Isu dan Implikasi' [KBSR – Some Issues and Implications], in S. Ibrahim (ed.) 1982, *Dari Pedagogi ke Politik*, [From Pedagogy to Politics] (Kuala Lumpur: Utusan Publication).

Avalos, B. (1980) 'Teacher Effectiveness: Research in the Third World – Highlights of a Review', *Comparative Education*, vol. 16, no. 1.

—— (1986) 'Qualitative/Popular Education Research in Latin America', paper presented to BERA Conference, Bristol, September 1986 (mimeo).

Baez, A.V. (1976) *Innovation in Science Education World-Wide* (Paris: UNESCO Press).

Bacchus, M.K. (1980) *Education for Development or Underdevelopment?* (Waterloo, Canada: Wilfrid Laurier University Press).

Ball, S.J. (1981a) 'The Sociology of Education in Developing Countries', *British Journal of Sociology of Education*, vol. 2, no. 3.

—— (1981b) *Beachside Comprehensive* (Cambridge University Press).

—— (1982) 'Competition and Conflict in the Teaching of English: A Socio-historical Analysis', *Journal of Curriculum Studies*, 14 (1): 1–28.

—— (1983) 'Case Study Research in Education: Some Notes and Problems', in M. Hammersley (ed.), *The Ethnography of Schooling* (Nafferton Books).

—— (1987) 'Relations, Structures and Conditions in Curriculum Change: A Political History of English Teaching 1970–1985', in I. Goodson (ed.), *International Perspectives in Curriculum History* (London: Croom Helm).

Barnes, D. and F. Todd (1977) *Communication and Learning in Small Groups* (London: Routledge & Kegan Paul).

Becher, T. and S. MaClure (1978) *The Politics of Curriculum Change* (London: Hutchinson).

Beeby, C.E. (1966) *The Quality of Education in Developing Countries* (Cambridge, Mass: Harvard University Press).

Beijing Normal University SMSGC Editorial Group* (1983) *Teaching Reference for Senior Middle School Geography, Books 1 and 2* (Beijing: People's Education Press).

Berger, P. (1974) *Pyramids of Sacrifice* (London: Pelican).

Berman, P. and M. McLaughlin (1976) 'Implementation of Curriculum Innovation', *Education Forum*, 3: 347–70.

——— (1979) *An Explanatory Study of School District Adaptation* (Santa Monica: Rand Corporation).

Blakemore, K. and B. Cooksey (1981) *A Sociology of Education for Africa* (London: Allen & Unwin).

Blau, P. (1955) *The Dynamics of Bureaucracy* (University of Chicago Press).

Blaug, M. (1973) *Education and the Employment Problem in Developing Countries* (Geneva: ILO).

Bloom, B.S. (1956) *Taxonomy of Educational Objectives* (London: Longman).

Bloom, B.S., G.F. Madaus and J.T. Hastings (1981) *Evaluation to Improve Learning* (McGraw Hill).

Boakye, J.K. and J. Oxenham (1982) *Qualifications and the Quality of Education in Ghanaian Rural Middle Schools*, Education Report no. 6, Institute of Development Studies, University of Sussex.

Bolam, R. (1978) 'The Management of Educational Change; Towards a Conceptual Framework', in A. Harris, M. Lawn and W. Prescott *Curriculum Innovation* (Milton Keynes: Open University).

Boud, D.J. *et al* (1985) 'The Physical Science Evaluation, Western Australia 1978–79: An Application of the Illuminative Model', in P. Tamir (ed.), *The Role of Evaluators in Curriculum Development* (London: Croom Helm).

Bowles, S. and H. Gintis (1976) *Schooling in Capitalist America* (New York: Basic Books).

Bowles, S., H. Gintis and J. Simmons (1976) 'The Impact of Education on Poverty: The US Experience', *International Development Review* no. 2.

Broadfoot, P. (1980) 'Rhetoric and Reality in the Context of Innovation: An English Case Study', *Compare*, 10 (2): 117–76.

Brooke, N. and J. Oxenham (1980) *The Quality of Education in Mexican Primary Schools. Research Reports*, Education Report no. 5, Institute of Development Studies, University of Sussex.

——— (1984) 'The Influence of Certification and Selection on Teaching and Learning', in J. Oxenham (ed.), *Education versus Qualifications?* (London: Allen & Unwin).

Brooke, N., J. Oxenham and A.W. Little (1978) *Qualifications and Employment in Mexico. Research Reports*, Education Report no. 1, Institute of Development Studies, University of Sussex.

Bude, U. (1980) 'Science Education Programme for Africa (SEPA), An Overview of Organization, Aim and Actions', in U. Bude (ed.), *Science for Self Reliance. The Science Education Programme for Africa* (Koln: Deutsche Stiftung Fur Internationale Entwicklung) DOK 1050 A IT 21-05-80.

Burrell, G. and G. Morgan (1979) *Sociological Paradigms and Organiza* *tional Analysis* (London: Heinemann Educational Books).
CARN (Classroom Action Research Network) Bulletins: no. 4 (1980) *Th* *Theory and Practice of Educational Action Research*; no. 6 (1984) *Actio* *Research in Schools: Getting it into Perspective*; no. 7 (1986) *Collaborativ* *Action Research*; no. 8 (1987) *Action Research in Development*.
Carnoy, M. (1974) *Education as Cultural Imperialism* (Longman).
Carr, W. and S. Kemmis (1983) *Becoming Critical: Knowing through Actio* *Research* (Victoria: Deakin University Press).
Cassen, R. *et al* (1986) *Does Aid Work?* (Oxford: Clarendon Press).
CCP (1985) *Decision of the Central Committee of the Communist Party o* *China on the Reform of the Educational Structure* (Beijing: Foreig* Languages Press).
Chambers, R. (1980) *Rural Poverty Unperceived: Problems and Remedies* World Bank Staff Working Paper no. 400.
———(1983) *Rural Development: Putting the Last First* (New York: Longman)
Chen Erzou* (1982) 'Explanatory Notes on the Newly Edited Senior Middl* School Geography Textbooks', *Kejing, Jiaocai and Jiaofa (Curriculum* *Teaching Materials and Teaching Methods)*, vol. 2.
Chen Yuanxian and Chu Zhenchung (1983)* *On Teaching and Learning* (Zhejiang Education Press).
Chenery, H. *et al* (1974) *Redistribution with Growth* (Oxford University Press).
Chin, R. and K.D. Benne (1969) 'General Strategies for Effecting Changes in Human Systems', in W.G. Bennis, K.D. Benne and R. Chin (eds), *The* *Planning of Change*, 2nd edn (New York: Holt, Rinehart & Winston).
China Geographical Association* (1982) *Communiqué on the Xiamen* *Conference*, September 1982.
Chu Zhaotang and Sun Dawn* (1980) 'Enquiring into the Senior Middle School Earth Science Curriculum', paper presented at the Hangzhou Conference, December 1980.
———(1982) *Geography Teaching Methods* (East China Normal University).
Chu Yaping* (1985) 'The Problem of Text Construction and Geography Curriculum of Primary and Middle Schools', *Teaching References for* *Middle School Geography* (Shenxi Normal University).
Clark, B.R. (1962) *Educating the Expert Society* (San Francisco: Chandler).
Cohen, L. and L. Manion (1980) *Research Methods in Education* (London: Croom Helm).
Cohn, C. and R.A. Rossmiller (1987) 'Research on Effective Schools: Implications for Less Developed Countries', *Comparative Education* *Review*, vol. 31, no. 3.
Commissiong F. (1979) 'Grade 10 and 11: Science Curriculum in Jamaica', in *Science Education for Progress – A Caribbean Perspective* (Regional Conference, Barbados, West Indies 19–22 April 1979) (London: International Council of Association for Science Education/ASE).
Coombs, P.H. (1968) *The World Educational: A Systems Analysis* (London: Oxford University Press).
——— (1985) *The World Crisis of Education: The View from the Eighties* (Oxford Univeristy Press).

Coombs, P.H. and Ahmed M. (1975) *Education for Rural Development* (New York: Praeger).
Cooper, B. (1984) *Innovation in English Secondary School Mathematics* (Falmer Press).
Corey, S.M. (1953) *Action Research to Improve School Practices*, Bureau of Publications, Teachers College (New York: Columbia University Press).
Crossley, M. (1984) 'The Role and Limitation of Small Scale Innovations in Educational Innovation', *Prospects*, vol. XIV, no. 4, UNESCO.
Crossley, M. and G. Vulliamy (1984) 'Case Study Research Methods and Comparative Education', *Comparative Education* (20) 2.
Curle, A. (1963) *Educational Strategy for Developing Countries* (London: Tavistock Publications).
Dalin, P. (1978) *Limits to Educational Change* (London: Macmillan Press).
Dalin, P. and V. Rust (1983) *Can Schools Learn?* (NFER-Nelson).
Day, C. (1984) 'External Consultancy: Supporting School-based Curriculum Development', in *CARN Bulletin no. 6* (Cambridge Institute of Education).
Delamont, S. (1976) *Explorations in Classroom Observation* (Wiley).
Deng Xiaoping* (1977) 'Respect Kowledge, Respect Trained Personnel', *Selected Works of Deng Xiaoping* (Beijing: Foreign Languages Press).
_____* (1978a) 'Speech at the Opening Ceremony of National Science Conference 27 March 1978', *Peking Review*, no. 12.
_____* (1978b) 'Speech at the Conference on Education', *Selected Works of Deng Xiaoping* (Beijing: Foreign Languages Press).
Depierre, R. (1987) 'Maoism in Recent French Educational Thought and Practice', in R. Hayhoe and M. Bastid (eds), *China's Education and the Industrialised World: Studies in Cultural Transfer* (New York: M.E. Sharpe).
Deraniyagala C., R.P. Dore and A.W. Little (1978) *Qualification and Employment in Sri Lanka. Research Reports*, Education Report no. 2, Institute of Development Studies, University of Sussex.
DES (1987) *Quality in Schools: The Initial Training of Teachers – A Survey of Initial Teacher Training in the Public Sector in England, Northern Ireland and Wales* (London: HMSO).
Dodd, W.A. (1969) *Education for Self-reliance: A Study of its Vocational Aspects* (New York: Teachers College Press, Columbia University).
Dore, R.P. (1976) *The Diploma Disease* (Unwin Education).
_____ (1977) *Underdevelopment in Theoretical Perspective*, Discussion Paper no. 109, Institute of Development Studies, University of Sussex.
Dore, R.P., R. Jolly, A. Little, B. Mook and J. Oxenham (1975) *Qualification and Selection in Educational Systems in Developing Countries: A Programme of Research*, Part 1: 'How Employers Use Qualifications and How Qualifications Affect Schools'; Part 2: 'Job Seekers and Job Placement Services', Discussion Papers nos 70 and 71, Institute of Development Studies, University of Sussex.
Dore, R.P. and A.W. Little (1982) *The Diploma Disease Film and Video* (Institute of Development Studies, University of Sussex).
Dore, R. and J. Oxenham (1984) 'Educational Reform and Selection for Employment – an Overview', in J.P.C. Oxenham (ed.), *Education versus Qualifications?* (London: Allen & Unwin).

Dowdeswell, W.H. (1967) 'The Nuffield Project I: Biology 11–16', *School Science Review* vol. XLVIII, no. 165: 323–31.

Durkheim, E. (1969) 'L'Evolution Pédagogique en France', Presses Universitaires France, translated in J. Karabel and A.H. Halsey *Power and Ideology in Education* (Oxford University Press).

Economist Intelligence Unit (1987) *Country Profile: Sudan* (Economist Publications).

Elliott, J. (1976) *Developing Hypotheses about Classrooms from Teachers' Practical Constructs* (Ford Teaching Project, Cambridge Institute of Education).

—— (1981) *Action Research: A Framework for Self-evaluation in Schools*, Working Paper no. 1, Schools Council Programme 2 'Teacher-pupil Interaction and the Quality of Learning' Project.

Elliott, J. and C. Adelman (1975) 'Teachers' Accounts and the Objectivity of Classroom Research', *London Educational Review*, vol. 4.

English, P.W. and R.C. Mayfield (eds) (1972) *Man, Space and Environment: Concepts in Contemporary Human Geography* (Oxford University Press).

Eraut, M. (1977) 'Some Perspectives on Consultancy in In-service Education', *British Journal of In-service Education*, vol. 4 no. 1–2.

—— (1985), 'In-Service Teacher Education', in *International Encyclopedia of Education Research and Studies*, vol. 5 (Oxford: Pergamon Press).

Eraut, M., L. Goad and G. Smith (1975) *The Analysis of Curriculum Materials*, Occasional Paper no. 2, University of Sussex Education Area.

Federal Republic of Nigeria (1979) *Implementation Committee for the National Policy on Education 1978–9: Blueprint* (Lagos: Federal Government Press).

—— (1981) *National Policy on Education (Revised)* (Lagos: Federal Government Press).

Flanders, T. (1980) *The Professional Development of Teachers* (Vancouver: British Columbia Teachers' Federation).

Foreign and Commonwealth Office (1986) *Year Book of the Commonwealth 1986* (London: HMSO).

Foster, G.M. (1973) *Traditional Societies and Technological Change*, 2nd edn (New York: Harper).

Foster, P.J. (1965) 'The Vocational School Fallacy in Development Planning', in C.A. Anderson and M.J. Bowman (eds) *Education and Economic Development* (London: Cass).

Frank, A.G. (1974) *Lumpenbourgeoisie; Lumpendevelopment: Dependence, Class and Politics in Latin America* (New York: Monthly Review Press).

Freire, P. (1972) *The Pedagogy of the Oppressed* (Harmondsworth: Penguin).

Fullan, M. (1982) *The Meaning of Educational Change* (New York: Teachers College, Columbia University).

—— (1985a) 'Curriculum Change', in *International Encyclopedia of Education Research and Studies*, vol. 2 (Oxford: Pergamon Press).

—— (1985b) 'Change Processes and Strategies at the Local Level', in *The Elementary School Journal*, vol. 85, no. 3.

Fullan, M. and A. Pomfret (1977) 'Research on Curriculum and Instruction Implementation', *Review of Educational Research* 47 (1): 335–97.

Gambian Ministry of Education (1975) *Republic of the Gambia Education Policy: 1976–1986* (Banjul: Government Printer).
_____ (1982) *Gambia Education Sector Study; Final Draft* (Banjul: Government Printer).

Gambian Ministry of Economic Planning and Industrial Development (1981) *Republic of Gambia Five-Year Plan for Economic and Social Development 1981/82–1985/86* (Banjul: Ministry of Economic Planning).

Gatewood, C.W. and E.S. Obourn (1963) 'Improving Science Education in the United States', *Journal of Research in Science Teaching*, vol. 1: 355–99.

Ge Wencheng* (1986) 'Thoughts on the Writing of Senior Middle School Geography Textbooks', paper presented in a teacher seminar on the writing of geography textbooks, Shanghai.

Glaser, B. and A. Strauss (1967) *The Discovery of Grounded Theory: Strategies for Qualitative Research* (Hawthorne, NY: Aldine Publishing Company).

Goodlad, J.I. *et al* (1966) *The Changing School Curriculum* (New York: The Fund for the Advancement of Science Education).

Goodson, I. (1983) *School Subjects and Curriculum Change* (London: Croom Helm).

Graham, S.F. (1966) *Government and Mission Education in Northern Nigeria, 1900–1919* – with special reference to the work of Hanns Vischer (Ibadan University Press).

Gross, N., J.B. Giacquinta and M. Bernstein (1971) *Implementing Organisational Innovations: A Sociological Analysis of Planned Change* (London: Harper & Row).

Guba, E.G. and Y.S. Lincoln (1981) *Effective Evaluation* (San Francisco: Jossey Bass).

Gumo, C. and U. Kann (1982) *A Review of the Development of the Kenya Teachers College*, Report no. 61, Institute of International Education, University of Stockholm.

Gunn, L.A. (1978) 'Why is Implementation so Difficult?', *Management Services in Goverment*, 33.

Guo Zhenchuan (1987) 'Implementation of the Geography Curriculum in Remote and Border Regions', oral report of the PEP Investigation Team, presented at the Hangzhou Conference, November 1987.

Guthrie, G. (1986) 'Current Research in Developing Countries: the Impact of Curriculum Reform on Teaching', *Teaching and Teacher Education*, (2) 1.

Haffenden, I (1991) 'Curriculum Innovation, Implementation and Purification: The Syechelles National Youth Service 1981–86' in K. Evans and I. Haffenden (eds) *Education for Young Adults: International Perspectives* (London: Routledge).

Hall, G.E. and S.F. Loucks (1977) 'A Developmental Model for Determining whether the Treatment is Actually Implemented', *American Educational Research Journal*, 3: 263–76.

Ham, C. and M. Hill (1984) *The Policy Process in the Modern Capitalist States* (Wheatsheaf Books).

Handy, C. (1985) *Understanding Organizations*, 3rd edn (Harmondsworth: Penguin).

310   *Bibliography*

Harding, H. (1984) 'The Study of Chinese Politics: Towards a Third Generation of Scholarship', *World Politics*, vol. 36, no. 2.

Harms, N.C. and R.E. Yager (1981) (eds), *What Research Says to the Science Teacher*, vol. 3 (Washington: National Science Teachers Association).

Havelock, R.G. (1969) *Planning for Innovation through Dissemination and the Utilisation of Knowledge* (Centre for Research on the Utilisation of Scientific Knowledge, Institute for Social Research, University of Michigan).

_____ (1970) *A Guide to Innovation in Education* (ISR, University of Michigan).

_____ (1973a) *Planning for Innovation through Dissemination and Utilization of Knowledge* (ISR, University of Michigan).

_____ (1973b) *The Change Agent's Guide to Innovation* (Englewood Cliffs, New Jersey: Educational Technology Publications).

Havelock, R.G. and A.M. Huberman (1977) *Solving Educational Problems: The Planning and Reality of Innovation in Developing Countries* (Paris: UNESCO).

Hawes, H. (1979) *Curriculum and Reality in African Primary Schools* (Longman).

He Bochuan* (1986) 'Hidden Crisis in Chinese Education', *Weilai Yu Fazhan (Future & Development)*, vol. 4.

He Dongchang* (1988) 'Rural Education should Serve Local Construction', *Zhongguo Jiaoyu Bao, (Chinese Education News)* 1 March 1988.

He Manhua* (1985) 'On Reforming Curriculum for Rural Schools', *Kejing, Jiaocai and Jiaofa, (Curriculum, Teaching Materials and Teaching Methods)*, 6: 61–5.

Heaver, R. (1982) *Bureaucratic Politics and Incentives in the Management of Rural Development*, World Bank Staff Working Paper no. 537.

Heyneman, S.P. and W.A. Loxley (1982) 'Influences on Academic Achievement across High- and Low-Income Countries: A Re-Analysis of IEA Data', *Sociology of Education*, 55.

_____ (1983) 'The Effect of Primary School Quality on Academic Achievement across Twenty-Nine High- and Low-Income Countries', *American Journal of Sociology*, 88.

Holmes, F. (1984) 'The Poverty of Dependence Theory', in C.B.W. Treffgarne (ed.), *Reproduction and Dependency in Education, Part 2*, Occasional Paper no. 7, University of London Institute of Education.

Hondebrink, J.G. (1981) 'Reform of Chemical Education in Holland', *Journal of Chemical Education* vol. 58, no. 11, November 1981.

Hopkins, D. (1985) *A Teacher's Guide to Classroom Research* (Milton Keynes: Open University Press).

Hopper, E. (1971) 'The Classification of Education Systems', in E. Hopper (ed.), *Readings in the Theory of Education Systems* (London: Hutchinson).

Hoyle, E. (1970) 'Planned Organisational Change in Education Research', *Education*, vol. 3.

Hu Yaobang* (1980) 'Opening Speech at the Second National Conference on Science and Technology', *Chinese Education 1949–1982*, Ministry of Education, People's Republic of China.

Hu Yongfai* (1986) 'Review and Preview of Geography Higher School Examination', *Dili Jiaoxue (Geography Teaching)*, vol. 2: 12–13.

Hua Guofeng* (1978) 'Raise the Scientific and Cultural Level of the Entire Chinese Nation', *Peking Review*, no. 13: 6–14.

Huberman, A.M. (1973) 'Understanding Change in Education: An Introduction', in *Experiments and Innovations in Education*, no. 4 (Paris: UNESCO).

Huberman, A.M. and M.B. Miles (1984) *Innovation up Close: How School Improvement Works* (London: Plenum Press).

Hurst, P. (1978) *Implementing Innovatory Projects*, paper commissioned by the World Bank for the Diversified Secondary Curriculum Project (Washington: World Bank).

_____ (1983) *Implementing Educational Change: A Critical Review of the Literature*, EDC Occasional Paper no. 5, University of London Institute of Education.

Husen, T. (1972) *Social Background and Educational Career* (Paris: OECD/ CERI).

Imahori, K. (1980) 'Problems of Innovation in Japanese Science Education', in P. Adey (ed.), *UK – Japan Science Education Seminar: Innovation in Science Education*, 8–12 September 1980 (London: The British Council/ Chelsea College, University of London).

Ivowi, U.M.O. (1982) *Science Curriculum in Nigerian Secondary Schools*, Occasional Paper no. 4. CESAC, University of Lagos.

Jackson, P.W. (1983) 'The Reform of Science Education: A Cautionary Tale', *Daedalus. Journal of the American Academy of Arts and Sciences*, vol. 112, no. 2: 143–66.

Kano State (1970) *Kano State Statistical Year Book 1970* (Kano: Military Governor's Office, Economic Planning Division).

_____ (1971) *Kano State Development Plan 1970–1974* (Kano State: Military Governor's Office, Economic Planning Division).

_____ (1976) *Education Review Committee Final Report* (The Galadanchi Report) (Kano: Government Printer).

_____ (1977) *Policy Statement 1977/78* (Kano: Government Printer).

_____ (1979) *Ministry of Education Kano State: Progress Report, 1968–1979*, compiled by Alhaji Imam Wali (Kano: Ministry of Education, Directorate Division).

_____ (1981) *Kano State – A Giant Leap* (Kano: Triumph Publishing Company).

_____ (1982) Law no. 10 of 1982, 'Science and Technical Schools Board Law', *1982 Kano State of Nigeria Gazette*, vol. 16, no. 11, 26 August 1982 (Kano: Government Printer).

_____ (1983) *Report of Committee on Problems and Prospects of Education in Kano State* (The Tijjani Ismai'l Report) (Kano: Institute for Higher Education/Kano State Polytechnic).

Kaplinsky, R. (1980) *Accumulation in the Periphery: A Special Case – The Seychelles* (Institute of Development Studies, University of Sussex).

Karabel, J. and A.H. Halsey (1977) *Power and Ideology in Education* (Oxford University Press).

Katz, D. and R. Kahn (1966) *The Social Psychology of Organisation* 2nd edn (New York: John Wiley).

KBSR Implementation Committee (1982) 'Minutes of Meeting on 9 February 1982', CDC, Malaysian Ministry of Education.

KBSR Technical Committee (1984) 'Minutes of KBSR Technical Committee Meeting on 28 May 1984', CDC, Malaysian Ministry of Education.

Keddie, N. (1971) 'Classroom Knowledge', in M.F.D. Young (ed.), *Knowledge and Control* (London: Collier Macmillan).

Kelly, P. (1963) 'The Biological Sciences Curriculum Study', *The School Science Review*, vol. XLIV, no. 153: 312–23.

Kelly, P.J. (1975) *Curriculum Diffusion Research Project Outline Report* (Centre for Science Education, University of London).

Kemmis, S. and R. McTaggart (1988) *The Action Research Planner*, 3rd edn (Victoria: Deakin University Press).

Kirk, J. and M.L. Miller (1986) *Reliability and Validity in Qualitative Research* (Beverly Hills: Sage).

Knamiller, G.W. (1984) 'The Struggle for Relevance in Science Education in Developing Countries', *Studies in Science Education*, vol. 11: 60–78.

Knowles, M. (1970) 'Andragogy: An Emerging Technology for Adult Learning', in M. Tight (ed.) (1983), *Education for Adults, Vol. I: Adult Learning and Education* (London: Croom Helm/Open University).

Kogan, M. (1975) *Educational Policy-making: A Study of Interest Groups and Parliament* (London: George Allen & Unwin).

Lacey, C. and I. Haffenden (1985) 'The Seychelles National Youth Service', in K. Lillis (ed.), *School and Community in Less Developed Areas* (London: Croom Helm).

Lazerson, M. *et al* (1984) 'New Curriculum, Old Issues', *Teachers College Record*, vol. 86, no. 2: 300–19.

Le Brun, O. and R. Murray (1980) 'The Seychelles National Youth Service: the Seed of a New Society' (unpublished Seychelles Government report).

Lefoka, J.P. and C.M. Chabane (1987) 'Teaching/Learning Strategies in Lesotho Primary School Classrooms', Institute of Education, National University of Lesotho, Roma (mimeo).

Leithwood, K.A. (1981) 'The Dimensions of Curriculum Innovation', *Journal of Curriculum Studies*, 13: 25–36.

Lethem, F. and L. Cooper (1983) *Managing Project-Related Technical Assistance: The Lessons of Success*, World Bank Staff Working Paper no. 586.

Letiche, H. (1987) *From Europe to the Teaching Team* (Delft: Eburon).

Lewin, K. (1946) 'Action Research and Minority Problems', *Journal of Social Issues*, vol. 2.

——— (1947) *Resolving Social Conflicts* (London: Harper & Row).

Lewin, K.M. (1980) 'Curriculum Renewal and Examination Reform: A Case Study from Malaysia', *IDS Bulletin*, vol. 11, no. 2: 34–41, Institute of Development Studies, University of Sussex.

——— (1981) *Science Education in Malaysia and Sri Lanka: Curriculum Development and Course Evaluation, 1970–1978*, unpublished D.Phil. thesis, University of Sussex.

——— (1984) 'Selection and Curriculum Reform', in J. Oxenham (ed.), *Education Versus Qualifications?* (London: Allen & Unwin).

——— (1985) 'Quality in Question: A New Agenda for Curriculum Reform in Developing Countries', *Comparative Education*, 21 (2).

——— (1987a) *Education in Austerity: Options for Planners* (Paris: International Institute for Educational Planning, UNESCO).

_____ (1987b) 'Science Education in China; Transformation and Change in the 1980s', *Comparative Education Review*, vol. 32, no. 2.

_____ (1988a) 'Curriculum Innovation in Asia: What's Right about the Past and What's Left for the Future?' Opening Address, Conference for the State Education Commission of China on Curriculum Development and Teacher Training, University of Hong Kong.

_____ (1988b) 'Perspectives on Planning: New Initiatives for the Nineties', *Educational Review*, vol. 40, no. 2.

_____ (1988c) 'Valuing the Vulnerable, Responding to Austerity', Conference Paper, Department of International and Comparative Education, University of London Institute of Education, March 1988.

_____ (1988d) 'The Organisational Response to Parsimony', *Compare*, vol. 18, no. 1.

_____ (1989) 'Educational Planning for Scientific and Technological Development', in *International Encyclopaedia of Education* (1988 supplement) (Oxford: Pergamon Press).

Lewin, K.M. and A.W. Little (1984) 'Examination Reform and Educational Change in Sri Lanka 1972–1982: Modernization or Dependent Underdevelopment?', in K. Watson (ed.), *Dependence and Interdependence in Education* (Croom Helm).

Lewin, K. and Wang Lu (1988) 'University Entrance Examinations in China: A Quiet Revolution', paper presented at British Comparative Education Society Annual Conference, 26 November 1988, published in P. Broadfoot, R. Murphy and H. Torrance (1990) *Changing Educational Assessment: International Perspectives and Trends* (Routlege).

Lewin, K.M. and D. Berstecher (1989) 'The Cost of Recovery; Are User Fees the Answer?' *IDS Bulletin*, vol. 20, no. 1, Institute of Development Studies, University of Sussex.

Lewin, K.M. and Xu Hui (1989) 'Rethinking Revolution: Reflections on China's 1985 Educational Reforms', *Comparative Education*, vol. 25, no. 1.

Lewis, L.J. (1954) *Educational Policy and Practice in British Tropical Areas* (London: Thomas Nelson).

Li Yudan* (1980a) 'Remarks on the 24th International Geographical Conference', paper presented at Hangzhou Conference, December 1980.

_____ (1980b) 'On Innovating in Human Geography – A Retrospective and Prospective Look at the Man-Land Relationship', paper presented at Hangzhou Conference, December 1980.

Likert, R. (1961) *New Patterns of Management* (London: McGraw Hill).

_____ (1966) *The Human Organisation* (New York: McGraw Hill).

Lillis, K.M. (1981) *Expatriates and Processes of Secondary Curriculum Innovation in Kenya*, unpublished D.Phil. thesis, University of Sussex.

_____ (1984) 'Africanising the School Literature Curriculum in Kenya: A Case Study in Curriculum Independency', in C.B.W. Treffgarne (ed.), *Reproduction and Dependency in Education: Part 2*, Occasional Paper no. 7, University of London Institute of Education.

_____ (1985) 'Processes of Secondary Curriculum Innovation in Kenya', *Comparative Education Review*, 29 (1).

Lillis, K.M. and D. Hogan (1980) 'The Diversification of Secondary Education: A Review of the Literature', *Development Research Digest*, no. 4, Winter 1980.

—— (1983) 'Dilemmas of Diversification: Problems Associated with Vocational Education in Developing Countries', *Comparative Education*, vol. 19, no. 1.

Little, A.W. (1978) *Types of Examination and Achievement*, Education Report no. 4, Institute of Development Studies, University of Sussex.

—— (1984) 'Education, Earnings and Productivity – The Eternal Triangle', in J. Oxenham (ed.), *Education versus Qualifications?* (London: Allen & Unwin).

Liu Bin* (1987) 'Implementation of Nine Year Compulsory Education should have a Sense of Emergency', *Guangming Ribao*, 11 January 1987.

Liu Shuren* (1980) 'On Reforming the Education Structure and Geography Education', paper presented at the Hangzhou Conference, December 1980.

Long, M. and B.S. Robertson (1972) *Teaching Geography* (London: Heinemann).

Lucas, A.M. (1972) ASEP, 'A National Curriculum Development Project in Australia', *Science Education*, vol. 56: 443–51.

Ma Li* (1985) 'Modification of the Teaching Requirement of Subjects is a Positive Measure to Raise the Quality of Junior Middle Schools', *Renmin Jiaoyu, (People's Education)*, vol. 9.

McClelland, D.C. (1961) *The Achieving Society* (New York: John Wiley).

McNiff, J. (1988) *Action Research: Principles and Practice* (Macmillan Education).

Maddock, M.N. (1981a) 'Science Education: An Anthropological Viewpoint', *Studies in Science Education*, vol. 8: 1–26.

—— (1981b) 'Science Education in the Philippines – The Decade of the 1970s', *Search*, vol. 2, no. 8: 253–9.

Malaysian Ministry of Education (1981) 'National Status Study – Joint Innovative Project on In-Service Primary Teacher Education' (Kuala Lumpur: Teacher Education Division and Curriculum Development Centre, Ministry of Education).

—— (1982) *Buku Panduan Am KBSR* [General Guide Book KBSR] (Kuala Lumpur: Dewan Bahasa dan Pustaka).

—— (1983) 'Peruntukan KBSR Bagi Sekolah-Sekolah Dalam Tahun 1984', [KBSR Grants for Schools in 1984] (Kuala Lumpur: CDC, Ministry of Education).

—— (1985) *Report of the Cabinet Committee to Review the Implementation of Educational Policy* (Kuala Lumpur: Berita Publishing).

—— (1986) *Final Report, UNESCO – The Joint Innovative Project on Raising the Achievement Level in Primary Education in Malaysia (1984–86)* (Kuala Lumpur: CDC, Ministry of Education).

Mancham, J. (1983) *Paradise Raped* (London: Methuen).

Marsh, C. and M. Huberman (1984) 'Disseminating Curricula: A Look from the Top Down', *Journal of Curriculum Studies*, vol. 16, no. 1.

Maslow, A. (1943) 'A Theory of Human Motivation', *Psychological Review* 50: 370–96.

Maybury, R.H. (1975) *Technical Assistance and Innovation in Science Education* (New York: Science Education/John Wiley).

Mayo, E. (1945) *The Social Problems of Industrial Civilisation* (Boston: Harvard University Press).

Millar, R.H. (1981) 'Science Curriculum and Social Control: a Comparison of some Recent Science Curriculum Proposals in the UK and the Federal Republic of Germany', *Comparative Education*, vol. 17, no. 1: 26–46.

Mohr, L.B. (1969) 'Determinants of Innovation in Organizations', *American Political Science Review*, (63) 1.

Morris, P. (1985) 'The Context of Curriculum Development in Hong Kong: An Analysis of the Problems and Possibilities', *Asian Journal of Public Administration*, 7 (1): 18–35.

Moss, S. (1974) 'Biology Curriculum Development in Malawi', *Journal of Biological Education*, vol. 8, no. 1: 20–31.

Namuddu, C. (1984) *The Structure of Classroom Communication in Selected Biology Lessons in some Secondary Schools in Kenya* (CEDDEA, Université Laval, Quebec).

Nation (1982) *Histoire d'un Lutte, d'une Combat et d'une Victoire, 1964–1982* (Seychelles Government Press).

Nigerian Educational Research Council (1985) *National Curriculum for Senior Secondary Schools*, (A) Biology, (B) Chemisty, (C) Physics (Kano: Educational Resource Centre).

Nixon, J. (1981) *A Teachers' Guide to Action Research* (London: Grant McIntyre).

Nwakoby, F. (1987) *The Educational Change Process in Nigeria: an Evaluation of the Junior Secondary School Innovation in Anambra State*, unpublished D.Phil. thesis, University of Sussex.

OECD (1973) *Case Studies of Educational Innovation; III At the School Level*, Centre for Educational Research and Innovation (Paris: OECD).

OECD/CERI (1972) *Styles of Curriculum Development* (Paris: OECD/CERI).

_____ (1973) *Case Studies of Curriculum Innovation* (Paris: OECD/CERI).

Orpwood, G.W.F. and J. Souque (1984) *Science Education in Canadian Schools, Summary of Background Study 52* (Ontario: Science Council of Canada).

Oxenham, J.C.P. (1984) (ed.), *Education versus Qualifications?* (Allen & Unwin).

_____ (1984) 'Employers, Jobs, and Qualifications', in J.C.P. Oxenham (ed.), *Education versus Qualifications?* (London: Allen & Unwin).

Papagiannis, G., S.J. Klees and N. Bickel (1982) 'Toward A Political Economy of Educational Innovation', *Review of Educational Research*, 52 (2): 245–90.

Parlett, M. and D. Hamilton (1972) *Evaluation as Illumination: A New Approach to the Study of Innovatory Programs*, Occasional Paper no. 9, Centre for Research in the Educational Sciences, University of Edinburgh.

_____ (1976) 'Evaluation as Illumination', in D. Tawney (ed.), *Evaluation Today: Trends and Implications* (Schools Council).

_____ (1977) 'Evaluation as Illumination', in D. Hamilton, D. Jenkins, C. King, B. Macdonald and M. Parlett (eds), *Beyond the Numbers Game* (MacMillan).

316   *Bibliography*

Patton, M.Q. (1980) *Qualitative Evaluation Methods* (Beverly Hills: Sage Publications).
Paulston, R.G. (1976) *Conflicting Theories of Educational and Social Change* (Centre for International Studies, Pittsburgh University Press).
People's Education Press* (1981) 'Explanatory Note on the Outline of Senior Middle School Geography', internal circular.
———* (1982) *Senior Middle School Geography*, Book I and Book 2, 1st edn.
———* (1983) *Teaching References for Senior Middle School Geography*, 1st edn.
People's Republic of China, Ministry of Education* (1982) 'On Offering Senior Middle School Geography', internal circular to schools.
Perak Department of Education (1986) 'Department Circular (J.Pel.Pk.(AM) 3955/21/8/Sj–7/Jld.II/(9)', 23 June 1986.
Pilder, W. (1968) 'The Concept of Utility in Curriculum Discourse 1918–1967', in Kirst and Walker (1971) 'An Analysis of Curriculum Policy-Making', *Review of Education Research*, 41 (5): 479–509.
Popper, K. (1966) *The Open Society and Its Enemies* (5th edn) (Routledge).
Pratt, D. (1980) *Curriculum Design and Development* (New York: Harcourt Brace Jovanovich).
Psacharopoulos, G. (1986) 'The Planning of Education: Where Do We Stand?', *Comparative Education Review*, vol. 30, no. 4.
Pu Tongshiu* (1985) 'The People's Education Press and I', *Retrospect and Prospect of the People's Education Press* (PEP).
Reid, W. (1986) 'Curriculum Theory and Curriculum Change: What can We Learn from History?', *Journal of Curriculum Studies*, 18 (2).
Reynolds, D. (1984) 'Ten Years On – A Decade of Research and Activity in School Effectiveness Research Reviewed', in D. Reynolds (ed.), *Studying School Effectiveness* (Falmer Press).
Richards, P. (1979) 'Community Environmental Knowledge in African Rural Development', *IDS Bulletin*, vol. 10, no. 2, Institute of Development Studies, University of Sussex.
Roethlisberger F.J. and W.J. Dickson (1939) *Management and the Worker* (Harvard University Press).
Rogers, C.R. (1969) *Freedom to Learn* (Ohio: Charles Merrill).
Rogers, E.M. (1971) *Adult Learning* (Milton Keynes: Open University).
Rogers, E.M. and F.F. Shoemaker (1971) *Communication of Innovation: A Cross-cultural Approach* (London: Collier Macmillan).
Saha, L.J. (1983) 'Social Structure and Teacher Effects on Academic Achievement: a Comparative Analysis', *Comparative Education Review*, vol. 27, no. 1.
Sapianchai, N. and T. Chewprececha (1984) 'Implementation of Thai High School Chemistry Curriculum', *Journal of Chemical Education*, vol. 61, no. 1: 44–7.
Sarason, S. (1971) *The Culture of the School and the Problem of Change* (Boston: Allyn & Bacon).
Schön, D.A. (1983) *The Reflective Practitioner* (London: Temple-Smith).
——— (1987) *Educating the Reflective Practitioner* (London: Jossey Bass).
Schools Council (1979) *Schools Council Development Project: Geography 16–19, Advanced Level Syllabus*.

Schram, S.R. (1984) 'Ideology and Policy in China Since the Third Plenum 1978–1984', *Research Notes and Studies*, no. 6, University of London Contemporary China Institute.

Scriven, M. (1972) 'Pros and Cons about Goal-Free Evaluation', in *Evaluation Comment*, vol. 3, no. 2.

Seers, D. (1983) *The Political Economy of Nationalism* (Oxford University Press).

Seychelles People's Progressive Front (1978) *Onward Socialism: SPPF Policy Statement* (Victoria, Mahé: Seychelles People's Progressive Front).

Seychelles Government (1978) *Republic of the Seychelles National Development Plan 1978–82* (Seychelles National Printing Company).

——— (1979) *Republic of the Seychelles National Development Plan 1979–83* (Seychelles National Printing Company).

——— (1980) *The Seychelles National Youth Service, What it Aims to Do, and How it will be Run* (Victoria, Mahé: Department of Youth and Community Development, Ministry of Education and Information).

Shanghai Normal University* (1979) 'Translated Syllabuses of Earth Science and Human Geography in Foreign Countries', document distributed at the Hangzhou Conference, December 1980.

Silverman, D. (1970) *The Theory of Organisations* (London: Heinemann).

Simmons, J. and L. Alexander (1978) 'Factors which Promote School Achievement in Developing Countries: A Review of the Research', in J. Simmons (ed.), *The Education Dilemma: Policy Issues for Developing Countries in the 1980s* (Oxford: Pergamon Press).

Skinner, B.F. (1948) *Walden Two* (New York: Macmillan).

Slater, D. (1985) 'The Management of Change: The Theory and the Practice', in M. Hughes, P. Ribbins and H. Thomas (1985) *Managing Education: The System and the Institution* (New York: Holt Rinehart and Winston).

Sleight, G.F. (1965) The Gambia Sessional Paper no. 8 of 1966; *The Development Programme in Education for the Gambia 1965–1976: A Survey of Education in the Gambia with Recommendations* (Bathurst: UNESCO Educational Planning Mission).

SLOG (1987) *Why do Students Learn? A Six Country Study of Student Motivation*, Research Report no. 17, Institute of Development Studies, University of Sussex.

Smawfield, D. (1984) 'Relevance Education through Education with Production: A Comparative Discussion with Special Reference to the Seychelles National Youth Service', unpublished M.Ed. seminar paper, University of Hull.

Smith, L. and P. Keith (1971) *Anatomy of Educational Innovation: Organisational Analysis of an Elementary School* (New York: Wiley).

Ste-Marie, L. (1982) 'Science Teaching at the Secondary Level: An Evaluation', in *Quebec Science Education: Which Directions?* The proceedings of a symposium sponsored by the Science Council of Canada and l'Association des professeurs de sciences du Québec, March 1982 (Ontario: Science Council of Canada).

Stenhouse, L. (1975) *An Introduction to Curriculum Research and Development* (London: Heineman Educational).

—— (1980) *Curriculum Research and Development in Action* (London: Heineman).

Stuart, J.S. *et al* (1985) *Case-studies in Development Studies Teaching in Lesotho Classrooms*, Research Report no. 9, Institute of Southern African Studies, National University of Lesotho.

Stufflebeam, D.L. *et al* (1971) *Educational Evaluation and Decision Making*, PDK National Study Committee on Evaluation (Illinois: Peacock Publishers).

Su Shaozhi and Feng Lanrui* (1979) 'The Problem of Stages in Socialist Development after the Proletariat has Taken Power', *Jingji Yanjiu* (Economic Research), 5: 14–19.

Su Xiaokang and Zhang Min* (1987) 'A Reflection of the Crisis in Primary and Middle School Education', *Renmin Wenxue [People's Literature]*, 9: 4–22.

Sun Dawen* (1985) 'Standardization of Examination and Reform of China's Geography High School Examination', Proceedings in the Annual Conference of Chinese Education Research Association, Qunming, August 1985.

Sunkel, O. (1979) 'The Development of Development Thinking' in J. Vilamil (1979) *Transnational Capitalism and National Development* (Harvester Press).

Sunkel, O. and E. Fuenzalida (1979) 'Transnationalism and its National Consequences' in J. Vilamil (1979) *Transnational Capitalism and National Development* (Harvester Press).

Suttmeier, R.P. (1981) 'Politics, Modernization and Science in China', *Problems of Communism*, Jan–Feb: 25–34.

Taba, H. (1962) *Curriculum Development: Theory and Practice* (Harcourt Brace Jovanovich).

Tang Sui Chen* (1985) 'Continue the Tradition of Serving Text Construction', *Retrospect and Prospect of the People's Education Press* (Beijing: PEP).

Taylor, D.C. (1982) 'The Rationale for Development Studies', in F. Schorn and A. Blair (eds) *Perspectives on Curriculum and Instruction: Teaching in Lesotho* (Morija, Lesotho: UNESCO).

Theisen, G.L., P. Achola and F.M. Boakari (1983) 'The Underachievement of Cross-national Studies of Achievement', *Comparative Education Review*, vol. 27, no. 1.

Thompson, A.R. (1981) *Education and Development in Africa* (Macmillan).

Tien, Wang and Li* (1980) 'Preliminary Suggestions on Establishing Senior Middle School Geography', paper presented at Hangzhou Conference, December 1980.

Tisher, R.P. *et al* (1972) *Fundamental Issues in Science Education*, (Sydney: John Wiley and Sons).

Toye, J. (1987) *Dilemmas of Development* (Blackwell).

Unger, J. (1982) *Educationa under Mao; Class and Competition in Canton Schools 1960–1980* (New York: Columbia University Press).

Van Rensburg, P. (1974) *Report from Swaneng Hill* (Uppsala: Dag Hammarskjold Foundation).

Villamil, J. (1979) *Transnational Capitalism and National Development* (Harvester Press).

Vulliamy, G., K.M. Lewin and D. Stephens (1990) *Doing Educational Research in Developing Countries: Qualitative Strategies* (Falmer Press).
Walker, R. and C. Adelman (1975) *A Guide to Classroom Observation* (Methuen).
Wang Wenzhan* (1986) 'Labour Technology is a Compulsory Middle Curriculum', *Renmin Jiaoyu [People's Education]*, vol. 6.
Waring, M. (1979) *Social Pressures and Curriculum Innovation – A Study of the Nuffield Foundation Science Teaching Project* (London: Methuen).
Watson, J.K.P. (1979) 'Curriculum Development: Some Comparative Perspectives', *Compare*, 9 (1).
Weber, M. (1947) *The Theory of Social and Economic Organisation*, (tr. A.M. Henderson and T. Parsons) (Illinois: Free Press of Glencoe).
Weiler, H.N. (1978) 'Education and Development: From the Age of Innocence to the Age of Scepticism', *Comparative Education*, vol. 14, no. 3.
——— (1976) 'The Myth of Subject Choice', in *British Journal of Sociology*, vol. 27, no. 2.
Williams, D.H. (1960) *A Short Survey of Education in Northern Nigeria* (Kaduna: Government Printer, Northern Region).
Woodhouse, H.R. (1984) 'Beyond the Hidden Curriculum in Nigeria', in C.B.W. Treffgarne (ed.), *Reproduction and Dependency in Education*, EDC Occasional Paper, no. 7, University of London Institute of Education.
Woods, P. (1986) *Inside Schools: Ethnography in Educational Research* (RKP).
Wright, C.A.H. (1988) 'Collaborative Action Research in Education (CARE) – reflections on an Innovative Paradigm' in *International Journal of Education*, vol. 8, no. 4.
Wu Jie* (1986) *On Teaching and Learning – A Historical Development of the Theories of Teaching and Learning* (Jilin Education Press).
Yang Zhihan* (1986) 'Summary of the Symposium on Primary and Middle School Teaching Plans jointly held by the State Education Commission and the Central Institute of Educational Research', *Kejing, Jiaocai, Jiaofa [Curriculum, Teaching Materials and Teaching Methods]* (People's Education Press), vol. 3.
Ye Lequn* (1987) 'Discussions on the Reform of the Primary and Middle School Curriculum', in Wu and Jiang Shao (eds), *Reform of General Education* (Beijing: People's Education Press).
Yin, R. (1982) 'Studying the Implementation of Public Programs', in W. Williams (ed.), *Studying Implementation* (New York: Chatham House).
Zaltman, G., R. Duncan and J. Holbeck (1973) *Innovations and Organizations* (New York: Wiley).
Zaltman, G., D. Florio and L. Sikorski (1977) *Dynamic Educational Change* (New York: Free Press, MacMillan).
Za'rour, G.I. and R. Jirmanus (1977) 'SCIS in a Lebanese School', *School Science and Mathematics*, vol. LXXVII, no. 5: 407–17.
Zhang Lianfeng* (1985) 'Foster and Enhance the Tradition of the People's Education Press', *Retrospect and Prospect of the People's Education Press* (Beijing: PEP).

Index

action research, 4, 5, 8, 9, 93, 94,
    129–30, 132–4, 141, 142,
    149–50, 151, 288
adult learning theories, 123
agents of change, see change agents
anthropological approach to field
    work, 160, 180
approaches to learning, 247–51
    see also teaching techniques;
        teaching methods
assessment
    continuous, 206
    of needs, 121, 122
    strategies/methods, 49–50, 298
    teacher assessment, 241
    see also examinations
attitude and behaviour change,
    172–4, 181
attitude change, 261–2, 264, 293
attitudes
    judged appropriate, 163, 215
    judged inappropriate, 164, 167,
        168, 179, 183
    of personnel on technical
        assistance projects, 154, 158,
        180
    of pupils towards manual work, 232
    of pupils towards school work,
        192, 207
    of pupils towards vocational
        subjects, 232
    of teachers towards the
        innovation, 47–8, 103
    of teachers towards inservice
        courses, 103, 111–14, 120
    see also perceptions

backwash effect of examinations,
    30, 49–52, 201, 207
benefits
    of innovations/projects, 11,
        16–19, 163–4
    of attitude and behaviour change,
        173

Bowles, S. and H. Gintis, 292
bureaucratic approaches to
    innovation, 285–7
Burrell, G. and G. Morgan, 64

'cascade' inservice training model,
    93, 285
Carnoy, M., 297
change
    agents, 18, 100, 288, 292, 302
    bottom-up, teacher-led, 216
    'change without change', 11, 25
    disruptive, 16–19
    endogenous v. externally-
        stimulated, 130, 216
    literature, 281–2, 291
    models, see strategies
    planned, 2, 7, 14, 18, 20, 215,
        216, 256, 267, 277, 281
    rates of, 16
    resistance/unwillingness to, 120,
        265, 279
    strategies, 13–15, 62, 78, 81, 90,
        130, 282–3
        normative–re-educative, 130,
            288, 289
        power–coercive, 21, 25, 43, 53,
            286
changes in teaching content and
    methods, 118–19
charismatic
    approaches to innovation,
        290–1
    individuals, 38, 290
Chin, R. and K. D. Benne, 130,
    286, 287, 288, 289
classroom
    interaction, 131
    observations, 65–6, 78, 93, 119,
        225, 259
    transactions, 243, 247–51
communication
    lack of/inadequate, 46, 181, 215,
        234–9, 246

management in the classroom,
244–7
theory, 122
confidentiality, 58, 180
conflict, 294–5, 296
among teachers, 270–1
between co-ordinators and
teachers, 273, 281
between expatriates and
nationals, 159, 163, 171
theories, 291, 294–6, 297, 300–1
see also consensus
consensus, 162, 167, 217, 273, 291,
294–6
consultation, 13, 165–9, 246
Coombs, P. H., 10
counterparting, 176, 177, 178, 182
crisis management, 19, 299
cross-cultural situations, 153, 160,
169, 179, 180, 181, 268, 274,
278, 281
cultural differences, *see* cross-
cultural situations
curriculum
conceptualisation of, 228–33
developers, 2, 55
linkages between universities and
schools, 34
linkages between school levels,
44
linkages between subjects, 244
materials, 242–3
modernisation, 21, 32, 36, 37,
52–3, 54, 55, 56
organisation and development,
274–7
reform, 7

data collection, 5, 28
see also qualitative data;
quantitative data
decision-making, 11, 166, 167, 236,
269, 271–3, 278
see also participation
Deng Xiaoping, 31, 32
dependence, 172, 182
of pupils on teachers, 192, 199,
200–1, 210
of national on expatriate staff, 280

dependency theory, 291, 292, 294,
297, 299, 302
diffusionist approaches to
innovation, 289–90
discovery learning, 119, 240
see also teaching techniques
Durkheim, E., 292

educational change, 12, 13–15, 16
see also change
educational change models, *see*
change strategies
educational facilities, 67–8
see also resources
educational innovation/change
literature, 3, 9, 27, 281–2
see also change literature
educational research, 2–5, 11
literature, 13
élites, 31, 177, 182, 210, 297–8,
300–1, 302
élitism, accusations of, 71, 74, 76–7
evaluation, 142, 147–9, 190, 286,
287, 302–3
continuous, 97, 98
illuminative, 5, 22, 27, 64–5, 89,
101, 224, 225, 256–9
objective, 225
responsive, 5
examinations
GCE O level, 73, 77, 83, 84, 188,
189, 190, 194, 198, 277
GCE O and A level, 194, 207
orientation of schools/teachers/
pupils towards, 196–7, 199,
201, 207–9, 213
requirements of, 50–1, 55
setting and marking of, 49, 50
for student selection, 76, 297–8
types of questions set, 50–1
expatriates, 75, 157–9, 163–72, 173,
174, 175–9, 180, 215, 216, 267,
272–3, 278, 280, 301
expectations
regarding the innovation, 11–12,
125, 268, 279
regarding roles, 115–16, 270–1,
272–3
v. reality, 80, 83–4, 116, 280

facilities, *see* resources
foreign staff, *see* expatriates
functionalist theories, 291, 292

generalisability (of research
  findings), 181, 191
generalisation (in the curriculum),
  222
goal displacement, 17, 284, 286
grounded theory, 10, 259

Handy, C., 116, 123, 169, 170, 175
Havelock, R. G., 287, 288, 289
human capital, 1
  theory, 31, 292, 293

illuminative evaluation, *see*
  evaluation
implementation
  barriers to, 21, 45, 54, 253–5
  gap, 45
  partial/inadequate, 17, 25, 45,
    54, 254, 285
  strategies, *see* change strategies
  structural problems of, 159
  v. adoption, 45
incentives, *see* motivation
information
  flows, 11, 19, 106, 122, 234,
    236–9, 252, 273, 278, 285,
    286
  see also communication;
    consultation
infrastructure, 16–17, 100, 155,
  159, 164, 165, 168, 273, 285
initiative
  in teachers, 242–3, 247–51
  in students, 246, 247
innovation literature, 7, 281–2, 291
  see also educational innovation
    literature
innovation models, 100, 282–3
  see also change strategies
innovation theory, 283
inquiry mode of teaching, 79, 83
  see also teaching techniques
inservice courses, 8, 10, 18, 93, 94,
  95, 100–1, 104–25
  effects on teachers of, 118–19

integrated approaches to teaching
  and learning, 97, 98, 215, 219,
  231, 239, 244
integrated curriculum, 243, 271
interaction
  in the classroom, 247, 251,
    258
  between inspectorate and
    colleges, 234
  among students, 246
  between students and teachers,
    79, 246, 258
  between trainers and teachers,
    110–11
interpretative paradigm, 64–5
interviews, 28–9, 56–7, 104, 131,
  154, 157–9, 212, 223–4, 225
  semi-structured, 29, 56, 179, 223,
    259
  types of questions asked in, 29
involvement, *see* participation

Katz, D. and R. Kahn, 284
key actors (in innovation), 28, 29,
  225
key personnel (in inservice
  courses), 18, 105–6, 107,
  109–10, 111, 114–18, 121
  credibility of, 116, 123–4
  roles of, 115–16, 123–4
knowledge transfer, 244
knowledge and skills transfer,
  176–9, 263

management
  of innovation implementation,
    234, 254–5, 269, 271–3
  of communication flow in
    classroom, 244–7
manpower
  needs, 21, 22, 23, 31, 62, 66–70,
    75, 84–8, 89–90, 293
  from overseas, 67; *see also*
    expatriates
  shortage of, 23, 67–9, 155
methodological constraints, 57
  see also research methods
modernisation theories, 291, 294,
  296, 297, 299, 300–1, 302

motivation, 150, 172, 192, 199–200, 210
to change, 302
lack of, 157, 163, 164–5, 183
theory, 124–5
multiplying effect, 106

negative power, 169
neo-Marxist theories, 291, 292, 295, 299, 300, 302
see also conflict theory, dependency theory
non-participant observation, 211, 278
normative–re-educative approach to innovation, *see* change strategies

O levels, *see* examinations
objectivity, 65, 160–1, 180
observation, *see* classroom observations
organisation theory, 162
organisational cultures, 12, 175–6
organisational pain, 17, 253, 288

Parlett, M. and D. Hamilton, 64, 256, 257
participant observer, 154, 215, 258, 278
participation
in change process, 15
of inspectors in curriculum innovation, 234, 236
of local staff in technical assistance projects, 165–8
of students in learning process/ innovation, 133, 137, 144, 247, 266, 267
of teachers in innovation process, 53, 55, 150, 238, 272–3, 275
of teachers in inservice courses, 110–11, 113–14, 123
perception gaps, 10, 153, 158, 160–79, 180, 181
perceptions, 5, 8, 22, 54, 154, 179, 181, 190–1, 192, 208, 216, 225, 230, 231, 301
differences in, 269–71, 273

of need for change, 253
of researcher's role, 252
of trainers' roles, 116, 124
of teachers' needs, 122
perceptual bias, 160
personality cult, 25
planned change, *see* change
planners, 7, 15–16
political issues/pressures, 21, 36–7, 53, 69–72, 90, 269
orientation of curriculum, 33, 36–7
rationale for change strategies, 90
power, 73–4, 265, 270, 290
within organisations, 285–6
relations between groups, 293, 295, 296, 302
power–coercive approach to innovation, *see* change strategies
pre-vocational subjects, 188, 189, 195, 221, 222, 227–8, 229, 230–1, 233, 240
problem-solving approaches to innovation, 288–9
process
approach to teaching and learning, 22, 81
see also teaching methods
helper, 2, 8, 116, 133, 288
v. content, 78–9, 93, 122, 123
v. product, 176

qualitative data, 56, 103, 135, 179
quantitative data, 65, 89, 103, 137
questionnaires, 103, 104, 212, 224, 225, 226, 252

rational–empirical approach to innovation, 284, 287, 293
reification, 284
relationships
between participants in innovation, 270–1
among students, 246–7, 258, 259
between teachers and students, 247, 258, 267–8
on technical assistance projects, 159–60, 161, 168

reliability of information, 58–9
research
  bias, 65
  ethnographic style of, 211
  methods, 5, 28, 56–60, 150, 191,
    212, 223–6, 251–3, 277–9
  multi-method approach to, 28,
    56, 102, 103–4; *see also*
    triangulation
  as part of innovation process,
    287–8
research, development, diffusion
  (RDD) approach to
  innovation, 56, 283, 284, 287
research paradigms, 5, 56
researcher role conflict, 252–3
resistance to change, 265, 279
resources
  availability/shortage of, 10–11,
    25, 48–9, 54, 163–4, 168,
    175, 178, 190, 201–4, 210,
    211, 222, 240–1
  human *v.* material, 163
  lack of hardware/equipment,
    82–3, 118, 201–2, 211,
    240–1
responsive evaluation, *see*
  evaluation
role
  ambiguity, 116, 123
  distortion, 169
  expectations, 198–201
  overload, 170
  status of interviewees, 59
  stress, 116, 123
  underload, 170
roles
  collaborator, 132
  performer, 169, 176
  process helper, 2, 8, 116, 133,
    288
  resource provider, 161
  solution giver, 116, 288
  and duties, 153, 169–72, 173,
    174–6
  of teachers/trainers, 198–201,
    210, 216, 268, 272

Schon, D. A., 143, 149–50

schooling systems
  two-track, 153, 185, 209
scientific approaches to innovation,
  287–8
selection procedures, 76–7
  see also examinations; élites
Silverman, D., 284
social interaction model of
  innovation, 289
staff development, 176, 178, 272
  see also counterparting;
  knowledge and skills
  transfer; teachers'
  professional development
status, 171, 172, 173, 174
Stufflebeam, D. L. *et al.*, 110,
  116
subjectivity
  of interpretive approach, 64
  of research findings, 181, 192
Sunkel, O., 299
sustainability (of project), 164
systems
  engineering, 56
  linkages, 255
  maintenance, 16, 175
  -oriented frames of reference, 5
  reforms, 9–10
  approach to innovation, 283–5

teacher shortage, 43, 44, 45, 52,
  240, 266–7
teacher training/teacher education,
  8, 35, 70, 151, 215, 240
teachers'
  professional development, 127,
    129
  competence, 241–2
  initiative (lack of), 242–3
  experience of the change process,
    256, 277
  expectations of the innovation,
    270–1
teachers as researchers, 127, 129,
  132–3, 141, 144–7, 150
teaching aids, 48–9, 82–3, 240, 241
  243
  see also resources
teaching materials, 40, 82–3

teaching methods
  activity based, 129, 140
  problem-oriented, 215, 243
  recall, 242, 248
  rote learning, 240
teaching strategies, 119
teaching techniques, 80
  discovery learning, 119, 240
  experimental approaches,
    240
  guided discovery, 79–80
  open-ended, 142
  see also approaches to learning;
    inquiry mode of teaching;
    process approach to teaching
technical assistance, 155, 183
  personnel, 158, 183

top-down implementation of
  innovations, 43, 53
training
  on-the-job, 176, 178–9
  see also counterparting; teacher
    training

values, 7, 13–15
  change in, 261
vocational skills, 189, 195
vocationally-oriented curriculum,
  210, 215, 219, 221, 228–9, 253,
  265
vocationally-oriented subjects, 197,
  204, 207, 210, 223, 298
  see also pre-vocational subjects